THE PRECARIAT

THE PRECARIAT

The new dangerous class

GUY STANDING

Bloomsbury Academic
An imprint of Bloomsbury Publishing Plc

B L O O M S B U R Y
LONDON · NEW DELHI · NEW YORK · SYDNEY

Bloomsbury Academic
An imprint of Bloomsbury Publishing Plc

50 Bedford Square
London
WC1B 3DP
UK

1385 Broadway
New York
NY 10018
USA

www.bloomsbury.com

BLOOMSBURY and the Diana logo are trademarks of Bloomsbury Publishing Plc

First published in 2011
Reprinted 2011 (three times), 2012 (three times), 2013
This edition first published 2014
Reprinted by Bloomsbury Academic 2014, 2015 (twice)

Cover designer: MP
Cover image: Construction Worker at Kings Cross by Colin Gray www.CGPGrey.com
CC licenced

British Library Cataloguing-in-Publication Data
A catalogue record for this book is available from the British Library.

ISBN: PB: 978-1-4725-3616-7
ePDF: 978-1-8496-6454-7
ePUB: 978-1-8496-6456-1

Library of Congress Cataloging-in-Publication Data
Standing, Guy.
The precariat: the new dangerous class/Guy Standing.
pages cm
"First published in [2011] by Bloomsbury Academic."
Includes bibliographical references.
ISBN 978-1-84966-351-9 (pbk.) – ISBN 978-1-84966-352-6 (hardback) –
ISBN 978-1-84966-454-7 (epdf) – ISBN 978-1-84966-456-1 (epub) 1. Precarious
employment. 2. Casual labor. 3. Minimum wage. I. Title.
HD5857.S73 2014
331.25'727–dc23
2014002708

Typeset Deanta Global Publishing Services, Chennai, India
Printed and bound in Great Britain

CONTENTS

Preface to the revised edition vi
Preface to the first edition x
List of abbreviations xii

1   The precariat 1

2   Why the precariat is growing 43

3   Who enters the precariat? 101

4   Migrants: Victims, villains or heroes? 153

5   Labour, work and the time squeeze 197

6   A politics of inferno 227

7   A politics of paradise 267

Bibliography 317
Index 327

PREFACE TO THE
REVISED EDITION

In August 2011, sparked by the killing of a young man by police, fires lit up the London skyline. Riots spread from Tottenham, in the city's north-east, to suburbs and cities around England, shocking, perplexing and enraging politicians and affluent folk watching the events on television.

What linked the riots to the event in Hamburg described in Chapter 1 of this book, of life imitating art? What linked them with the EuroMayDay parades that had taken place in 25 European cities and Tokyo, involving hundreds of thousands of demonstrators, unreported by the mainstream media? What linked them to the demonstrations that swept the city squares of the Middle East in 2011, precipitated by the self-immolation of a young Tunisian graduate, reduced to selling goods off a barrow? And to the shop burning and demonstrations in Athens' Constitution Square, coupled with the *den plirono* ('refuse to pay') movement across Greece? And to the Occupy Movement, the seething anger of the *indignados* in Spain and Portugal, the *tentifada* actions of 250,000 people in Tel Aviv later that year, to the student riots and fires in Santiago, the four nights of riots around Stockholm in 2012, the surge of protest by what the Turkish Prime Minister called *çapulcu* ('riff-raff') in Istanbul in June 2013, and to the huge protests across Brazil shortly afterwards?

Although some will say they all had separate causes and characteristics, which they did, they were all, partially, the stirrings of the *precariat* – the phase of *primitive rebels*, when protests and reactions are by people who know more about what they are against than what they are for. That will change. The first stage of any new social movement is the emergence of a sense of common identity. The energies unleashed in the city squares, streets, internet cafes and other public spaces have generated an identity that is becoming a social force.

As a result of the collective outpourings of 2011, we may surmise that more in the precariat, when they look in a mirror in the morning, do not see a failure or a shirker, but someone who shares a common predicament with many others. This is a necessary change from isolation, self-pity or self-loathing to collective strength, knowing that the economic institutions want a large precariat.

Those in it have lives dominated by insecurity, uncertainty, debt and humiliation. They are becoming denizens rather than citizens, losing cultural, civil, social, political and economic rights built up over generations. The precariat is also the first class in history expected to endure labour and work at a lower level than the schooling it typically acquires. In an ever more unequal society, its relative deprivation is severe.

Pain and anomie will grow. There will be more 'days of rage'. But it is not enough to be angry. While some are listening to ugly populist, simplistic voices, others are rediscovering their humanity and desire for society. Across the world, there is an energy building around the precariat. It is organizing, and struggling to define a new forward march.

Other developments since *The Precariat* was written have served to strengthen the argument that the precariat is emerging as a new mass class with transformative potential. These developments include the continued pursuit of austerity in the industrialized world, which is pushing more and more people into the precariat, and an intensification of what is described in the book as 'the politics of inferno', including the growth of commodified and populist politics and Edward Snowden's brave revelations on the extent of the surveillance state.

A second book, *A Precariat Charter: From Denizens to Citizens*, published alongside this revised edition of *The Precariat*, attempts to take the debate forward by discussing the impact on the precariat of the austerity era and the disturbing utilitarian thinking that underpins it. *A Precariat Charter* goes on to set out a series of policies aimed at addressing the precariat's insecurities and aspirations, proposed not as a manifesto but as a starting point for the construction of a new precariat agenda.

That book also responds to those critics of *The Precariat* who argue that nothing has changed and that the precariat is not a class. These criticisms come mainly from those wedded to a particular brand of Marxism, for whom capitalism is unchanging. But global capitalism is profoundly different from national industrial capitalism. There is a vast amount of evidence to show how labour relations and patterns of work, and systems of social protection, regulation and redistribution, have evolved in the globalization era, in the process generating a new class structure that is far from a simplistic division between capitalists and 'workers'.

In terms that Marxist critics would presumably accept, the precariat can be defined as having distinctive relations of production, distinctive relations of distribution and distinctive relations to the state, producing a distinctive class consciousness. It is a class-in-the-making because it is internally divided at present. As a 'dangerous' class, it must become a class-for-itself in order to abolish itself. In other words, it must become sufficiently united to have the political strength to pressurize the state into creating the social and economic conditions that would remove its precariousness. These are outlined in *A Precariat Charter*.

The precariat will also need new forms of organization to press its demands. Some on the left have felt uncomfortable with the comments made on trade unions in *The Precariat*; I will just say that, although I have long been a member and supporter of trade unions, that involvement has convinced me that their ethos must adapt to the twenty-first century. Unions must escape from 'labourism', the elevation of subservient labour above the freedom to pursue occupation (Standing 2009).

Another criticism of *The Precariat* has been an alleged lack of data to support its principal theses. In fact, the book was founded on over two decades of empirical and conceptual research that yielded several technical books and reports as well as journal articles, some of which are cited. *The Precariat* was an attempt to distil this work into an approachable narrative. Ironically, many readers who are not social scientists have shown a greater understanding of the concepts – and the realities of labour and work in the early twenty-first century – than some academics and commentators steeped in old paradigms.

It remains to thank the numerous people from all over the world who have contacted me with their reactions, in many cases relating their experiences and perspectives. I have tried to respond personally to as many as possible and apologize to those to whom I have not. Their insights and ideas have fed into *A Precariat Charter*. As Karl Marx famously said, the point is not to interpret the world, it is to change it.

Guy Standing

January 2014

PREFACE TO THE
FIRST EDITION

This book is about a new group in the world, a class-in-the-making. It sets out to answer five questions: What is it? Why should we care about its growth? Why is it growing? Who is entering it? And where is the precariat taking us?

That last question is crucial. There is a danger that, unless the precariat is understood, its emergence could lead society towards a politics of inferno. This is not a prediction. It is a disturbing possibility. It will only be avoided if the precariat can become a class-for-itself, with effective agency, and a force for forging a new 'politics of paradise', a mildly utopian agenda and strategy to be taken up by politicians and by what is euphemistically called 'civil society', including the multitude of non-governmental organisations that too often flirt with becoming quasi-government organisations.

We need to wake up to the global precariat urgently. There is a lot of anger out there and a lot of anxiety. But although this book highlights the victim side of the precariat more than the liberating side, it is worth stating at the outset that it is wrong to see the precariat in purely suffering terms. Many drawn into it are looking for something better than what was offered in industrial society and by twentieth-century labourism. They may no more deserve the name of Hero than Victim. But they are beginning to show why the precariat can be a harbinger of the Good Society of the twenty-first century.

The context is that, while the precariat has been growing, globalisation's hidden reality has come to the surface with the 2008 financial shock. Postponed for too long, global adjustment is pushing the high-income countries down as it pulls the low-income countries up. Unless the inequalities wilfully neglected by most governments in the past two decades are radically redressed, the pain and repercussions could become explosive. The global market economy may eventually raise living standards everywhere – even its critics should wish that – but it is surely only ideologues who can deny that it has brought economic insecurity to many, many millions. The precariat is in the front ranks, but it has yet to find the Voice to bring its agenda to the fore. It is not 'the squeezed middle' or an 'underclass' or 'the lower working class'. It has a distinctive bundle of insecurities and will have an equally distinctive set of demands.

In the early stages of writing the book, a presentation of the themes was made to what turned out to be a largely ageing group of academics of a social democratic persuasion. Most greeted the ideas with scorn and said there was nothing new. For them, the answer today was the same as it was when they were young. More jobs were needed, more decent jobs. All I will say to those respected figures is that I think the precariat would have been unimpressed.

There are too many people to thank all of them individually for helping in the thinking behind the book. However, I would like to thank the many groups of students and activists who have listened to presentations of the themes in the sixteen countries visited during its preparation. One hopes their insights and questions have filtered into the final text. Suffice it to add that the author of a book like this is mainly a conveyor of the thoughts of others.

Guy Standing

November 2010

LIST OF ABBREVIATIONS

AARP	American Association of Retired Persons
AFL-CIO	American Federation of Labor/Congress of Industrial Organizations
BBVA	Banco Bilbao Vizcaya Argentaria
BIEN	Basic Income Earth Network
CBT	Cognitive behavioural therapy
CCT	Conditional cash transfer
CIA	Central Intelligence Agency
CRI	Crime Reduction Initiatives
EHRC	Equality and Human Rights Commission (UK)
EU	European Union
GCSE	General Certificate of Secondary Education
IMF	International Monetary Fund
LIFO	Last-in, first-out
NGO	Non-governmental organisation
NIC	Newly industrialising country
OECD	Organisation for Economic Co-operation and Development
RMI	*Revenu minimum d'insertion*
SEWA	Self-Employed Women's Association of India
UKBA	UK Border Agency
UMP	*Union pour un Mouvement Populaire*

1

The precariat

In the 1970s, a group of ideologically inspired economists captured the ears and minds of politicians. The central plank of their 'neo-liberal' model was that growth and development depended on market competitiveness; everything should be done to maximise competition and competitiveness, and to allow market principles to permeate all aspects of life.

One theme was that countries should increase labour market flexibility, which came to mean an agenda for transferring risks and insecurity onto workers and their families. The result has been the creation of a global 'precariat', consisting of many millions around the world without an anchor of stability. They are becoming a new dangerous class. They are prone to listen to ugly voices, and to use their votes and money to give those voices a political platform of increasing influence. The very success of the 'neo-liberal' agenda, embraced to a greater or lesser extent by governments of all complexions, has created an incipient political monster. Action is needed before that monster comes to life.

The precariat stirs

On 1 May 2001, 5,000 people, mainly students and young social activists, gathered in Milan's city centre for what was intended to be an alternative May Day protest march. By 1 May 2005, their ranks had swollen to well over 50,000 – over 100,000, according to some estimates – and 'EuroMayDay' had become pan-European, with hundreds of thousands of people, mostly young, taking to the streets of cities across continental Europe. The demonstrations marked the first stirrings of the global precariat.

The ageing trade unionists who normally orchestrated May Day events could only be bemused by this new parading mass, whose demands for free migration and a universal basic income had little to do with traditional unionism. The unions saw the answer to precarious labour in a return to the 'labourist' model they had been so instrumental in cementing in the mid-twentieth century – more stable jobs with long-term employment security and the benefit trappings that went with that. But many of the young demonstrators had seen their parents' generation conform to the Fordist pattern of drab full-time jobs and subordination to industrial management and the dictates of capital. Though lacking a cohesive alternative agenda, they showed no desire to resurrect labourism.

Stirring first in Western Europe, EuroMayDay soon took on a global character, with Japan becoming a notable centre of energy. It started as a youth movement, with educated disgruntled Europeans alienated by the competitive market (or neo-liberal) approach of the European Union project that was urging them on to a life of jobs, flexibility and faster economic growth. But their Eurocentric origins soon gave way to internationalism, as they saw their predicament of multiple insecurities linked to what was happening to others all over the world. Migrants became a substantial part of the precariat demonstrations.

The movement spread to those with non-conventional lifestyles. And all the time there was a creative tension between the precariat as victims, penalised and demonised by mainstream institutions and policies, and the precariat as heroes, rejecting those institutions in a concerted act of intellectual and emotional defiance. By 2008, the EuroMayDay demonstrations were dwarfing the trade union marches on the same day. This may have gone largely unnoticed by the wider public and politicians, but it was a significant development.

At the same time, the dual identity as victim/hero made for a lack of coherence. A further problem was a failure to focus on struggle. Who or what was the enemy? All the great movements throughout history have been class based, for better or for worse. One group interest (or several) has fought against another, the latter having exploited and oppressed the former. Usually, the struggle has been about use and control over the key assets of the production and distribution system of the time. The precariat, for all its rich tapestry, seemed to lack a clear idea of what those assets were. Their intellectual heroes included Pierre Bourdieu (1998), who articulated precarity, Michel Foucault, Jürgen Habermas, and Michael Hardt and Tony Negri (2000), whose *Empire* was a seminal text, with Hannah Arendt (1958) in the background. There were also shades of the upheavals of 1968, linking the precariat to the Frankfurt School of Herbert Marcuse's (1964) *One Dimensional Man*.

It was liberation of the mind, a consciousness of a common sense of insecurity. But no 'revolution' comes from simple understanding.

There was no effective anger yet. This was because no political agenda or strategy had been forged. The lack of a programmatic response was revealed by the search for symbols, the dialectical character of the internal debates, and tensions within the precariat that are still there and will not go away.

Leaders of the EuroMayDay protesters did their best to paper over the cracks, literally as in their visual images and posters. Some emphasised a unity of interests between migrants and others (*migranti e precarie* was a message emblazoned on a Milan EuroMayDay poster of 2008) and between youth and the elderly, as sympathetically juxtaposed on the Berlin EuroMayDay poster of 2006 (Doerr, 2006).

But as a leftish libertarian movement, it has yet to excite fear, or even interest, from those outside. Even its most enthusiastic protagonists would admit that the demonstrations so far have been more theatre than threat, more about asserting individuality and identity within a collective experience of precariousness. In the language of sociologists, the public displays have been about pride in precarious subjectivities. One EuroMayDay poster, done for a Hamburg parade, blended in a pose of defiance four figures into one – a cleaner, a care worker, a refugee or migrant and a so-called 'creative' worker (presumably like the person who designed the poster). A prominent place was given to a carrier bag, held up as an iconic symbol of contemporary nomadism in the globalising world.

Symbols matter. They help unite groups into something more than a multitude of strangers. They help in forging a class and building identity, fostering an awareness of commonality and a basis for solidarity or *fraternité*. Moving from symbols to a political programme is what this book is about. The evolution of the precariat as the agency of a politics of paradise is still to pass from theatre and visual ideas of emancipation to a set of demands that will engage the state rather than merely puzzle or irritate it.

A feature of the EuroMayDay demonstrations has been their carnival atmosphere, with salsa music and posters and speeches built around mockery and humour. Many of the actions linked to the loose network behind them have been anarchic and daredevilish, rather than strategic or socially threatening. In Hamburg, participants have been given advice on how to avoid paying bus fares or cinema tickets. In one stunt in 2006, which has gone into the folklore of the movement, a group of about 20 youths wearing carnival masks and calling themselves names such as Spider Mum, Multiflex, Operaistorix and Santa Guevara raided a gourmet supermarket in mid-morning. They filled a trolley with luxury food and drink, posed to take photographs of themselves and then walked out, having handed the woman at the till a flower with a note explaining that they produced wealth but did not enjoy any of it. The episode was life imitating art, based on the film *The Edukators*. The group known as the Robin Hood gang has never been caught. They posted a note on the internet announcing that they had distributed the food to interns, whom they singled out as among the most exploited precarious workers in the city.

Scarcely intended to win friends or influence mainstream society, the antics of groups like this bring to mind historical analogies. We may be at a stage in the evolution of the precariat when those opposed to its central features – precariousness of residency, of labour and work and of social protection – are akin to the 'primitive rebels' that have emerged in all the great societal transformations, when old entitlements have been stripped away and social compacts tossed aside. There have always been Robin Hoods, as Eric Hobsbawm (1959) famously celebrated. They have usually flourished in a period before a coherent political strategy to advance the interests of the new class has taken shape.

Those who participate in the EuroMayDay parades and in companion events in other parts of the world are just the tip of the precariat. There is a much larger element living in fear and insecurity. Most would not identify with the EuroMayDay demonstrations. But that does not make them any less part of the precariat. They are floating, rudderless and potentially angry, capable of veering to the extreme right or extreme left politically and backing populist demagoguery that plays on their fears or phobias.

The precariat stirred

In 1989, the city of Prato, a short distance from Florence, was almost entirely Italian. For centuries, it had been a great manufacturing centre of textiles and garments. Many of its 180,000 residents were linked to those industries, generation after generation. Reflecting the old values, this Tuscan town was solidly left in its politics. It seemed the embodiment of social solidarity and moderation.

That year, a group of thirty-eight Chinese workers arrived. A new breed of garment firms began to emerge – owned by Chinese immigrants and a few Italians with links to them. They imported more and more Chinese labourers, many coming without work visas. While noticed, they were tolerated; they added to the flourishing economy and did not place demands on public finances since they were not receiving any state benefits. They kept to themselves, penned in an enclave where the Chinese factories were located. Most came from one city, coastal Wenzhou in Zhejiang Province, an area with a long history of entrepreneurial migration. Most came via Frankfurt on three-month tourist visas and continued to work clandestinely after the visas expired, putting themselves in a vulnerable and exploitable position.

By 2008, there were 4,200 Chinese firms registered in the city and 45,000 Chinese workers, making up a fifth of the city's population (Dinmore, 2010a, b). They were producing 1 million garments every day, enough to dress the world's population in 20 years, according to calculations by municipal officials. Meanwhile, undercut by the Chinese and buffeted by competition from India and Bangladesh, local Italian firms shed workers in droves. By 2010, they employed just 20,000 workers, 11,000 fewer than in 2000. As they shrank, they shifted more workers from regular to precarious jobs.

Then came the financial shock, which hit Prato in much the same way as it hit so many other old industrial areas of Europe and North America. Bankruptcies multiplied, unemployment rose, resentments turned nasty. Within months, the political left had been swept from power by the xenophobic Northern League. It promptly instituted a crackdown on the Chinese, launching night-time raids on their factories and 'sweatshops', rounding up workers and demonising them, just as the League's political ally, Prime Minister Silvio Berlusconi, spoke of his determination to defeat 'the army of evil', as he described illegal immigrants. A shaken Chinese ambassador hurried from Rome and said that what was going on reminded him of the Nazis in the 1930s. Bizarrely, the Chinese government seemed reluctant to take the migrants back.

The problems were not just caused by intolerant locals. The nature of the enclave contributed. While Prato's old factories struggled to compete, leaving Italian workers to seek alternative sources of income, the Chinese built up a community within a community. Chinese gangs reportedly organised the exodus from China and ran the enclave, albeit vying for control with gangs from Russia, Albania, Nigeria and Romania, as well as with the Mafia. And they were not just restricting themselves to Prato. Chinese gangs were linking up with Chinese companies in investing in Italian infrastructural projects, including a proposed multibillion Euro 'China terminal' near the port of Civitavecchia.

Prato has become a symbol of globalisation and the dilemmas thrown up by the growth of the precariat. As those Chinese sweatshops spread, Italians lost their proletarian roles and were left to scramble for a precariat job or none at all. Then the migrant part of the precariat was exposed to retribution from the authorities, while dependent on dubious networks within their enclave community. By no means unique, Prato reflects an undertow of globalisation.

Globalisation's child

In the late 1970s, an emboldened group of social and economic thinkers, subsequently called 'neo-liberals' and 'libertarians' (although the terms are not synonymous), realised that their views were being listened to after decades of neglect. Most were young enough not to have been scarred by the Great Depression or wedded to the social democratic agenda that had swept the mainstream after the Second World War.

They disliked the state, which they equated with centralised government, with its planning and regulatory apparatus. They saw the world as an increasingly open place, where investment, employment and income would flow to where conditions were most welcoming. They argued that unless European countries, in particular, rolled back the securities that had been built up since the Second World War for the industrial working class and the bureaucratic public sector, and unless the trades unions were 'tamed', de-industrialisation (a new concept at the time) would accelerate, unemployment would rise, economic growth would slow down, investment would flow out and poverty would escalate. It was a sobering assessment. They wanted drastic measures, and in politicians like Margaret Thatcher and Ronald Reagan they had the sort of leaders willing to go along with their analysis.

The tragedy was that, while their *diagnosis* made partial sense, their *prognosis* was callous. Over the next 30 years, the tragedy was compounded by the fact that the social democratic political parties that had built up the system the neo-liberals wished to dismantle, after briefly contesting the neo-liberals' diagnosis, subsequently lamely accepted both the diagnosis and the prognosis.

One neo-liberal claim that crystallised in the 1980s was that countries needed to pursue 'labour market flexibility'. Unless labour markets were made more flexible, labour costs would rise and corporations would transfer production and investment to places where costs were lower; financial capital would be invested in those countries, rather than 'at home'. Flexibility had many dimensions: wage flexibility meant speeding up adjustments to changes in demand, particularly downwards; employment flexibility meant easy and costless ability of firms to change employment levels, particularly downwards, implying a reduction in employment security and protection; job flexibility meant being able to move employees around inside the firm and to change job structures with minimal opposition or cost; skill flexibility meant being able to adjust workers' skills easily.

In essence, the flexibility advocated by the brash neo-classical economists meant systematically making employees more insecure, claimed to be a necessary price for retaining investment and jobs. Each economic setback was attributed in part, fairly or not, to a lack of flexibility and to the lack of 'structural reform' of labour markets.

As globalisation proceeded, and as governments and corporations chased each other in making their labour relations more flexible, the number of people in insecure forms of labour multiplied. This was not technologically determined. As flexible labour spread, inequalities grew, and the class structure that underpinned industrial society gave way to something more complex but certainly not less class based. We will come back to this. But the policy changes and the responses of corporations to the dictates of the globalising market economy generated a trend around the world that was never predicted by the neo-liberals or the political leaders who were putting their policies into effect.

Millions of people, in affluent and emerging market economies, entered the precariat, a new phenomenon even if it had shades of the past. The precariat was not part of the 'working class' or the 'proletariat'. The latter terms suggest a society consisting mostly of workers in long-term, stable, fixed-hour jobs with established routes of advancement, subject to unionisation and collective agreements, with job titles their fathers and mothers would have understood, facing local employers whose names and features they were familiar with.

Many entering the precariat would not know their employer or how many fellow employees they had or were likely to have in the future. They were also not 'middle class', as they did not have a stable or predictable salary or the status and benefits that middle-class people were supposed to possess.

As the 1990s proceeded, more and more people, not just in developing countries, found themselves in a status that development economists and anthropologists called 'informal'. Probably they would not have found this a helpful way of describing themselves, let alone one that would make them see in others a common way of living and working. So they were not working class, not middle class, not 'informal'. What were they? A flicker of recognition would have occurred in being defined as having a *precarious* existence. Friends, relatives and colleagues would also be in a temporary status of some kind, without assurance that this was what they would be doing in a few years' time, or even months or weeks hence. Often they were not even wishing or trying to make it so.

Defining the precariat

There are two ways of defining what we mean by the precariat. One is to say it is a distinctive socio-economic group, so that by definition a person is in it or not in it. This is useful in terms of images and analyses, and it allows us to use what Max Weber called an 'ideal type'. In this spirit, the precariat could be described as a neologism that combines an adjective 'precarious' and a related noun 'proletariat'. In this book, the term is often used in this sense, though it has limitations. We may claim that the precariat is a *class-in-the-making*, if not yet a *class-for-itself*, in the Marxian sense of that term.

Thinking in terms of social groups, we may say that, leaving aside agrarian societies, the globalisation era has resulted in a fragmentation of national class structures. As inequalities grew, and as the world moved towards a flexible open labour market, class did not disappear. Rather, a more fragmented global class structure emerged.

The 'working class', 'workers' and the 'proletariat' were terms embedded in our culture for several centuries. People could describe themselves in class terms, and others would recognise them in those terms, by the way they dressed, spoke and conducted themselves. Today they are little more than evocative labels. André Gorz (1982) wrote of 'the end of the working class' long ago. Others have continued to agonise over the meaning of that term and over the criteria for classification. Perhaps the reality is that we need a new vocabulary, one reflecting class relations in the global market system of the twenty-first century.

Broadly speaking, while the old classes persist in parts of the world, we can identify seven groups. At the top is an 'elite', consisting of a tiny number of absurdly rich global citizens lording it over the universe, with their billions of dollars, listed in Forbes as among the great and the good, able to influence governments everywhere and to indulge in munificent philanthropic gestures. Below that elite comes the 'salariat', still in stable full-time employment, some hoping to move into the elite, the majority just enjoying the trappings of their kind, with their pensions, paid holidays and enterprise benefits, often subsidised by the state. The salariat is concentrated in large corporations, government agencies and public administration, including the civil service.

Alongside the salariat, in more senses than one, is a (so far) smaller group of 'proficians'. This term combines the traditional ideas of 'professional' and 'technician' but covers those with bundles of skills that they can market, earning high incomes on contract, as consultants or independent own-account workers. The proficians are the equivalent of the yeomen, knights and squires of the Middle Ages. They live with the expectation and desire to move around, without an impulse for long-term, full-time employment in a single enterprise. The 'standard employment relationship' is not for them.

Below the proficians, in terms of income, is a shrinking 'core' of manual employees, the essence of the old 'working class'. The welfare states were built with them in mind, as were the systems of labour regulation. But the battalions of industrial labourers who formed the labour movements have shrivelled and lost their sense of social solidarity.

Underneath those four groups, there is the growing 'precariat', flanked by an army of unemployed and a detached group of socially ill misfits living off the dregs of society. The character of this fragmented class structure is discussed elsewhere (Standing, 2009). It is the precariat that we want to identify here.

Sociologists conventionally think in terms of Max Weber's forms of stratification – class and status – where class refers to social relations of production and a person's position in the labour process (Weber, [1922] 1968). Within labour markets, apart from employers and self-employed, the main distinction has been between wage workers and salaried employees, the former covering piece-rate and time-rate suppliers of labour, with images of money-for-effort, and the latter supposedly being rewarded by trust and compensation-for-service (Goldthorpe, 2007, Vol. 2, Ch. 5; McGovern, Hill and Mills, 2008, Ch. 3). The salariat has always been expected to be closer to managers, bosses and owners, while wage workers are inherently alienated, requiring discipline, subordination and a mix of incentives and sanctions.

By contrast with class, the idea of status has been associated with a person's occupation, with higher status occupations being those that are closer to professional services, management and administration (Goldthorpe, 2009). A difficulty is that within most occupations there are divisions and hierarchies that involve very different statuses.

In any case, the division into wage labour and salaried employee, and ideas of occupation, break down when considering the precariat. The precariat has *class* characteristics. It consists of people who have minimal trust relationships with capital or the state, making it quite unlike the salariat. And it has none of the social contract relationships of the proletariat, whereby labour securities were provided in exchange for subordination and contingent loyalty, the unwritten deal underpinning welfare states. Without a bargain of trust or security in exchange for subordination, the precariat is distinctive in class terms. It also has a peculiar *status* position, in not mapping neatly onto high-status professional or middle-status craft occupations. One way of putting it is that the precariat has 'truncated status'. And, as we shall see, its structure of 'social income' does not map neatly onto old notions of class or occupation.

Japan illustrates the problems confronting students of the precariat. It has had a relatively low level of income inequality (making it a 'good country', according to Wilkinson and Pickett (2009)). But inequality runs deep in terms of status hierarchy and has been intensified by the proliferating precariat, whose economic plight is underestimated by conventional measures of income inequality. Higher status positions in Japanese society entail a set of rewards providing socio-economic security that is worth far more than can be measured by monetary incomes alone (Kerbo, 2003: 509–12). The precariat lacks all those rewards, which is why income inequality is so seriously understated.

The descriptive term 'precariat' was first used by French sociologists in the 1980s, to describe temporary or seasonal workers. This book will use a different notion, but temporary labouring status comprises a central aspect of the precariat. We just have to remember that temporary employment contracts are not necessarily the same as doing temporary labour.

Some try to give the precariat a positive image, typifying a romantic free spirit who rejects norms of the old working class steeped in stable labour, as well as the bourgeois materialism of those in salaried 'white-collar' jobs. This free-spirited defiance and nonconformity should not be forgotten, for it does figure in the precariat. There is nothing new in youthful and not so youthful struggles against the dictates of subordinated labour. What is more novel is a welcoming of precarious labour and work style by 'old agers', opting for such an existence after a long period of stable labour. We consider them later.

The meaning of the term has varied as it has come into popular parlance. In Italy, the *precariato* has been taken to mean more than just people doing casual labour and with low incomes, implying a precarious existence as a normal state of living (Grimm and Ronneberger, 2007). In Germany, the term has been used to describe not only temporary workers but also the jobless who have no hope of social integration. This is close to the Marxian idea of a *lumpenproletariat* and is not what will be meant in this book.

In Japan, the term has been used as synonymous with 'the working poor', although it evolved as a distinctive term as it became associated with the Japanese May Day movement and so-called 'freeter unions', made up of young activists demanding better working and living conditions (Ueno, 2007; Obinger, 2009). Japan has produced a group of young workers known as 'freeters' – a name peculiarly combining 'free' and *Arbeiter*, German for worker – who have been pushed into a work style of casual labour.

It is not right to equate the precariat with the working poor or with just insecure employment, although these dimensions are correlated with it. The precariousness also implies a lack of a secure work-based identity, whereas workers in some low-income jobs may be building a career. Some commentators have linked the idea to lacking control over their labour. This is complicated, since there are several aspects of work and labour over which a person may have control – skill development and use, amount of time required to labour, the timing of work and labour, labour intensity, equipment, raw materials and so on. And there are several types of control and controller, not just the standard supervisor or manager standing over the worker.

To assert that the precariat consists of people who have no control over their labour or work would be too restrictive, since there is always ambivalence and implicit bargaining over effort, cooperation and application of skills, as well as scope for acts of sabotage, pilfering and boondoggling. But aspects of control are relevant to an assessment of their predicament.

Perhaps an equally interesting line of delineation is associated with what may be called 'status discord'. People with a relatively high level of formal education, who have to accept jobs that have a status or income beneath what they believe accord with their qualifications, are likely to suffer from status frustration. This sentiment has been prevalent in the youth precariat in Japan (Kosugi, 2008).

For our purposes, the precariat consists of people who lack the seven forms of labour-related security, summarised in the Box, that social democrats, labour parties and trades unions pursued as their 'industrial citizenship' agenda after the Second World War, for the working class or industrial proletariat. Not all those in the precariat would value all seven forms of security, but they fare badly in all respects.

FORMS OF LABOUR SECURITY UNDER INDUSTRIAL CITIZENSHIP

Labour market security – Adequate income-earning opportunities; at the macro-level, this is epitomised by a government commitment to 'full employment'.

Employment security – Protection against arbitrary dismissal, regulations on hiring and firing, imposition of costs on employers for failing to adhere to rules and so on.

Job security – Ability and opportunity to retain a niche in employment, plus barriers to skill dilution, and opportunities for 'upward' mobility in terms of status and income.

Work security – Protection against accidents and illness at work, through, for example, safety and health regulations, limits on working time, unsociable hours, night work for women, as well as compensation for mishaps.

Skill reproduction security – Opportunity to gain skills, through apprenticeships, employment training and so on, as well as opportunity to make use of competencies.

Income security – Assurance of an adequate stable income, protected through, for example, minimum wage machinery, wage indexation, comprehensive social security, progressive taxation to reduce inequality and to supplement low incomes.

Representation security – Possessing a collective voice in the labour market, through, for example, independent trade unions, with a right to strike.

In discussions of modern labour insecurity, most attention is given to employment insecurity – lack of long-term contracts and absence of protection against loss of employment. That is understandable. However, job insecurity is also a defining feature.

The difference between employment security and job security is vital. Consider an example. Between 2008 and 2010, thirty employees of France Telecom committed suicide, resulting in the appointment of an outsider as the new boss. Two-thirds of the 66,000 employees had civil service tenure, with guaranteed employment security. But the management had subjected them to systematic job insecurity, with a system called 'Time to Move' that obliged them to change offices and jobs abruptly every few years. The resulting stress was found to be the main cause of the suicides. Job insecurity mattered.

It also matters in the civil service. Employees sign contracts that give them much-envied employment security. But they also agree to be allocated to positions as and when their managers decide. In a world of rigorous 'human resources management' and functional flexibility, the shifting around is likely to be personally disruptive.

Another feature of the precariat is precarious income and a pattern of income that is different from that of all other groups. This can be demonstrated using the concept of 'social income'. People everywhere obviously have to survive on the income they receive. That may be a flow of money or income in kind, in terms of what they or their families produce. It can be measured by what they could anticipate receiving should they need it. Most people in most societies have several sources of income, although some may rely on just one.

The composition of social income can be broken into six elements. The first is self-production, the food, goods and services produced directly, whether consumed, bartered or sold, including what one might grow in a garden or household plot. Second, there is the money wage or the money income received from labour. Third, there is the value of support provided by the family or local community, often by way of informal mutual insurance claims. Fourth, there are enterprise benefits that are provided to many groups of employees. Fifth, there are state benefits, including social insurance benefits, social assistance, discretionary transfers, subsidies paid directly or through employers, and subsidised social services. Finally, there are private benefits derived from savings and investments.

Each of these can be subdivided into forms that are more or less secure or assured, and which determine their full value. For instance, wages can be divided into forms that are fixed on a long-term contractual basis and forms that are variable or flexible. If someone receives a salary that provides the same income each month for the next year, the income received this month is worth more than the same money income derived from a wage that is dependent on the vagaries of the weather and an employer's undetermined production schedule. Similarly, state benefits can be divided into universal 'citizenship' rights, alongside insurance benefits, which are dependent on past contributions and are thus, in principle, 'assured', and more discretionary transfers that may or may not be available depending on unforeseen circumstances. Enterprise benefits may be subdivided into elements that everybody in a firm receives, elements that depend on status or past service and elements given discretionarily. The same is true of community benefits, which can be divided into family or kinship claims and claims that can be made on the wider community for support in times of need.

The precariat can be identified by a distinctive structure of social income, which imparts a vulnerability going well beyond what would be conveyed by the money income received at a particular moment. For instance, in a period of rapid commercialisation of the economy of a developing country, the new groups, many going towards the precariat, find that they lose traditional community benefits and do not gain enterprise or state benefits. They are more vulnerable than many with lower incomes who retain traditional forms of community support and are more vulnerable than salaried employees who have similar money incomes but have access to an array of enterprise and state benefits. A feature of the precariat is not the level of money wages or income earned at any particular moment but the lack of community support in times of need, lack of assured enterprise or state benefits, and lack of private benefits to supplement money earnings. We will consider the effects of this in Chapter 2.

Besides labour insecurity and insecure social income, those in the precariat lack a work-based *identity*. When employed, they are in career-less jobs, without traditions of social memory, a feeling they belong to an occupational community steeped in stable practices, codes of ethics and norms of behaviour, reciprocity and fraternity.

The precariat does not feel part of a solidaristic labour community. This intensifies a sense of alienation and instrumentality in what they have to do. Actions and attitudes, derived from precariousness, drift towards opportunism. There is no 'shadow of the future' hanging over their actions, to give them a sense that what they say, do or feel today will have a strong or binding effect on their longer-term relationships. The precariat knows there is no shadow of the future, as there is no future in what they are doing. To be 'out' tomorrow would come as no surprise, and to leave might not be bad, if another job or burst of activity beckoned.

The precariat lacks occupational identity, even if some have vocational qualifications and even if many have jobs with fancy titles. For some, there is a freedom in having no moral or behavioural commitments that would define an occupational identity. We will consider the image of the 'urban nomad' later, and the related one of 'denizen', the person who is not a full citizen. Just as some prefer to be nomadic, travellers not settlers, so not all those in the precariat should be regarded as victims. Nevertheless, most will be uncomfortable in their insecurity, without a reasonable prospect of escape.

Labour, work, play and leisure

The precariat's historical antecedents were the *banausoi* of ancient Greece, those required to do the productive labour in society (unlike slaves, who laboured only for their owners). The *banausoi*, regarded by their superiors as 'cramped in body' and 'vulgar in mind', had no opportunity to rise up the social scale. They worked alongside the *metics* (resident aliens), admitted craftsmen with limited rights. With the slaves, these two groups did all the labour, without expectation that they could ever participate in the life of the *polis*.

The ancient Greeks understood better than our modern policy makers the distinctions between work and labour and between play and leisure, or what they called *schole*. Those who did labour were non-citizens. Citizens did not do labour; they indulged in *praxis*, work in and around the home, with family and friends. It was 'reproductive' activity, work done for its own sake, to strengthen personal relationships, to be combined with public participation in the life of the community. Their society was inequitable by our standards, particularly in the treatment of women. But they understood why it was ridiculous to measure everything in terms of labour.

A contention in this book is that a primary objective in overcoming the 'downside' of the precariat as the twenty-first century advances should be to rescue work that is not labour and leisure that is not play. Throughout the twentieth century, the emphasis was on maximising the number of people doing labour, while denigrating or ignoring work that was not labour. The precariat is expected to do labour, as and when required, in conditions largely not of its own choosing. And it is expected to indulge in a lot of play. As argued in Chapter 5, it is also expected to do much unremunerated work-for-labour. But its leisure is regarded as incidental.

Varieties of precariat

However one defines it, the precariat is far from being homogeneous. The teenager who flits in and out of the internet café while surviving on fleeting jobs is not the same as the migrant who uses his wits to survive, networking feverishly while worrying about the police. Neither is similar to the single mother fretting where the money for next week's food bill is coming from or the man in his 60s who takes casual jobs to help pay medical bills. But they all share a sense that their labour is instrumental (to live), opportunistic (taking what comes) and precarious (insecure).

One way of depicting the precariat is as 'denizens'. A denizen is someone who, for one reason or another, has a more limited range of rights than citizens do. The idea of the denizen, which can be traced back to Roman times, has usually been applied to foreigners given residency rights and rights to ply their trade, but not full citizenship rights.

The idea can be extended by thinking of the range of rights to which people are entitled – civil (equality before the law and right to protection against crime and physical harm), cultural (equal access to enjoyment of culture and entitlement to participate in the cultural life of the community), social (equal access to forms of social protection, including pensions and health care), economic (equal entitlement to undertake income-earning activity) and political (equal right to vote, stand for elections and participate in the political life of the community). A growing number of people around the world lack at least one of these rights, and as such belong to the 'denizenry' rather than the citizenry, wherever they are living.

The concept could also be extended to corporate life, with corporate citizens and denizens of various types. The salariat can be seen as citizens with at least implicit voting rights in the firm, covering a range of decisions and practices that the other group of citizens, the shareholders and owners, implicitly accept while having their own explicit voting rights on the strategic decisions in the firm. The rest of those connected to corporations – the temps, casuals, dependent contractors and so on – are denizens, with few entitlements or rights.

In the wider world, most denizens are migrants of one kind or another, and they will be considered later. However, one other category stands out – the large layer of people who have been criminalised, the convicted. The globalisation era has seen a growth in the number of actions deemed to be criminal. More people are arrested and more are incarcerated than ever before, resulting in more people being criminalised than ever before. Part of the expansion of criminalisation is due to petty crime, including behavioural reactions to social assistance schemes that create immoral hazards, situations in which deprived people risk penalising themselves if they tell the truth and thus fall foul of some bureaucratic rule.

Temporary career-less workers, migrant denizens, criminalised strugglers, welfare claimants ... the numbers mount up. Unfortunately, labour and economic statistics are not presented in a way that could allow us to estimate the total number of people in the precariat, let alone the number in the varieties that make up its ranks. We have to build a picture on the basis of proxy variables. Let us consider the main groups that make up the precariat, bearing in mind that not all of them fit neatly; the identifying characteristic is not necessarily sufficient to indicate that a person is in the precariat.

For a start, most who find themselves in temporary jobs are close to being in the precariat because they have tenuous relations of production, low incomes compared with others doing similar work and low opportunity in occupational terms. The number with a temporary tag to their job has grown enormously in the flexible labour market era. In a few countries, such as the United Kingdom, restrictive definitions of what constitutes temporary work have made it hard to identify the number in jobs without employment protection.

But in most countries, the statistics show that the number and share of national labour forces in temporary statuses have been rising sharply over the past three decades. They have grown rapidly in Japan, where by 2010 over a third of the labour force was in temporary jobs, but the proportion may be highest in South Korea, where on reasonable definitions more than half of all workers are in temporary 'non-regular' jobs.

While being in a temporary job is an indication of a person being in a career-less job, that is not always the case. Indeed, those we are calling proficians exult in a project-oriented existence in which they move from one short-term project to another. And long-term jobs in which someone must do the same few tasks over and over again are hardly aspirational. Having a temporary job is fine if the social context is satisfactory. But if the global economic system requires a lot of people to have temporary jobs, then policy makers should address what makes them precarious.

Currently, having a temporary job is a strong indicator of a kind of precariousness. For some it may be a stepping stone to the construction of a career. But for many it may be a stepping stone *down* into a lower income status. Taking a temporary job after a spell of unemployment, as urged by many policy makers, can result in lower earnings for years ahead (Autor and Houseman, 2010). Once a person enters a lower rung job, the probability of upward social mobility or of gaining a 'decent' income is permanently reduced. Taking a casual job may be a necessity for many, but it is unlikely to promote social mobility.

Another avenue into the precariat is part-time employment, a tricky euphemism that has become a feature of our tertiary economy, unlike industrial societies. In most countries, part-time is defined as being employed or remunerated for less than 30 hours a week. It would be more accurate to refer to *so-called* part-timers, since many who choose or are obliged to take a part-time job find that they have to work more than anticipated and more than they are being paid for. Part-timers, often women, who step off a career ladder, may end up more exploited, having to do much uncompensated work-for-labour outside their paid hours, and more self-exploited, having to do extra work in order to retain a niche of some sort.

The growth in part-time jobs has helped conceal the extent of unemployment and underemployment. Thus, in Germany, shifting more people into 'mini-jobs' has maintained the illusion of high employment and led some economists to make foolish claims about a German employment miracle after the financial crash.

Other categories overlapping with the precariat are 'independent contractors' and 'dependent contractors'. There is no equivalence with the precariat here, since many contractors are secure in some respects and have a strong occupational identity. One thinks of the self-employed dentist or accountant. But differentiating dependent from independent contractors has caused headaches for labour lawyers everywhere. There have been interminable debates over how to distinguish between those who provide services and those who provide service labour, and between those dependent on some intermediary and those who are concealed employees. Ultimately, distinctions are arbitrary, hinging on notions of control, subordination and dependence on other 'parties'. Nevertheless, those who are dependent on others for allocating them to tasks over which they have little control are at greater risk of falling into the precariat.

Another group linked to the precariat is the growing army in call centres. These are ubiquitous, a sinister symbol of globalisation, electronic life and alienated labour. In 2008, the United Kingdom's Channel 4 presented a television documentary called 'Phone Rage', highlighting the mutual misunderstandings between young call-centre staff and angry customers. According to the programme, on average, people in the United Kingdom spent a full day each year talking to call centres, and the amount of time was rising.

Then there are interns, a peculiarly modern phenomenon whereby recent graduates, current students or even pre-students work for a while for little or no pay, doing petty office jobs. Some French commentators have equated the precariat with interns, which is inaccurate but indicative of the unease with which the phenomenon is regarded.

Internships are potentially a vehicle for channelling youths into the precariat. Some governments have even launched intern programmes as a form of 'active' labour market policy designed to conceal unemployment. In reality, efforts to promote internships are often little more than costly, inefficient subsidy schemes. They have high administrative costs and use people to do little of lasting value, either to the organisations or the interns themselves, despite rhetoric about acclimatising people to organisational life and learning on the job. We will consider interns later.

In sum, one way of looking at the precariat is seeing how people come to be doing insecure forms of labour that are unlikely to assist them to build a desirable identity or a desirable career.

Precariatisation

Another way of looking at the precariat is in terms of process, the way in which people are 'precariatised'. This ungainly word is analogous to 'proletarianised', describing the forces leading to proletarianisation of workers in the nineteenth century. To be precariatised is to be subject to pressures and experiences that lead to a precariat existence, of living in the present, without a secure identity or sense of development achieved through work and lifestyle.

In this sense, part of the salariat is drifting into the precariat. The case of Japan's legendary 'salaryman' is illustrative. This twentieth-century worker, with lifetime employment in one enterprise, emerged through a highly paternalistic model of labourism that prevailed until the early 1980s. In Japan (and elsewhere), the gilded cage can easily become a leaden cage, with so much employment security that the outside becomes a zone of fear. This is what happened in Japan and in other East Asian countries that adopted a similar model. To fall out of the company or organisation became a visible sign of failure, a loss of face. In such circumstances, the pursuit of personal development easily gives way to a petty politics of deference to those higher in the internal hierarchy and of opportunistic scheming.

This was taken to its limit in Japan. The company became a fictitious family so that the employment relationship became 'kintractship', in which the employer 'adopted' the employee and in return expected something close to a gift relationship of subservience, filial duty and decades of intensified labour. The result was a culture of service overtime and the ultimate sacrifice of *karoshi*, death from overwork

(Mouer and Kawanishi, 2005). But since the early 1980s, the share of the Japanese labour force in the salariat has shrunk dramatically. Those still clinging on are under pressure, many being replaced by younger workers and by women with none of their employment security. The precariat is displacing salaryman, whose pain is revealed by an alarming rise in suicides and social illnesses.

The Japanese transformation of salaryman may be an extreme case. But one can see how someone psychologically trapped in long-term employment loses control and drifts closer to a form of precarious dependency. If the 'parent' becomes displeased, or is unable or unwilling to continue the fictive parental role, the person will be plunged into the precariat, without the skills of autonomy and developmental prowess. Long-term employment can *deskill*. As elaborated elsewhere (Standing, 2009), this was one of the worst aspects of the era of labourism.

Although one must beware of stretching the definition too far, another feature of precariatisation is what should be called fictitious occupational mobility, epitomised by the postmodernist phenomenon of 'uptitling', elegantly satirised by *The Economist* (2010a). Someone in a static, going-nowhere job is given a high-sounding epithet to conceal precariat tendencies. People are made into 'chief' or 'executive' or 'officer' without having an army to lead or a team to forge. The US occupational body, characteristically giving itself the inflated title of the International Association of Administrative Professionals (having been the more modest National Secretaries Association), reported that it had over 500 job titles in its network, including 'front-office coordinator', 'electronic document specialist', 'media distribution officer' (paper boy/girl), 'recycling officer' (bin emptier) and 'sanitation consultant' (lavatory cleaner). The United States does not have a monopoly on titling ingenuity; it is happening everywhere. The French now tend to call cleaning ladies the more prestigious *techniciennes de surface*.

The Economist attributed the proliferation of job titles to the post-2008 recession, inducing a substitution of new fancy titles for wage rises, and to the increasing internal complexity of multinational corporations. But this is not just a recent outbreak of hyperbole. It reflects the growth of the precariat, in which fictitious symbols of occupational mobility and personal development have to cover up for a sterility of work. Flattened job structures are concealed by title inflation. *The Economist* put it nicely:

> The cult of flexibility is also inflationary. The fashion for flattening hierarchies has had the paradoxical effect of multiplying meaningless job titles. Workers crave important sounding titles, much as superannuated politicians are made Chancellor of the Duchy of Lancaster or Lord President of the Council. Everybody, from the executive suite downward, wants to fluff up their resumé as a hedge against being sacked.

This points to a deeper malaise. *The Economist* concluded its perceptive review by noting, 'The benefits of giving people a fancy new title are usually short-lived. The harm is long-lasting'. It felt that the practice induced cynicism and that fancy titles can make the possessors more expendable. It is surely just as much the other way round. It is because people are in expendable posts that the titles they are given might as well demonstrate it.

The precariatised mind

One does not have to be a technological determinist to appreciate that technological landscapes shape the way we think and behave. The precariat shows itself as not yet a class-for-itself partly because those in it are unable to control the technological forces they face. There is growing evidence that the electronic gadgetry that permeates every aspect of our lives is having a profound impact on the human *brain*, on the way we think and, more alarmingly still, on our capacity to think. It is doing so in ways that are consistent with the idea of the precariat.

The precariat is defined by short-termism, which could evolve into a mass incapacity to think long term, induced by the low probability of personal progress or building a career. Peer groups may accentuate this by threatening to ostracise those who do not conform to the behavioural norms. Unwritten rules on what is done and not done impose heavy costs on the nonconformist.

The internet, the browsing habit, text messaging, Facebook, Twitter and other social media are all operating to rewire the brain (Carr, 2010). This digital living is damaging the long-term memory consolidation process that is the basis for what generations of humans have come to regard as intelligence, the capacity to reason through complex processes and to create new ideas and ways of imagining.

The digitised world has no respect for contemplation or reflection; it delivers instant stimulation and gratification, forcing the brain to give most attention to short-term decisions and reactions. Although this has certain advantages, a casualty is the 'literate mind' and the idea of individuality. There is a move away from a society made up of individuals with distinctive combinations of knowledge, experience and learning to one in which most people have socially constructed, rapidly acquired views that are superficial and veer towards group approval rather than originality and creativity. Fancy terms abound, such as 'continuous partial attention' and 'cognitive deficits'.

This may seem exaggerated. But it is becoming harder to deny that mental, emotional and behavioural changes are taking place and that this is consistent with the spread of precariatisation. The literate mind – with its respect for the deliberative potential of 'boredom', of time standing still, for reflective contemplation and a systematic linking of the past, present and an imagined future – is under threat from the constant bombardment of electronically prompted adrenalin rushes.

The ability to focus has to be learned and can equally be lost or distorted. Some evolutionary biologists claim that electronic devices are returning the human to its primitive state, of being wired to respond instinctively and rapidly to signals of danger and opportunity, whereas the scholarly mind was actually the historical aberration. This interpretation of a biological regression is surely depressing, with enormous evolutionary implications.

The electronic environment permits and encourages multitasking, a feature of the tertiary society that will be considered later. Research has shown that those who, from habit, inclination or necessity, indulge in extensive multitasking dissipate energies and are less productive on any specific task than those who do much less of it. The multitaskers are prime candidates for the precariat, since they have more trouble in focusing and more difficulty in shutting out irrelevant or distracting information (Richtel, 2010). Unable to control their use of time, they suffer from stress, which corrodes the capacity to maintain a developmental mind, that sense of reflective learning with a longer-term perspective.

In sum, the precariat suffers from information overload without a lifestyle that could give them the control and capacity to sift the useful from the useless. We will see how the neo-liberal state is dealing with this later.

Anger, anomie, anxiety and alienation

The precariat experiences the four A's – anger, anomie, anxiety and alienation. The anger stems from frustration at the seemingly blocked avenues for advancing a meaningful life and from a sense of relative deprivation. Some would call that envy, but to be surrounded and constantly bombarded with the trappings of material success and the celebrity culture is bound to induce seething resentment. The precariat feels frustrated not only because a lifetime of flexi-jobs beckons, with all the insecurities that come with them, but also because those jobs involve no construction of trusting relationships built up in meaningful structures or networks. The precariat also has no ladders of mobility to climb, leaving people hovering between deeper self-exploitation and disengagement.

One example, cited in *The Observer* (Reeves, 2010), is a 24-year-old woman social worker, earning £28,000 a year and working a 37.5-hour week, in theory. She was doing 'quite a few late nights' because some families could not be visited in the daytime, spending more

time working on her own and doing more work from home. She told
the paper:

> My great frustration is that I've been told for a long while I'm good
> enough to progress to the next level, and I've taken on tasks beyond
> my job role, but there's no recognition of that. I just have to wait
> until a post becomes available. I think that happens to quite a few
> people. From the team I started with, I'm the only social worker
> left. And a lot of them have left due to issues of career support
> and progression. We do a tough, responsible job and if that was
> recognised it might keep us in the job longer.

This woman is linked to the precariat by lack of progression and her
appreciation of it. She was self-exploiting in the hope of mobility,
doing more work-for-labour. Her fleeing colleagues had realised that
the mirage of promotion was just that.

Ever since at least the work of Emile Durkheim, we have understood
that anomie is a feeling of passivity born of despair. This is surely
intensified by the prospect of artless, career-less jobs. Anomie comes
from a listlessness associated with sustained defeat, compounded by
the condemnation lobbed at many in the precariat by politicians and
middle-class commentators castigating them as lazy, directionless,
undeserving, socially irresponsible or worse. For welfare claimants to
be told that 'talking therapies' are the way forward is patronising and
easily seen as such by those exhorted to opt for them.

The precariat lives with anxiety – chronic insecurity associated
not only with teetering on the edge, knowing that one mistake or
one piece of bad luck could tip the balance between modest dignity
and being a bag lady, but also with a fear of losing what they possess

even while feeling cheated by not having more. People are insecure in the mind and stressed, at the same time 'underemployed' and 'overemployed'. They are alienated from their labour and work, and are anomic, uncertain and desperate in their behaviour. People who fear losing what they have are constantly frustrated. They will be angry but usually passively so. The precariatised mind is fed by fear and is motivated by fear.

Alienation arises from knowing that what one is doing is not for one's own purpose or for what one could respect or appreciate; it is simply done for others, at their behest. This has been regarded as a defining feature of the proletariat. But those in the precariat experience several special injections, including a feeling of being fooled – told they should be grateful and 'happy' that they are in jobs and should be 'positive'. They are told to be happy and cannot see why. They experience what Bryceson (2010) has called 'failed occupationality', which can only have an adverse psychological effect. People in such circumstances are likely to experience social disapproval and a profound lack of purpose. And lack of occupation creates an ethical vacuum.

The precariat is not fooled. They face a barrage of exhortations. But does the intelligent mind succumb so easily? In *Smile or Die*, Barbara Ehrenreich (2009) attacked the modern cult of positive thinking. She recalled how in the United States in the 1860s two quacks (Phineas Quimby and Mary Eddy) set up the New Thought Movement, based on Calvinism and the view that belief in God and positive thinking would lead to positive outcomes in life. Ehrenreich traced this through into modern business and finance. She described how motivational conferences had speakers telling short-term contract workers who had been made redundant to be good team players, defined as 'a positive person' who 'smiles frequently, does not complain and gratefully submits to whatever the boss demands'. One could go further and wonder if some do not adopt the old Chinese adage: 'Bow so low that the Emperor does not see you smile'. But grating of teeth is more likely to be the response to the alienating twaddle that the precariat has to put up with.

There are other reactions apart from repressed rage. For instance, the precariat may fall into a corrosive zone of deception and illusion, illustrated by a South Korean interviewed by the *International Herald Tribune* (Fackler, 2009). The reporter noted,

> With his clean, white university sweatshirt and shiny cell phone, Lee Changshik looks the part of a manager at a condominium development company, the job that he held until the financial panic last year – and the job that he tells his friends and family he still holds.

Carefully not telling anybody, he had gone to labour on a crab boat. 'I definitely don't put crab fisherman on my resume', said Mr Lee. 'This work hurts my pride'. He added that in phone conversations he avoided talking about his job and avoided meeting friends or relatives in case this came up. Another man working on the crab boats said he did not tell his wife; another told his wife that he was away in Japan rather than admit what he was doing. Such tales of status decline are familiar enough. It is the feeling that they are endemic, a structural feature of the modern labour market, that should cause alarm.

Those in the precariat lack self-esteem and social worth in their work; they must look elsewhere for that esteem, successfully or otherwise. If they succeed, the disutility of the labour they are required to do in their ephemeral unwelcome jobs may be lessened, as status frustration will be lessened. But the ability to find sustainable self-esteem in the precariat is surely deflated. There is a danger of feeling a sense of constant engagement but of being isolated amidst a lonely crowd.

Part of the problem is that the precariat experiences few trusting relationships, particularly through work. Throughout history, trust has evolved in long-term communities that have constructed institutional frameworks of fraternity. If one experiences confusion from not knowing one's station in life, trust becomes contingent and fragile (Kohn, 2008). If human beings have a predisposition to trust and to cooperate, as social psychologists surmise, then an environment of infinite flexibility and insecurity must jeopardise any sense of cooperation or moral consensus (Haidt, 2006; Hauser, 2006). We do what we can get away with, acting opportunistically, always on the edge of being amoral. This is easier to rationalise when every day we hear of the elite and celebrities breaking moral codes with impunity and when there is no shadow of the future in our dealings.

In a flexible labour market, individuals fear making or being locked into long-term behavioural commitments, since they may involve costs and actions that could not be subject to desirable reciprocities. The young will not wish to be tied by economic commitments to their parents if they fear they might have to support them long into old age, with a shrinking state and increasing longevity raising the prospective costs of doing so. The withering of an inter-generational bargain is matched by more contingent sexual and friendship relationships.

Stability builds stability

If everything is commodified – valued in terms of costs and financial rewards – moral reciprocities become fragile. If the state removes labourist forms of social insurance that created a substantive, if inequitable, social solidarity system, without putting anything comparable in its place, then there is no mechanism to create alternative forms of solidarity. To build one, there must be a sense of stability and predictability. The precariat lacks both. It is subject to chronic uncertainty. Social insurance thrives when there is a roughly equal probability of upward and downward mobility, of making gains and making losses. In a society in which the precariat is growing, and in which social mobility is limited and declining, social insurance cannot flourish.

This highlights a feature of the precariat at the moment. It has yet to solidify as a class-for-itself. One may depict a process of 'falling' into the precariat or of being dragged into a precariatised existence. People are not born in it and are unlikely to identify themselves as members with a glow of pride. Fear, yes; anger, probably; sardonic humour, perhaps; but not pride. This is a contrast with the traditional industrial working class. It took time to become a class-for-itself but, when it did, it engendered a robust pride and dignity that helped make it a political force with a class agenda. The precariat is not yet at that stage, even if a few in its ranks display a defiant pride, in their parades, blogs and comradely interactions.

A good society needs people to have empathy, a capacity to project oneself into another's situation. Feelings of empathy and competition are in constant tension. People in incipient competition conceal from others knowledge, information, contacts and resources, in case revealing them would take away a competitive edge. Fear of failure, or of being able to achieve only a limited status, easily leads to disavowal of empathy.

What induces empathy? It may arise from a shared sense of alienation or insecurity, or even shared poverty. Evolutionary biologists generally agree that empathy is more likely within small stable communities, in which people know each other and engage with each other on a regular basis (see, e.g., De Waal, 2005). For many centuries, occupational communities fostered empathy, with apprenticeship being a primary mechanism for building up an appreciation of reciprocity, bolstered by guild rules of self-regulation. Everywhere that model has been eroded by globalisation, even in Africa (Bryceson, 2010). The precariat has a feeling of being in a diffuse, unstable international community of people struggling, usually in vain, to give their working lives an occupational identity.

Once jobs become flexible and instrumental, with wages insufficient for a socially respectable subsistence and a dignifying lifestyle, there is no 'professionalism' that goes with belonging to a community with standards, ethical codes and mutual respect among its members based on competence and respect for long-established norms of behaviour. Those in the precariat cannot be professionalised because they cannot specialise and they cannot construct a steady improvement in depth of competence or experience. They face uncertainty of returns to any specific form of work and have little prospect of 'upward' social mobility.

The precariat has a weakened sense of 'social memory'. It is part of humanity to define ourselves by what we do and to do what we are. The social memory arises from belonging to a community reproduced over generations. At best it provides a code of ethics and a sense of meaning and stability, emotional and social. There are deeply rooted class and occupational dimensions to this. It extends to what we aspire to be. There are socially constructed barriers to aspiration. For instance, in most societies a working-class child would be laughed at for aspiring to be a banker or lawyer; a middle-class child would be frowned on for aspiring to be a plumber or a hairdresser. You do not do what you are not. We all define ourselves by what we are not, as much as by what we are, by what we could not be, as much as by what we could be. The precariat does not exist by itself. It is also defined by what it is not.

Policies promoting labour flexibility erode processes of relational and peer-group interaction that are vital for reproducing skills and constructive attitudes to work. If you expect to change what you are doing at almost any time, to change 'employer' at short notice, to change colleagues, and above all to change what you call yourself, work ethics become constantly contestable and opportunistic.

Observers such as Haidt (2006) argue that work ethics can only be imposed and enforced from within society. This is expecting too much. Ethics stem from smaller, more identifiable communities, such as an occupational group, kinship group or social class. The flexibility regime implicitly rejects work ethics ground out by strong occupational communities.

A Gallup survey in Germany in 2009 found that only 13 per cent of all employed felt committed to their job, with 20 per cent of employees being resolutely disengaged (Nink, 2009). Given all those exhortations to be flexible and mobile, to go for jobs as the source of happiness, it is surely healthy to be disengaged, particularly in uncertain times. But given the significance of work in our lives, that is surely not good enough.

In sum, the mix of rising anger, anomie, anxiety and a
comprises the inevitable flip side of a society that has made 'fle
and insecurity cornerstones of the economic system.

Concluding remarks

Although we cannot give anything like precise figures, we may guess that at present, in many countries, at least a quarter of the adult population is in the precariat. This is not just a matter of having insecure employment, of being in jobs of limited duration and with minimal labour protection, although all this is widespread. It is being in a status that offers no sense of career, no sense of secure occupational identity and few, if any, entitlements to the state and enterprise benefits that several generations of those who saw themselves as belonging to the industrial proletariat or the salariat had come to expect as their due.

This is the reality of a system that waxes lyrical about and fosters a way of living based on competitiveness, meritocracy and flexibility. Human society has not been built over the centuries on permanent incessant change; it has been based on the slow construction of stable identities and rather 'rigid' spheres of security. The gospel of flexibility tells people that the enemy of flexibility is rigidity. A lesson of the Enlightenment is that the human being should be in control of his or her destiny, not God or natural forces. The precariat is told that it must answer to market forces and be infinitely adaptable.

The outcome is a growing mass of people – potentially all of us outside the elite, anchored in their wealth and detachment from society – in situations that can only be described as alienated, anomic, anxious and prone to anger. The warning sign is political disengagement.

Why should those who do not think they are part of it care about the growth of the precariat? There is the altruistic reason, which is that we would not wish to be there ourselves and therefore would wish better for those facing such an existence. But there are other reasons too. Many of us fear falling into the precariat or fear that our family and friends will do so. The elite and the smugger parts of the salariat and proficians may think that, in a world of diminished social mobility, they themselves will remain comfortable and immune. But they might be alarmed by the thought that the precariat is an emerging dangerous class. A group that sees no future of security or identity will feel fear and frustration that could lead to it lashing out at identifiable or imagined causes of its lot. And detachment from the mainstream of economic affluence and progress is conducive to intolerance.

The precariat is not a class-for-itself, partly because it is at war with itself. One group in it may blame another for its vulnerability and indignity. A temporary low-wage worker may be induced to see the 'welfare scrounger' as obtaining more, unfairly and at his or her expense. A long-term resident of a low-income urban area will easily be led to see incoming migrants as taking better jobs and leaping to head the queue for benefits. Tensions within the precariat are setting people against each other, preventing them from recognising that the social and economic structure is producing their common set of vulnerabilities. Many will be attracted by populist politicians and neo-fascist messages, a development already clearly visible across Europe, the United States and elsewhere. This is why the precariat is the dangerous class and why a 'politics of paradise' is needed that responds to its fears, insecurities and aspirations.

2

Why the precariat is growing

To understand why the precariat is growing one must appreciate the nature of the Global Transformation. The globalisation era (1975–2008) was a period when the economy was 'disembedded' from society as financiers and neo-liberal economists sought to create a global market economy based on competitiveness and individualism.

The precariat has grown because of the policies and institutional changes in that period. Early on, the commitment to an open market economy ushered in competitive pressures on industrialised countries from newly industrialising countries (NICs) and 'Chindia' with an unlimited supply of low-cost labour. The commitment to market principles led inexorably towards a global production system of network enterprises and flexible labour practices.

The objective of economic growth – making us all richer, it was said – was used to justify rolling back fiscal policy as an instrument of progressive redistribution. High direct taxes, long used to reduce inequality and to provide economic security for low earners, were presented as disincentives to labour, save and invest, and as driving investment and jobs abroad. And a reorientation of social protection from social solidarity to dealing with poverty and with people deemed social failures ushered in a trend to means-tested social assistance and from that to 'workfare'.

A central aspect of globalisation can be summed up in one intimidating word, 'commodification'. This involves treating everything as a commodity, to be bought and sold, subject to market forces, with prices set by demand and supply, without effective 'agency' (a capacity to resist). Commodification has been extended to every aspect of life – the family, education system, firm, labour institutions, social protection policy, unemployment, disability, occupational communities and politics.

In the drive for market efficiency, barriers to commodification were dismantled. A neo-liberal principle was that regulations were required to prevent collective interests from acting as barriers to competition. The globalisation era was not one of *de-regulation* but of *re-regulation*, in which more regulations were introduced than in any comparable period of history. In the world's labour markets, most new regulations were directive, telling people what they could and could not do, and what they had to do to be beneficiaries of state policy.

The attack on collective institutions encompassed firms as social institutions, trades unions as representatives of employees, occupational communities as guilds of crafts and professions, education as a force for liberation from self-interest and commercialism, the family as an institution of reciprocity and social reproduction, and the civil service as guided by an ethics of public service.

This concoction splintered labour arrangements and created a class fragmentation, made more striking by the 'tertiarisation' of work and labour associated with a decline in manufacturing and a drift to services. This chapter fleshes out this picture, not exhaustively but in enough detail to appreciate why the precariat is becoming a global class.

The global transformation

Since the 1970s, the world economy has become integrated, to the extent that developments in one part of the world almost instantly affect what happens elsewhere. In the 1970s, movements on one stock exchange were matched by similar movements in others only in a minority of cases; today, they move in tandem. In the 1970s, trade was a small part of national income in many countries and took place mainly in complementary goods; today it involves goods and services flowing in all directions with an increasing share consisting of parts of goods and services, much within multinationals' own networks. Relative labour costs have become a much greater part of the trading process.

Capital and associated employment are flowing from Organisation for Economic Co-operation and Development (OECD) countries to emerging market economies. This will continue. Capital per person in China, India, Indonesia and Thailand is three per cent of that in the United States. Productivity in these economies will rise for many years simply by the construction of more machines and infrastructure. Meanwhile, industrialised countries will become *rentier* economies, in which average real wages will not rise or be a means of reducing inequality.

The emerging market economies will continue to be a primary factor in the growth of the precariat. There will be no reversal of this aspect of globalisation. It is folly for those worried about inequality and economic insecurity in today's rich countries to imagine that an effective response to the financial shock of 2008 and the subsequent economic crisis would be to retreat into protectionism. Regrettably, however, as we shall see, governments have reacted in ways that have merely intensified the insecurities and inequalities that underpinned the crisis.

The emergence of Chindia

Globalisation marked the emergence of what we may call 'Chindia', which has profoundly changed social and economic life everywhere. The combination of China and India is not quite right; they are countries with different cultures and structures. However, for our purposes, Chindia makes a convenient short-form metaphor.

Before globalisation, the labour markets of economies open to trade and investment had about 1 billion workers and job seekers (Freeman, 2005). By 2000, the labour force of those countries had risen to 1.5 billion. Meanwhile, China, India and the ex-Soviet bloc had entered the global economy, adding 1.5 billion. So the labour supply in the globalising economies trebled. The newcomers came with little capital and with very low wages, altering the world's capital-labour ratio and weakening the bargaining position of workers outside Chindia. Since 2000, other emerging market countries have added to the supply, including Vietnam, Indonesia, Cambodia and Thailand, with Bangladesh and others entering the picture. A new term has become popular, 'China Plus One', implying that multinationals will hedge their strategy by having plants in at least one other country as well as China. Vietnam, with 86 million people, is a leading candidate, with real wages that have stayed constant for two decades. In 2010, a textile worker there earned US$100 per month, a tiny fraction of wages in the United States or Germany, for example.

Symbolising the speed of change, for 40 years Japan was the world's second largest economy after the United States, and in 2005, in dollar terms, China's gross domestic product (GDP) was still half as big as Japan's. In 2010, China overtook Japan and was closing on the United States. India is racing up behind, growing prodigiously year on year.

China's growth has been led by state investment, notably in infrastructure, and by foreign direct investment. Multinationals have rushed in, using surrogates from around China. They have herded hundreds of thousands of workers into hastily built industrial parks, housing them in dormitory compounds, forcing them to work so intensively that most leave within three years. They might fit the image of an industrial proletariat, but they are treated as a disposable itinerant labour force. Pressure to raise wages has grown. But they are so low that they will long remain a small fraction of wages in rich industrialised countries, as will unit labour costs, especially as productivity is rising sharply.

China has contributed to global income inequality in several ways. Its low wages have put downward pressure on wages in the rest of the world and widened wage differentials. It has kept its own wages remarkably low. As growth accelerated, the share of wages in national income fell for 22 consecutive years, falling from a low 57 per cent of GDP in 1983 to just 37 per cent in 2005. This makes China the most 'capitalistic' large economy in history.

Foxconn, the world's largest contract manufacturer, epitomises the connivance of multinationals in the abuses in the industrial parks that have sprung up in China. A subsidiary of Taiwan's Hon Hai Precision Industry Company, it employs 900,000 people in China. Half are in 'Foxconn City' in Shenzhen, with its fifteen-storey manufacturing buildings, each dedicated to one customer, such as Apple, Dell, HP, Nintendo and Sony. Foxconn City expanded by using a strategy of hiring rural-urban migrants for pitifully low wages, expecting labour turnover of 30–40 per cent a year as successive cohorts burnt themselves out.

Its working arrangements helped increase the global precariat. The low wages and labour intensity (including 36 hours of overtime a month), belatedly brought to the world's attention by a spate of suicides and attempted suicides in 2009 and 2010, forced firms elsewhere to try to compete by cutting wages and opting for flexible labour.

Those suicides had an effect. Following adverse publicity and unofficial strikes, Foxconn raised wages. But one outcome will be cuts in free lodging and food as well as in the extensive recreation facilities. The immediate reaction of Foxconn to the suicides was paternalistic. It surrounded its buildings with nets to catch people if they jumped, hired counsellors for distressed workers, brought in Buddhist monks to calm them and considered asking employees to sign 'no suicide' pledge notes. Silicon Valley celebrities in California expressed concern. But they had no reason for surprise. They had made billions of dollars from the ridiculously low-cost products.

Foxconn is a metaphor for globalisation. It will change its model, raising wages in its primary zone, cutting enterprise benefits, moving more production to lower cost areas and shifting to more precarious employees. The great engine of outsourcing will outsource itself. However, Foxconn and the Chinese development model have accelerated changes in the rest of the world to a structure in which the precariat will become the centre of attention.

Commodification of the firm

An aspect of globalisation that has attracted less attention but which has contributed to the growth of the precariat is the way companies themselves have become commodities, to be bought and sold through mergers and acquisitions. Although long part of capitalism, these used to be quite rare. The frenzy with which firms are now traded, split up and repackaged is a feature of global capitalism. And corporations are increasingly owned by foreign shareholders, led by pension and private equity funds.

The commodification of companies means that commitments made by today's owners are not worth as much as they used to be. The owners could be out tomorrow, along with their management teams and the nods-and-handshakes that make up informal bargains about how labour is done, how payments should be honoured and how people are treated in moments of need.

In 1937, Ronald Coase set out a theory that was to earn him a Nobel Prize in Economics. He argued that firms, with their hierarchies, were superior to atomised markets made up solely of individuals; they reduced the transaction costs of doing business, one reason being that they fostered long-term relationships based on trust. This reasoning has collapsed. Now that opportunistic buyers can amass vast funds and take over even well-run companies, there is less incentive to form trust relationships inside firms. Everything becomes contingent and open to re-negotiation.

For years academic journals were full of articles on national 'varieties of capitalism'. These are fusing into one global hybrid, closer to the Anglo-Saxon shareholder model than to the German stakeholder model, as Japan's example illustrates. The 'Japanese miracle' in the 1960s and 1970s was based on the firm as a social institution, with rigid hierarchies, lifetime employment, seniority-based wages and company unions. This was suited to a country entering the world economy from a low-income base. But the model's rigidities hindered its adaptability in the globalisation era.

Eventually, the government rewrote corporate law to move towards the US model, enabling firms to introduce performance-related wages, share options, outside directors, promotions based on competence rather than age, pursuit of shareholder value and the hiring of salaried employees in mid-career. The firm was being commodified, orchestrated by financial capital and by owners – shareholders not managers. It was not fully Americanised, but the trend was clear.

The proportion of shares held by foreigners rose nearly sixfold between 1990 and 2007. Issuing shares became common, leaving firms open to takeover. Until the late 1990s, there were fewer than 500 mergers and acquisitions a year; in 2006, there were nearly 3,000. The change was due to a reform that allowed companies to use shares to buy other firms, while accounting reforms obliged firms to be more transparent. In 2007, a law allowed 'triangular mergers', enabling foreign companies to use shares to buy Japanese firms via subsidiaries.

The takeover threat led companies to curb lifetime employment, mainly through staff attrition without replacement by regular employees. The proportion of firms describing themselves as 'shareholder focused' rose to 40 per cent in 2007, while the share saying they were 'worker focused' fell to just 13 per cent.

Other countries have commodified the firm in similar ways, thereby making life more insecure for employees. Even those in the salariat can now find that overnight they have lost employment and other forms of security because their firm has been taken over or declared bankrupt prior to restructuring. For their part, as a partial defence, companies want more flexible labour forces so that they can respond quickly to external threats.

Commodification has also made the division of labour within enterprises more fluid. If activities can be done more cheaply in one location, they are 'offshored' (within firms) or 'outsourced' (to partner firms or others). This fragments the labour process; internal job structures and bureaucratic 'careers' are disrupted, due to uncertainty over whether jobs people might have expected to do will be offshored or outsourced.

The disruption feeds into the way skills are developed. The incentive to invest in skills is determined by the cost of acquiring them, the opportunity cost of doing so and the prospective additional income. If the risk increases of not having an opportunity to practise skills, investment in them will decline, as will the psychological commitment to the company. In short, if firms become more fluid, workers will be discouraged from trying to build careers inside them. This puts them close to being in the precariat.

The firm is becoming more portable than employees, in terms of its ability to switch activities. Many employees cannot relocate easily. They may have a partner earning an income, children locked into a school trajectory, elderly relatives to care for. This risks disrupting occupational careers, tending to push more into a precariat existence.

For a growing number of workers in the twenty-first century, it would be folly to regard a firm as a place for building a career and gaining income security. There would be nothing wrong with that, if social policy were adapted so that all those working for companies are able to have basic security. At present, that is far from being the case.

The sirens of labour flexibility: Labour re-commodification

The pursuit of flexible labour relations has been the major direct cause of the growth of the global precariat. How flexibility has grown globally has been considered elsewhere (Standing, 1999b). Here we will just highlight aspects accelerating the growth of the precariat by thinking of the main forms – numerical, functional and wage – of flexibility.

The flexibility drive is unfinished business, as is shown every time there is an economic dip, when commentators trot out the same call for more. It is a process of labour re-commodification, making the labour relationship more responsive to demand and supply, as measured by its price, the wage. This has meant eroding all seven forms of labour security identified in Chapter 1. Too many commentators concentrate on one aspect, the reduction of employment security by making it easier to fire employees, reducing the costs of dismissal and facilitating the use of casual and temporary employees. Although this is part of the process, diminishing employment security is used to increase other forms of flexibility.

Stable employees are more inclined to organise collectively, since they are more secure and confident in taking on their employers. Employment security goes with representation security. Similarly, being a citizen worker means feeling in control of one's occupational development. Without other forms of security employees have no skill security, since they fear being shifted around, instructed to do tasks outside their personal plans or aspirations.

The key point is that flexible labour relations are an imperative in the global labour process. We must understand what is entailed, not with an atavistic desire to reverse the changes but to identify what would be needed to make them tolerable.

Numerical flexibility

For three decades, making it easier to fire workers has been advocated as a way of boosting jobs. This, it is argued, will make potential employers more inclined to employ workers since it will be less costly to be rid of them. Weak employment security has been depicted by the International Monetary Fund (IMF), the World Bank and other influential bodies as necessary to attract and retain foreign capital.

Governments have accordingly competed with one another in weakening employment protection and have made it easier to employ workers with no such protection.

The dominant image of the precariat stems from numerical flexibility, through what were long called 'atypical' or 'non-standard' forms of labour. Mainstream companies are contracting out much of their labour, while preserving a small salariat (corporate citizens) whose loyalty they value and with whom they share a key asset – *knowledge*, the rent-seeking capacity of tertiary firms. If knowledge is shared too widely, companies lose control of the asset. The salariat are citizens with voting rights in their firms, consulted or taken into account in a range of decisions. These rights are implicitly accepted by the owners or major shareholders, who have voting rights on the strategic decisions of the enterprise or organisation.

A feature of flexibility is the growing use of temporary labour, which allows firms to change employment quickly, so that they can adapt and alter their division of labour. Temporary labour has cost advantages: wages are lower, experience-rated pay is avoided, entitlement to enterprise benefits is less and so on. And there is less risk; taking on somebody temporarily means not making a commitment that might be regretted, for whatever reason.

Where services predominate, labour tends to be project oriented rather than continuous. This brings more fluctuation in labour demand, making use of temporary labour almost necessary. There are also less tangible factors promoting its growth. People on temporary contracts can be induced to labour harder, especially if the jobs are more intense than regulars have been doing. Regulars may resent change. Those on temporary contracts can also be put in forms of underemployment more easily, paid less for fewer hours in down periods, for example. They can be controlled through fear more easily. If they do not put up with demands placed on them, they can be told to leave, with minimal fuss and cost.

Temporary workers are used to extract concessions from others, who are warned that they will be displaced if they do not adapt. For instance, chambermaids working for Hyatt Hotels in the United States, with contracts stipulating eight-hour days and regular routines, suddenly found they were working alongside agency temps pressurised to work 12-hour days and to clear more rooms (30 per shift). The regulars were being replaced.

The most striking example is the withering of Japan's salaryman model. Companies have put a freeze on hiring youths in lifetime positions and have turned to temporary contracts. Paid much less, the temporaries are denied training opportunities and benefits. Some factories even oblige workers to wear jumpsuits of different colours according to their employment status, a case of life imitating fiction, bringing to mind the alphas and epsilons of Aldous Huxley's *Brave New World*.

A simple reason for using more temporaries is that other firms are doing so, conferring a cost advantage. Competitiveness through use of temporary labour is increasingly important in the global system as companies seek to emulate what is done in other countries and by market leaders in their sector – a pattern known as 'the dominance effect'. Multinationals try to establish their employment model in places where they set up subsidiaries, usually edging out local practices. Thus McDonald's 'best practice' model involves deskilling, removal of long-serving employees, union busting, and lower wages and enterprise benefits. Others follow suit. Observers have highlighted the repertoires of labour practices on which managers can draw (Amoore, 2000; Sklair, 2002; Elger and Smith, 2006; Royle and Ortiz, 2009). Some use 'yellow unions' – set up and run by employers – to defeat independent unions. A global model is emerging in which corporate, technological and political factors influence the choice of tactics. To imagine sustained effective resistance is fanciful.

Another example is Walmart, the United States' largest and standard-setting retailer and the source of the fortunes of four of its richest ten people. It thrives on a sophisticated just-in-time process in which controlling labour costs through extreme labour flexibility has made it one of the most detested models in the world. Temporary labour is the essence of the system. Object to what goes on and you are out.

The shift to temporary labour is part of global capitalism. It has been accompanied by a growth of employment agencies and labour brokers, which have helped firms to shift faster to temporaries and to the contracting out of much of their labour. Temporary agencies are giants shaping the global labour process. Switzerland-based Adecco, with 700,000 people on its books, has become one of the world's biggest private employers. Pasona, a Japanese staffing agency set up in the 1970s, sends out a quarter of a million workers every day on short-term contracts. Pasona's founder says flexibility is beneficial for firms and workers, and dismisses the old norm of long-term employment as sentimental. 'Be a regular worker – and be exploited for the rest of your life', he told *The Economist* (2007). Like European and American agencies, Pasona has established dozens of subsidiaries dealing with outsourcing projects and production in Asian countries and the United States.

Traditionally, temporary agencies focused on clerical staff and menial jobs, such as cleaning and hospital auxiliaries. Then some hit on the lucrative sphere of 'welfare claimants'. They are now going increasingly into the professional arena, regarded as higher margin business. For instance, Adecco is shifting from 20 per cent professional, and 80 per cent clerical and blue-collar, to one-third professional.

The growth of temporary labour, multinational employment agencies and seedy labour brokers that figure in countries such as South Africa has been facilitated by legislative changes and has been legitimised by bodies such as the International Labour Organisation, which reversed its opposition to private employment agencies in the 1990s. In Japan, a 1999 law overturned a ban on temporary contracts and allowed private employment agencies in more areas; after 2004, they were allowed in manufacturing. These reforms undoubtedly contributed to the growth of the Japanese precariat. In Italy, the precariat was enlarged by the Treu law of 1997, which introduced temporary contracts, and by the 2003 Biagi law, which allowed private recruitment agencies. One country after another has acknowledged the pressure of globalisation in extending temporary labour.

It has accompanied what goes under the clumsy term of 'triangulation'. Labour law and collective bargaining were constructed on the basis of direct relationships between employers and employees. But who is responsible when a third party becomes an intermediary? Who is in control, the final employer or the intermediary? The blurring of boundaries of decision-making and responsibility adds to the precariousness. There is extensive case law to delight the minds of lawyers. But temporaries themselves know only that they report to two masters.

The situation is often murky. In Ontario, Canada, for instance, under a law governing temporary help agencies, when temps sign on they waive their rights to choose worksites and type of work, surrendering control over their 'labour power' and commodifying themselves, to the extent of paying the agency a fee for registering with it. This is a route to a second-class citizenship with truncated rights. A life in temping is a curtailment of control over time, as the temp must be on call; the time someone must put aside for labour exceeds the time in it.

So the trend towards temporary labour is strong. In some countries, notably the United Kingdom and the United States, very little employment is classified as temporary because short-term employees are not counted, even though they have no employment security and are temporary in all but name. Successive British governments extended the period during which employees have no security and reduced the employers' cost of ending contracts. It was casualisation by stealth. Elsewhere, in efforts to defend the 'standard employment relationship', unions, governments and employer bodies permitted temporaries alongside regular employees, creating dualistic labour forces.

The temporary share shows no sign of declining. On the contrary, the financial shock of 2008 and the recession that followed gave firms an excuse to rid themselves of 'permanent' employees and to welcome more temps. By 2010, temps in Japan accounted for over a third of the labour force and over a quarter of prime-age workers. In January 2009, 500 recently dismissed homeless workers set up a tent village in the centre of Tokyo. When politicians and TV crews congregated there, the city government reacted by finding them accommodation in unused public buildings. Although the gesture only lasted a week, it raised awareness of the precariat, underscoring the widespread lack of social protection. The image still held that families and companies looked after people, meaning the state did not need to do so. The stigma had persisted, so that an unemployed person could not easily ask for support. The incident heralded a societal shift of perceptions. The precariat was suddenly real.

In the United States, following the shock, firms resorted to a tactic that had figured after the 1991 collapse of the Soviet system, putting regular employees on 'contract status' to avoid fixed costs. In the Soviet case, millions of workers were put on 'unpaid leave', while firms retained their work history books. This gave the impression that employment was holding up, but it impoverished the workers, many of whom died. In the United States, the transfer of employees onto temporary contracts made them ineligible for health insurance, paid vacations and so on. It would be an exaggeration to say the United States was going down the Soviet route, but the tactics pushed workers into the precariat, resulting in much personal suffering.

Europe is also fostering temporary employment. In Germany, millions of workers have been added to the temporary category (*Zeiterbeit*). In the United Kingdom, the Labour government opposed and then delayed implementation of the EU Directive giving workers, hired through temporary agencies, rights equal to those of permanent staff, with the same pay, vacations and basic conditions. It wanted to keep the United Kingdom an attractive site for foreign investment. However, it confirmed the precarious status of all those with temporary contracts.

Spain meanwhile has become the epitome of a multi-tier labour market, with half of its workforce on temporary contracts. In 2010, the OECD estimated that 85 per cent of the jobs lost in Spain following the financial crash were temporary. It claimed permanent employees were being kept in jobs because it was costly to dismiss them. But the high costs of salaried staff had already induced the shift to temporaries as well as to outsourcing and employment of migrants. Government and trades unions had reacted to the earlier pressure for flexibility by preserving securities for regular workers and creating a buffer of temporaries. This not only led to a multi-tier labour force but resentment by the precariat towards the unions that had looked after their own members at its expense.

Another facet of numerical flexibility is the growth of part-time jobs. Reasons include the changing position of women and the shift to services. It is also partly involuntary. In the United States, the Bureau of Labour Statistics estimated in mid-2009 that over 30 million people were in part-time jobs 'of necessity', more than twice as many as the number counted as unemployed, which made for an adjusted unemployment rate of 18.7 per cent. A vast proportion of those jobs will remain part-time and low paid even if the economy picks up.

The term part-time can be misleading, since much of what is counted as part-time is anything but. As we shall discuss in Chapter 5, there are many ways by which firms pay people as part-timers but expect them to work more hours than are remunerated. As one woman told the *Wall Street Journal* (Maher, 2008), 'I have part-time status with full-time hours'. Many have to take two part-time jobs just to pay the bills or as insurance against loss of one of them.

Numerical flexibility has also been associated with outsourcing and offshoring. The financial shock accelerated the global drift to contract out labour, even as production and employment were shrinking. Managements became desperate to find ways of reducing costs. One way was to switch less urgent deliveries to shipping, which permitted more offshoring, previously limited by a need for expensive air transport. Companies also did more 'near-sourcing' and 'near-shoring'. Employment security in all of this is a mirage.

Finally, there are wheezes such as 'zero-hour contracts', whereby somebody is given a contract but left unsure how many hours, if any, they will be required to work or how much if anything they will be paid. Another wheeze is 'unpaid furloughs', a euphemism for lay-offs, sometimes for months at a time, sometimes as a regular weekly day off, unpaid. It is a lever of flexibility. Another wheeze is the use of interns. The number in this novel status has expanded since the shock. Governments have given subsidies and encouragement. Like furloughs, they do good things for the employment and unemployment counts; most of the costs are borne by interns and their families.

When all the intricacies of numerical flexibility are considered, the outcome is insecure working lives for a growing number near the precariat. Every year, about a third of employees in OECD countries leave their employer for one reason or another. In the United States, about 45 per cent leave their jobs each year. The image of long-term employment is misleading, even though a minority still have it. A third of the job turnover is accounted for by the creation and ending of firms.

In the 1960s, a typical worker entering the labour market of an industrialised country could have anticipated having four employers by the time he retired. In those circumstances, it made sense to identify with the firm in which he was employed. Today a worker would be foolish to do so. Now, a typical worker – more likely to be a woman – can anticipate having nine employers before reaching the age of 30. That is the extent of the change represented by numerical flexibility.

Functional flexibility and job insecurity

The essence of functional flexibility is to make it possible for firms to change the division of labour quickly without cost and to shift workers between tasks, positions and workplaces. With global competition, and an ongoing technological revolution, it is understandable why companies want this and why governments want to help. However, it has brought painful changes that have expanded the precariat. Whereas numerical flexibility generates employment insecurity, functional flexibility intensifies job insecurity.

A facilitating change came with the strengthening of managerial prerogative over work arrangements, the subject of struggle in the 1970s and 1980s, when employers wrested control from unions and professional bodies. In subjecting employees to more subordination, it marked an advance of 'proletarianisation' (Standing, 2009), but paradoxically it was necessary for 'precariatisation'. Establishing administrative control over the division of labour allowed managements to create flexible arrangements that included weaker lines of occupational progression.

As more enterprises became multinational, managements could switch jobs and functions between plants within their network and their supply chains. New terms came into the lexicon of management and labour analysis. Outsourcing became a catch-all for overlapping processes. Having control of the division of labour made it easier to *offshore* (shift employees or tasks to a plant in another country) and *inshore* (shift between plants within a country), and to switch between outsourcing and insourcing whenever advantageous.

A profit-maximising manager or an engineer might see this switchability as desirable. But consider the implications for the workers subject to it. Most never had control over building a career, so there should be no romanticising some golden age (Sennett, 1998; Uchitelle, 2006). But now, many more have no control at all. The strengthening of management prerogative means job insecurity is the new norm. How can people construct a career and build an occupational profile when they can be moved at short notice or when the next rungs on an occupational ladder are suddenly outsourced?

A related trend is the spread of individual contracts, as part of the 'contractualisation' of life. In industrial society, the norm was a collective contract, set by collective bargaining, perhaps extended to other firms in a sector. But as unions and collective bargaining have shrunk, individualised contracts have grown. For a brief time, fewer workers were covered by any contracts, but the trend to individual contracts is strengthening. They allow firms to provide different treatments, degrees of security and status, so as to channel some workers into the salariat, some into stable jobs, some into a precariat status, increasing divisions and hierarchies. Individualised contracts allow employers to tighten conditions to minimise the firm's uncertainty, enforced through the threat of penalties for breaking a contract.

Individual contracts have become more of a global trend since China enacted its Labour Law of 1994 and its Labour Contract Law of 2008, which entrenched fixed-term and open-term contracts. These will boost outsourcing and triangulation as firms learn to minimise the costs that come with contracts. As China is the world's most dynamic and largest labour market, these developments mark a move to a multi-layered global labour force in which privileged salariats will work alongside a growing precariat.

Individual contracts, casualisation and other forms of external flexibility come together in another clumsy term, 'tertiarisation'. This is more than is conveyed by 'the tertiary sector', which implies a shift to services. For decades the world's production and employment have been shifting to services. The popular term 'de-industrialisation' is misleading, since it implies an erosion and loss of capacity, whereas much of the change has been consistent with technological advances and the changing nature of production. Even in Germany, an export powerhouse, the share of manufacturing in output and employment has shrunk to under 20 per cent. In France, the United Kingdom and the United States, it is much lower.

Tertiarisation summarises a combination of forms of flexibility, in which divisions of labour are fluid, workplaces blend into home and public places, hours of labour fluctuate and people can combine several work statuses and have several contracts concurrently. It is ushering in a new system of control, focusing on people's use of time. One influential way of looking at it has been the Italian school, drawing on Marxism and Foucault (1977), which depicts the process as creating a 'social factory', with society an extension of the workplace (Hardt and Negri, 2000).

That image is not quite right. The factory is the symbol of industrial society, in which labour was defined in blocks of time, with mass production and mechanisms of direct control in fixed workplaces. This is unlike today's tertiary system. The flexibility involves more work-for-labour; a blurring of workplaces, home places and public places; and a shift from direct control to diverse forms of indirect control, in which increasingly sophisticated technological mechanisms are deployed.

Part of the functional flexibility and tertiarisation has been a growth of distance working, which breaks up groups of employees and tends to isolate them. Of course, many workers welcome the chance to work from home. At IBM, a pioneer in distance working, 45 per cent of employees do not come into the office regularly, saving the company US$100 billion annually (Nairn, 2009). Employees increasingly have 'roaming profiles', allowing them to transfer settings and files to whichever computer workstation they are using, including portable laptops. Virtual workplaces have proliferated, with employees working 'at home' or wherever they want. Such arrangements save money on offices, give a company access to a broader pool of talent (and retain women after childbearing), allow it to operate extended days, reduce office politics and colleague interruptions, and are more environmentally friendly. Drawbacks include lack of informal information sharing and less *esprit de corps*.

Teleworkers are also vulnerable to being pushed off the employee payroll, for tax and social contribution purposes. Or part of their labour may not show up in the records, perhaps to disguise the extent of work or the income, or to increase the exploitation of the person supplying the service. This shadow labour is inevitable in a tertiary market economy.

Occupational dismantling

In addition to functional flexibility and distance work, changes in occupational structures have disrupted the capacity of people to control and develop their occupational potential. In the globalisation era, governments quietly dismantled the institutions of 'self-regulation' of professions and crafts, and in their place erected elaborate systems of state regulation. These removed the capacity of occupational bodies to set their own standards, to control entry to their occupation, to establish and reproduce their ethics and ways of doing things, to set rates of pay and entitlements, to establish ways of disciplining and sanctioning members, to set procedures for promotion and for other forms of career advancement, and much else.

The onslaught on occupational self-regulation was part of the neo-liberal agenda. Milton Friedman – architect of monetarism and, after Friedrich Hayek, the most influential economist guiding Thatcher, Reagan and Chile's Pinochet – cut his intellectual teeth in 1945 with a book attacking the medical profession (Friedman and Kuznets, 1945). The neo-liberals wanted regulations to block any collective voice. Occupational bodies were high on the hit list.

State regulation has intensified via occupational licensing and a shift in licensing to state entities insisting on adherence to competition and market-based practices. Occupational bodies became subject to antitrust rules. Occupations that set their own rules were seen as market distorting, by acting monopolistically. So more people were subjected to occupational licensing and obliged to conform to market practices.

The changes have been dramatic. In the United States today, over 1,000 occupations are subject to licensing, covering more than

20 per cent of the labour force. The spread of licensing elsewhere has been as extensive. And whereas one might presume that ministries of labour or their equivalents would be responsible for regulation of occupational practices, the trend has been to transfer responsibility to finance ministries. The US Supreme Court and the Federal Trade Commission set the trend in the 1970s, removing the exemption of professions from antitrust rules. Gradually, competition and financial institutions have come to rule what occupations can and cannot do. In Australia, all occupations come under the Competition and Consumer Commission; in Belgium and the Netherlands, professions are subject to regulation by their competition authorities. In the United Kingdom, government-dominated boards have made competition and consumer interests the ruling principles.

Market regulation has accompanied liberalisation of occupations, orchestrated to some extent by international regulatory devices such as the General Agreement on Trade in Services of the World Trade Organisation and the European Union's Services Directive. National markets are being opened to foreign competition in occupational 'services' in countries that previously had national jurisdictions over who could practise being a lawyer, accountant, architect, plumber or whatever.

Even occupations that were bastions of the salariat and profician classes conceal precariat tendencies, through truncated 'careers'. In the financial sector, most people are in short-term jobs. A trading room of 1,000 people may contain fifty over the age of 40 and just ten aged over 50. A career might peak after just five years. A few become winners, wallowing in money. Some go into the salariat in administrative jobs. Some fizzle out, drifting into the precariat. It is no surprise that the post-2008 scene in the United States produced part-time mini-financiers doing deals from their bedrooms or kitchens for a few clients, imagined as well as real. Stratification is going deep into all sorts of occupations.

With job insecurity the flip side of functional flexibility and linked to re-regulation of occupations, enterprises can stratify workers almost along class lines, shunting less effective performers into dead-end or deskilling jobs while reserving salaried posts that preserve occupational credentials for favourites. Although stratifying decisions may be grounded in assessments of capacities, control of occupational structures by managers and administrative rules increases the scope for diverting people from a professional niche into a precariat channel. This may feed back into learning decisions. Why invest in an occupational skill if I have no control over how I can use and develop it?

The regulations are splintering occupations, breeding para-professions bound for the precariat. According to the first National Strategic Skills Audit issued in 2010, England's fastest-growing jobs over the past decade included a few modern professions and crafts – conservation officers, town planners, psychologists and hairdressers – but mainly consisted of semi-professional jobs, such as paramedics, legal associates and teachers' assistants. This reflects the weakening of occupational communities and their division into elites and precariats, the latter unable to climb to higher ranks. The process was encapsulated by the United Kingdom's Legal Services Act of 2007, dubbed the 'Tesco law', which permits standardised legal services to be offered, including through supermarkets, by legal assistants with minimal training and no chance of becoming real lawyers.

Finally, there is an emerging sphere of occupational restructuring that reflects the commodification of firms, which will accelerate precariat tendencies. This is the commodification of management, epitomised by the growth of interim managers hired out through agencies or by themselves for short-term assignments. If management school directors persist in thinking that management should not be a profession, they should not be surprised if many interim managers drift from being high-status proficians to disposable members of the precariat.

Wage system flexibility: Restructuring social income

One imperative of globalisation is wage flexibility. The term conceals a raft of changes that have propelled the growth of the precariat. In essence, not only has the level of income received by most workers gone down but their income insecurity has gone up. This can be seen through the prism of social income, as presented in Chapter 1.

Social income is being restructured. First, wages in industrialised countries have stagnated, in many countries for several decades. Wage differentials have widened enormously, including differentials between regular employees and those near the precariat. For instance, in German manufacturing, wages of permanent workers have risen, while wages of those with 'atypical' contracts have fallen. In Japan, temporary employees receive wages that are 40 per cent of those paid to salarymen doing similar jobs, and they are denied the biannual bonuses worth about 20 per cent of total pay. Temporaries even have to pay more for company canteen meals. When wages revived after the recession of 2008–10, wages of the shrinking salariat rose while those of temps fell even further.

Unlike others, the precariat relies largely on money wages. In the twentieth century, the salariat and the proletariat came to rely largely on other forms of remuneration. There was a shift from wages to enterprise and state benefits, mainly for full-time employees. The shift was greatest in the Soviet Union and in China, where the *danwei* ('iron ricebowl') system gave employees of state enterprises 'cradle-to-grave' benefits and services, provided they stayed compliant. The shift from money wages also occurred in welfare states, with more state benefits in Western Europe and more enterprise benefits in the United States and Japan. It also occurred in developing countries where the 'modern sector' copied what was happening elsewhere.

Some, such as Esping-Andersen (1990), have called the shift from wages 'labour decommodification', implying that workers were less reliant on the market for income. This is misleading in that entitlement to most benefits was dependent on regular participation in the labour market or on having a 'breadwinner' in a stable job. A more accurate description is 'fictitious decommodification'. Workers had to comply with market dictates to obtain those forms of social income, which is not the same as saying income was freed from the market.

In any event, globalisation has reversed the trend from wages to benefits. While the salariat retained, and continued to gain, an array of enterprise benefits and privileges, with bonuses, paid medical leave, medical insurance, paid holidays, crèches, subsidised transport, subsidised housing and much else, the shrinking 'core' has been losing them bit by bit. The precariat was deprived of them altogether.

This is how wage flexibility has shaped the precariat. Employer contributions and provision of benefits and services had come to comprise a large part of labour costs, particularly in industrialised countries. Faced by competition from Chindia, firms have been offloading those costs, by outsourcing and offshoring and by converting more of the workforce into the precariat, notably by using temporaries denied entitlement to benefits.

This is labour *re-commodification*, since remuneration is concentrated on money wages. It goes with the more contingent nature of employment and the pursuit of competitiveness. While one could give numerous examples, what has been happening in the United States captures the story. While the salariat have retained enterprise benefits, core workers have been tipped towards the precariat. The share of US-based firms offering health care benefits fell from 69 per cent in 2000 to 60 per cent in 2009. In 2001, employers paid 74 per cent of their employees' health costs; by 2010, they were paying 64 per cent. In 1980, US employers paid 89 per cent of contributions towards retirement benefits; by 2006, that had fallen to 52 per cent (Dvorak and Thurm, 2009). By 2009, only a fifth of US employees had company-based pensions.

The main reason was that American firms were trying to cut costs to adjust to the globalisation crisis. In 2009, US employers still offering health insurance were paying on average US$6,700 per employee a year, twice as much as in 2001. One response has been to offer core employees 'high-deductible health care plans', where they must pay the first tranche of medical costs up to a specified amount. Ford dropped its 'no deductible' plan in 2008, requiring employees and family members to pay the first US$400 before insurance compensation started and to pay 20 per cent of most medical bills. This was dismantling part of their income.

Meanwhile, the promise of a company pension is being taken away from those being pushed into the precariat. Corporations are rushing to cut pension obligations and other 'legacy costs', financial commitments to former employees living out their retirement years. The widely used 401(k) retirement plans have usually allowed employers to make variable contributions. In 2009, over a third of US firms cut back or eliminated matching payments to those plans. Even the American Association of Retired Persons (AARP), the non-profit advocacy group for people over 50, did that for its own employees. Some firms, such as the computer company Unisys, raised their contributions when closing or freezing old-style pension schemes so as to defuse resentment, only to suspend them later. Enterprise pensions are in free fall.

This has undermined mutual commitment by employer and employee. Ford, for generations the epitome of US capitalism, has frequently suspended contributions; between 2001 and 2009 it contributed for only two-and-a-half years. Salaried employees hired after 2003 have no company pensions at all. Ford claimed it switched to self-managed retirement accounts to give workers portability, claiming that younger workers 'don't think of a career with one company any more'. In reality, the firm was cutting labour costs and transferring the risks and costs to workers. Their lives were being made more precarious.

In the great car-producing areas of Michigan, abandonment of enterprise benefits was slowed by government subsidies and by labour intensification, the heart of lean production. But as benefits have been chipped away, the ranks of the precariat have been swelled by what would once have been considered the most unlikely of sources. As employment in car firms slumped, falling by three-quarters between 2000 and 2009, a group emerged called 'GM gypsies', car workers who moved around the country as one plant after another closed.

If company pensions, on which the social compact of twentieth-century capitalism was constructed, are being whittled away, so are state pensions, led by the United Kingdom. The UK state pension today is worth 15 per cent of average earnings and declining, and the age of entitlement is to rise to 68 from 65. One predicts the age of entitlement will recede to 70 or more. The Turner report of the Pensions Commission, accepted by the Labour and Conservative parties, proposed a three-part deal – stay in employment for longer, save more and then have a very modest state pension to help out. This was intended to halt the rise in means testing. But unless the basic pension rises, and means testing is reduced, the incentive to save will be enfeebled. There is no incentive for low-income earners to save, since if they do they will lose their pension entitlement.

Another aspect of social income restructuring is the shift from fixed to flexible pay. Here again, flexibility means an advantage for employers and increased risk and insecurity for wage earners. One demand of twentieth-century labour movements was for a stable predictable wage. But global capitalism wants to adjust wages quickly. If it cannot do so, it will go to where it thinks it can. In 2009, US firms on average were setting aside almost double the share of their payroll for variable pay, such as performance awards, as they did in 1994 (Dvorak and Thurm, 2009).

In the recession of the early 1980s, concession bargains proliferated as unions and employees gave up entitlement to benefits in return for wage rises. Now, concession bargains are more one sided. Benefits are taken away from the lower ranks of workers so that wages rise as a share of income, but wages stagnate. In 2009, Ford's workers gave up cost-of-living allowances and lost holiday pay and college scholarships for their children as well as tuition assistance. The same wage sustained a much more precarious existence. And there has been a further push to increase all forms of flexibility, including occupational dismantling. Thus, Ford reached a collective agreement with the United Auto Workers that froze entry-level wages, had a no-strike clause and paid current workers a bonus for agreeing to the concessions. This followed similar deals in GM and Chrysler, which also reduced the number of job classifications, in GM's case to just three skilled trade classifications.

Such developments are part of a process of adjustment around the world. The circle is closing. As workers in China agitated for higher wages and better conditions, multinationals grandly conceded large money wage increases but took enterprise benefits away. Foxconn's penned workers in Shenzhen had received subsidised food, clothing and dormitory accommodation. In June 2010, on the day he announced a second big rise in wages, the head of Foxconn said, 'today we are going to return these social functions to the government'. The company was shifting to money wages, giving the impression that workers were gaining a lot (a 96 per cent wage increase), but changing the form of remuneration and character of the labour relationship. The global model was coming to China.

The precariat experiences the full force of wage flexibility. Its wages are lower, more variable and more unpredictable. The variability is unlikely to correlate positively with personal needs. When those in the precariat have above-normal financial needs, as when they have an illness or family setback, they are also likely to be receiving a below-average income. And their economic uncertainty is intensified by the way credit markets work. Not only is the cost of obtaining loans higher, reflecting lack of creditworthiness, but also the need for them is higher, inducing many in desperation to take money from loan sharks at unsustainably high rates of interest and with unrealistic repayment schedules.

There are many studies, and quite a few novels, that show how in poor communities one form of income insecurity accentuates others. Those on precarious incomes, particularly if moving in and out of short-term low-paid jobs and dealing with the unfriendly complexities of the welfare system, easily drift into chronic debt.

For years, the impact of social income restructuring and wage stagnation was cushioned by state subsidies. We consider those later. But the stagnant earnings and economic insecurity of those being tilted towards the precariat were also concealed by cheap credit, subsidised by governments in most OECD countries. Middle-class families were enabled to consume more than they earned, disguising the fact that earned incomes were declining. They had a false private benefit income. The crash shattered the illusion that all were gaining from the second Gilded Age of rampant growth. Suddenly, millions of Americans and Europeans felt closer to the precariat.

In short, social income under global capitalism is increasingly insecure. While companies are 'travelling light', this translates into multi-layered income insecurity for the precariat. And the restructuring of income means that *costs* of living are rising for those in economic insecurity. A market society characterised by uncertainty and volatility makes it advisable to take out insurance, rewards those who do so and penalises those who cannot. Those with temporary contracts not only have a higher probability of financial need but also find it harder and more costly to take out insurance.

A final aspect of the post-globalisation restructuring of social income is that, whereas before the welfare state, individuals and families relied heavily on informal mechanisms of community help, these are no longer there. They were weakened by the growth of state and enterprise benefits. For several generations, people came to think there was no need for them, so they faded. But as firms offloaded enterprise benefits and as the state went for means-tested benefits, there was no community support to fall back on. 'When you need them, they don't help you', one 59-year-old unemployed Spaniard unable to obtain help from relatives told the *Financial Times* (Mallet, 2009). The family reciprocity system had broken down.

In sum, the precariat is faced by a unique combination of circumstances. Unlike the old proletariat and the salariat, it has no enterprise benefits to give income security and no contributions-based social protection. And while it must rely on money wages, these are lower and more variable and unpredictable than those of other groups. Income and benefit inequalities are mounting, with the precariat left further behind and dependent on an enfeebled community system of social support.

Precarious unemployment

Unemployment is part of life in the precariat. But there has been a revision of attitudes that has made it harder to handle. In the pre-globalisation era, unemployment was seen as due to economic and structural factors. The unemployed were unfortunate, in the wrong place at the wrong time. Unemployment benefit systems were built on the principle of social insurance; everybody contributed, so that those with a low probability of becoming unemployed subsidised those with a higher probability.

That model has collapsed, even if the fiction continues in some countries. Fewer workers are in a position to make contributions or have them made on their behalf, and fewer qualify under contribution rules. But in any case official attitudes to unemployment have radically changed. In the neo-liberal framework, unemployment became a matter of individual responsibility, making it almost 'voluntary'. People came to be regarded as more or less 'employable' and the answer was to make them more employable, upgrading their 'skills' or reforming their 'habits' and 'attitudes'. This made it easy to go to the next stage of blaming and demonising the unemployed as lazy and scroungers. We will consider where that has led in Chapter 6. Here we just want to capture how unemployment has affected the precariat.

The first recession of the globalisation era in the early 1980s led to a change in official attitudes towards the lower reaches of the labour market where the precariat was emerging and a change in attitude among those losing jobs. In the United Kingdom, flexible wages and precarious jobs combined with high unemployment led working-class youths, in particular, to embrace 'the dole' as authenticating their disdain of the lousy jobs on offer, a rejection caught by pop bands such as UB40, whose name (unemployment benefit form 40) and band members were drawn from the dole queues. This may have affected only a minority of youths growing up in declining working-class areas, but it helped change official attitudes, providing an excuse to resurrect an image of the idle irresponsible poor.

The real problem was the flexible labour market. If wages are driven down and more jobs become precarious, unemployment benefits become relatively more attractive. In recognition, governments in industrialised countries lowered benefits, made them harder to obtain and harder to retain. That did away with the insurance character and the avowed purpose of providing an adequate income to compensate for temporary 'interruption of earning power', as William Beveridge (1942: 7) had put it. But 'unemployment traps' became more widespread, since the loss of benefits entailed in taking a low-paying job pushed the effective 'tax' rate to near or even above 100 per cent.

A vicious circle led governments in ugly directions. As wages fell, and as low-paid temporary jobs became the norm for the lower end of labour markets, the income replacement rate of benefits rose. Middle-class commentators lamented the 'excessive generosity' of benefits and claimed that, as 'work did not pay', benefits should be cut. To help make work 'pay', governments introduced in-work benefits and earned-income tax credits, a recipe for distortions and inefficiencies. But the unemployment trap remained, leading policy makers to take steps towards coercing the unemployed to take jobs, however unpleasant and poorly paid.

Global reform of unemployment benefits has acted as a breeding ground for the precariat. While not identical in all countries, the trend has been similar. The biggest change has been in the image of unemployment. Now it is depicted as reflecting a lack of employability, personal failings and excessive wage or job expectations. The benefits regime is based on ascertaining whether a person deserves to receive anything, and this has become an agenda for requiring a person to behave in certain ways in order to deserve assistance.

While unemployment insurance still holds sway in a few countries, entitlement conditions have been tightened everywhere; periods for entitlement have been shortened and benefits have been cut. In most countries, only a minority of the unemployed receive benefits and the minority is shrinking. And means-tested benefits have expanded, with all sorts of behavioural conditions attached to them.

In the United States, to be entitled to unemployment benefits, usually someone must have been employed full-time for at least a year in his or her last job. More than half the unemployed (57 per cent in 2010) do not qualify. The situation is worse, since many who do not qualify drop out of the labour force altogether. Two-thirds of recipients say they fear their benefit will expire before they can obtain a job. By 2010, poverty among the unemployed and underemployed was worse than at any time since the 1930s, with one in nine Americans living on food stamps. There were six registered seekers for every job vacancy, up from 1.7 before the crisis, and long-term unemployment accounted for 40 per cent of the total, much more than in previous recessions. It was the only recession since the Great Depression of the 1930s to have wiped out all the job growth from the previous cyclical upturn.

The rich world's job-generating machine is running down. This pre-dates the shock of 2008. In the United States, GDP growth slowed between the 1940s and 2000s but employment growth slowed much more. In the 1940s, non-agricultural employment rose by nearly 40 per cent; the increase was less in the 1950s, accelerated slightly in the 1960s, fell to 28 per cent in the 1970s and 20 per cent in the 1980s and 1990s. But in the 2000s, employment actually fell by 0.8 per cent. Work was not 'disappearing' but the global market was leaving American workers behind.

In the globalising labour market, recessions accelerate the growth of the precariat. Now that there are more temps and other unprotected workers, there is more scope for rapid labour shedding in the first phase of a recession. The days are gone when large numbers of workers were laid off, retaining their jobs until demand picked up. Those on the margins lose their jobs first. However, they may not have appeared in the employment statistics before the recession or in the unemployment statistics subsequently. This helps explain why some European countries with high clandestine and migrant employment experienced only small rises in recorded unemployment and modest declines in employment after 2008.

Firms have used the recession to transfer more labour into the zone of the precariat and to restructure in other ways, including greater resort to offshoring and outsourcing. Successive recessions in the United States have been followed by more anaemic labour market recovery, alongside a huge rise in long-term unemployment. When economic growth revived after the recessions of the 1970s and early 1980s, employment expanded immediately and was substantial. When it restarted after the recession of 2008–9, there was no job expansion at all for over a year. Indeed, the 'sunbelt' states went on shedding jobs, arousing fears of a 'job-loss recovery'.

In Germany, some of the unemployed simply disappeared from the country; many East Europeans left because they could obtain community support in their home countries and because, coming from EU member countries, they could return when jobs picked up. By contrast, migrants losing precarious jobs in the United States dared not go home, for fear of being blocked from returning. Perversely, it might help the US unemployment rate if it was easier for migrants to leave and to return.

In general, recessions tip more people into the precariat, partly because those who lose jobs slip into a lower income-earning stream on re-employment. US studies (such as Autor and Houseman, 2010) have found that taking up temporary jobs after unemployment tends to lower annual incomes and long-term earnings. This is a reason for the unemployed to resist pressure to take the first job offered to them. It is not laziness or scrounging but merely common sense.

Meanwhile, the unemployed have been turned into a treatment category. The trend to making everything subject to contract has been extended to them. In some countries, the unemployed are renamed 'clients' and have to sign contracts, accepting certain obligations and penalties for failure to comply. Almost by definition, they are under duress when they sign. Contracts signed in such circumstances would normally be moot in common law. But we will consider where that has led later.

The unemployed also experience a form of tertiarisation. They have multiple 'workplaces' – employment exchanges, benefit offices, job-search training offices – and have to indulge in a lot of work-for-labour – filling in forms, queuing, commuting to employment exchanges, commuting in search of jobs, commuting to job training and so on. It can be a full-time job being unemployed, and it involves flexibility, since people must be on call almost all the time. What politicians call idleness may be no more than being on the end of the phone, chewing nails nervously hoping for a call.

The precarity trap

A labour market based on precarious labour produces high transaction costs for those on the margins. These costs include the time it takes to apply for benefits if they become unemployed, the lack of income in that period, the time and costs associated with searching for jobs, the time and cost in learning new labour routines, and the time and cost involved in adjusting activities outside jobs to accommodate the demands of new temporary jobs. The total may be substantial by comparison with expected earnings. This creates what could be called a 'precarity trap'.

A UK study in 2010 by Reed in Partnership, a firm helping unemployed find jobs, found that the average cost of obtaining a job, with clothes, travel, child care, training and so on, came to £146, a considerable amount for people who may have been unemployed for a long time or been through a series of temporary low-paid jobs. In the first month of a job the cost was a further £128. If there is the prospect of just a temporary low-paid job, the disincentive implied by the precarity trap is much greater than the conventional poverty trap to which so much attention has been paid. Reed in Partnership's chief executive commented, 'A large proportion of the people we work with cannot afford the cost of even paying travel costs to get to an interview'.

A person living on a stream of temporary jobs has a risk-strewn existence. Consider a woman who has a temporary job and adjusts her living expenses to equal the wage she earns. Then the job ends. She has minimal savings. She has to wait for several weeks – it may be much more – before she can obtain any state benefits. In that time, she adjusts her living standards downwards, but she may have to borrow or go into debt by delaying payment for rent and so on. There may be an additional factor. People doing temporary jobs typically do not rush to apply for benefits. It is often done reluctantly, after hardships have set in. So, debts and obligations to relatives, friends and neighbours mount, and the loan sharks lurk. The precariat trap becomes more formidable.

If our woman is fortunate, she may obtain state benefits with which to pay off some of the debts and gain some financial relief. But then suppose she is offered another temporary low-paying job. She hesitates. Some benefits might continue for a while, under rules to help 'make work pay' and reduce the standard 'poverty trap'. But she knows that when the job ends she will once again face daunting transaction costs. The reality is that she cannot afford to take the job because, in addition to the cost in lost benefits while the job lasts, there is the cost of getting back on benefits. That is the precarity trap.

The precarity trap is intensified by the erosion of community support. While being in and out of temporary low-wage jobs does not build up entitlement to state or enterprise benefits, the person exhausts the ability to call on benefits provided by family and friends in times of need. This is compounded by debt and interludes of social illness that may include drug taking and petty crime, such as shoplifting. It is made worse by the stress of insecurity and the indignity of constantly having to try to sell oneself to agencies and potential employers. Without an underpinning of economic security, the flexible labour market is bound to create those outcomes.

The financial shock

On top of the longer term changes towards the unemployed, the financial meltdown of 2008–9 accelerated the growth of the global precariat by putting more pressure on firms to cut labour costs through flexibility measures and prompting government policies that encouraged them.

Predictably, the precariat initially bore the brunt of the shock. Temporary employees were the easiest to make redundant, simply by not renewing contracts. Randstad, the world's second largest staffing company, reported sharp declines across Europe in 2008, observing that firms were more inclined to cut jobs than in previous recessions. But as the recession proceeded, it became clear it was a lever for expanding the precariat. Adecco, the world's biggest temporary employment agency, reported that the regrowth of employment was concentrated on temporary labour (Simonian, 2010).

In the United Kingdom, the impact of the crisis was notable for the drop in the number of employees, whereas the number of self-employed hardly fell. In the first year of the recession, full-time jobs plummeted by over 650,000 while part-time jobs rose by 80,000, with 280,000 part-timers saying they could not obtain a full-time job. Unemployment rose by more than employment fell, mainly due to the inflow of young labour force entrants and a rise in the labour force participation rate of elderly workers facing reduced pensions and savings.

In the United States, firms responded to the crisis by cutting long-term employees and replacing others by technological changes or by outsourcing, partly to avoid a repeat of the costs of making people redundant. A survey in 2010 concluded that at least a quarter of the 8.4 million jobs eliminated in the United States since the recession began would not return (Izzo, 2010).

After the job cuts, measured labour productivity soared, which was interpreted as a reflection of employers pressurising employees to labour more, curbing job creation. This may be only part of the story, since the shock may have accelerated outsourcing and resort to more shadow labour. For instance, there has been a boom in outsourcing of legal processing. Pangea3, an India-based leader in this emerging market, doubled its revenue in a year. While UK and US law firms were struggling, cutting recruitment and making lawyers redundant or putting them on furloughs, the recession was a boon for lawyers in India.

Traditionally, major recessions lead to reductions in inequality, but this time income differentials went on widening, in general and within particular sectors. Thus, the crisis led to growing inequality between the fortunes of top law firms and those of others. The elite guarded incomes and status by laying off some of the salariat and limiting career opportunities of others, while enlarging the number of legal auxiliaries with all the insecurities of the precariat. Leading financial and economic service companies also benefited from class differentiation, since opting for reputation and bigness is the risk-averse strategy at a time of insecurity. While the legal profession is undergoing the most profound restructuring, all professions are being pushed in the same direction, of having fewer protected insiders alongside a growing number in insecure career-less positions.

Putting employees on unpaid leave, or furloughs, has grown in the United States at the same time as unpaid overtime. In 2010, twenty US states required employees to take unpaid time off and over 200,000 public sector workers were 'furloughed' every week, typically told to take Friday off, without pay. For many it was liberating, despite the income loss, enabling them to spend more time with their family; 'Furlough Friday' became a staple part of life around the country. But it was a step in pushing employees out of the comfort zone of the salariat.

Furloughs have spread in Europe too. One major British firm asked employees to take two weeks unpaid leave and had a 95 per cent take-up. Others offered two months off at 50 per cent of salary. British Airways gave all staff the opportunity to work part-time; many said they wished to do so and work for charity in the time made available. It was also a bonanza for the new occupation of 'life coach', eager to counsel people on how to reorganise their lives.

In 2009, a Spanish bank, BBVA, offered to let staff take as much as five years off at 30 per cent of salary. This gave the average employee at least £12,000, with health care added. The bank was doing that rather than pay six weeks of severance pay for every year worked. It acknowledged that many employees might have difficulty readjusting when they returned, but that problem seemed far away.

Another bank in another country highlighted the dualistic treatment of the salariat and precariat post-2008. In response to the banking crisis, which left it heavily subsidised by the UK government, Lloyds Banking Group cut over 20,000 jobs. In October 2010, it announced that it had 'mitigated the impact on permanent staff with a significant release of temporary and contract staff'. Next time around, no doubt, the bank will have more temps and others who can be easily let go.

Dismantling the public sector

The final frontier for the precariat is the public sector, long the trailblazer for labour standards and stable employment. It provided a high social income, with benefits accounting for a large share of compensation, coupled with bureaucratic rules and an ethic of service.

For generations, the civil service deal was that, while earnings never reached the giddy heights of the private commercial sectors, public employees had employment security if not job security, as well as standard-setting pensions, health care benefits and so on. But as civil servants carried out their political masters' instructions to flexibilise private labour markets, the gap between their privileged security and the remainder of society became glaring. It was only a matter of time before the public sector itself became a prime target for flexibilisation. That time came with the shock of 2008, even though erosions had started long before.

The attack began with moves to commercialise, privatise and contract out services. Temporary contracts and part-time employment with inferior wages and benefits crept in. Then governments moved against the sector as a whole. Public pensions were declared 'unaffordable' and 'unfair'; governments used comparisons with the private economy to justify cutting public wages. It did not help that fiscal stimulus packages, quantitative easing and subsidies created bulging public deficits. That was not the fault of the public sector, but it became an easy target for budget cuts. Insecure private sectors looked on without solidarity. Financial markets too insisted on public spending cuts as evidence that governments were on 'the right track'. This is driving the erosion of the public salariat.

Globally, the public sector is being turned into a zone of the precariat. Nowhere is this more so than in the United States, where neo-liberal economic zealotry has created a fiscal perfect storm. Cities have been pushed into chronic debt by a straitjacket of fiscal rules demanding a low-tax 'balanced budget' regime. For years, public employees defended their wages through their unions and collective agreements, while the private sector suffered declining wages and shrinking benefits. Their unions remained strong. In 2008, 37 per cent of government workers were unionised, nearly the same as in 1980, whereas private unionisation had fallen from 20 to 7 per cent. In 2009, for the first time, public sector workers made up more than half of all union members in the country. They had defended their members well, but the widening inequality between public and private sectors made for rising resentment.

The crisis was used to cut public sector job security, through intensifying functional flexibility. Administrators began insisting that public employees should perform tasks other than those they were employed to do. A city administrator in Arkansas said, with evident pride, 'I pay more money to less people and maximise their use with more tasks' (Bullock, 2009). The court clerk now did marketing and handled the website, firefighters doubled as ambulance drivers, and workers at the water treatment plant were paid extra to stand in for truck drivers. A survey of cities and counties found that many were planning to take advantage of the crisis to rearrange work in similar ways.

Everywhere, the political right used the recession to intensify a campaign to cut public sector wages, benefits and employment security. Characteristically, in commenting on the United States, *The Economist* (2009) claimed that 'public sector workers are spoiled rotten', on the grounds that on average they earned 21 per cent more than those in the private sector and were 24 per cent more likely to have access to health care. Some 84 per cent of state and local government workers still had a defined-benefit pension plan, guaranteeing retirement income based on years of 'service' and final salary, compared with only 21 per cent of private sector workers. The figures could have been interpreted as showing how miserly private firms had become. Or the comparison could have been made with what the elite and private salariat were receiving.

Public employees now face an onslaught on their pensions, which will worsen the income prospects of their precariat offspring. Again the US situation is most alarming. The National Association of State Budget Officers warned that US states would face huge budget deficits due to pension liabilities. Anti-public sector critics were helped by media stories of a few former senior public employees living in opulence on their pensions.

The United States is only the harbinger. The attack on the public sector is part of the post-2008 adjustment across all industrialised countries. In Greece, under a centre-right government, 75,000 civil servants were added to the already huge public sector between 2004 and 2009. Once the crunch came in 2010, the public salariat was slashed, feeding the Greek precariat. The government also announced it would remove barriers to entry to some professions, lowering their wages to reduce public spending. In Italy, pressure on the civil service was also growing. In October 2009, 40,000 police officers marched through Rome to demand better pay and new police cars. Because of a freeze on hiring, the average age of Italian policemen had risen to 45. They were not alone; millions of civil servants were losing employment security. In Portugal, 50,000 civil servants protested in February 2010 against a pay freeze, but the government went ahead with a rundown of public services. In Ireland, forced to accept a Eurozone bailout in late 2010, the hard-won gains of the public sector (and its sometimes anachronistic perks) were being stripped away in a matter of months.

In the United Kingdom, as in the United States, two-thirds of all new jobs in the decade before 2008 were in the public sector. Cutting it will enlarge the precariat simply by altering the public-private share of employment. But the intention is to turn more of the public sector into the zone of the precariat through privatisation, outsourcing and casualisation.

An aspect of the attack is the effort to turn over more services to civil society or non-governmental organisations (NGOs). In the United Kingdom, this is presented as a way to reduce the Big State and generate the Big Society. But it is a way to obtain services on the cheap, transferring activities done by professional employees to those on precarious contracts and 'volunteers'. Entities registered as charities have become major employers, with 464,000 full-time staff in 2009. More than half their income comes from government contracts to supply public services. But charity employees are not well paid and have precarious contracts. Subsidised by gifts from private donors, they make social services cheaper, undercutting public equivalents and legitimising poor contractual relations for 'volunteers'. This makes the sector particularly vulnerable in a recession. When donations dry up, these quasi-public employees can feel close to being in the precariat themselves. It was no surprise that as the recession deepened many of them left to work in supermarkets. In effect, contracting out services is expanding the precariat while undermining small charities.

Governments are also acting more like commercial firms in their treatment of civil servants, pursuing functional and employment flexibility. For example, they are saving on office space by decentralising and flexibilising the labour of their employees. In the United States, a law passed in 2000 obliged federal government and its agencies to establish networking policies. By 2006, 140,000 federal employees, 19 per cent, were doing jobs from alternative worksites. This is precariatisation, isolating employees and limiting their space and opportunity for collective action.

In 2009, 24,000 Spanish civil servants – 10 per cent of the total – were labouring partly from home, on condition that they had to come to the office for 50 per cent of their labour time. Remote working has also been introduced in Italy, where the public sector is notorious for absenteeism. An innovator in the United Kingdom was Winchester City Council, which consolidated its four office locations into two and installed a web-based booking system to let employees reserve desk space or meeting rooms as they saw fit. This 'hot desking' is depersonalising the office, since it is no longer 'my office'. The psychological effect is of interest, since the increased instrumentality of the workplace will reduce a sense of attachment both to the firm or organisation and to the workforce as an entity to be defended.

In sum, the public sector, so long the bastion of the salariat and standard setter for decent labour, is fast being turned into a zone of flexibility in which the precariat can grow.

The subsidy state: Bane of the precariat

One scarcely noticed aspect of globalisation was the spread of subsidies. This may be one of the great 'con tricks' of economic history, since much has gone to capital and to high-income earners in the form of 'tax reliefs', 'tax holidays' and 'tax credits'. If a rich person in the United Kingdom, for instance, wishes to avoid tax on part of their income, they need to do no more than put it in a personal pension plan, deferring the income while saving 40 per cent of it. Someone in the precariat hardly has the same opportunity.

Consider what happened after the crash of 2008. Interventions to prop up banks globally in 2008–9 came to US$14,000 billion, according to the Bank of England. This is probably an understatement. Meanwhile, amid feverish lobbying by corporations, Western governments launched a vast range of subsidy schemes, in what should be called subsidy protectionism. Unbowed by its disastrous performance leading up to the crash, when it had indulged in financial speculation, US motor company GM said it would go 'subsidy shopping' and shift production and jobs to where governments offered the biggest subsidies.

Subsidies are integral to industrial policy, usually presented as backing 'winners'. In reality, such subsidies have been used to prop up big firms or sectors under pressure, preserving structures containing important political constituencies. But subsidies will not arrest the international re-division of labour as jobs are transferred from high-cost countries to low-cost high-productivity areas. While they may prolong some old-style employment, they do so at the cost of denying support to others. They rarely benefit the most insecure groups in society.

Subsidies introduced during the 2008–9 crisis to stimulate car sales benefited car buyers relative to others and car labourers relative to other workers. They were certainly not the poorest or most precarious. Ecologically, such subsidies favour resource use at the expense of resource conservation. Then there are subsidies for enterprise benefits; these lower the demand for workers doing low-productivity services.

And, as will be shown, enterprise benefits are a burden on youth since old agers and migrants are more prepared to labour without them.

Labour subsidies, including earned-income tax credits and marginal employment subsidies, are also in reality subsidies to capital, enabling companies to gain more profits and pay lower wages. They have no economic or social equity justification. The rationale for the main labour subsidy, tax credits, is that as the poor and less educated in rich countries face the stiffest competition from low-cost labour in developing countries, governments need to subsidise low wages to provide adequate incomes. But while intended to offset wage inequality, these subsidies encourage the growth or maintenance of low-wage precariat jobs. By topping up wages to something like subsistence, tax credits take pressure off employers, giving them an incentive to continue to pay low wages. Cheap labour means firms are also under less pressure to be efficient. Tax credits and other labour subsidies are the twenty-first-century equivalent of the Speenhamland system, a landlord-inspired subsidy introduced in Berkshire in 1795 that became notorious for causing rural pauperisation across England.

The folly has yet to be realised. Governments going down the tax credit route will have to run faster merely to stand still, since downward pressure on wages is growing as other emerging markets join Chindia. As a *Financial Times* leader (2010a) opined, without drawing this logical conclusion,

If Britain is to continue to offer a generous welfare net while wages at the bottom are stagnant, low-income workers may soon find that living on benefits is only slightly less profitable than working. To make sure that work still pays, the government will have to increase its subsidy on their wages via the tax credits system.

It added that, to limit rising costs, the government would have to tighten rules on who is 'deserving of support'. This it promptly did.

Within a year of the crash, sixteen OECD countries introduced wage subsidies, hiring bonuses or public works jobs to stem the rise in unemployment. While Spain had a huge public works programme, the United Kingdom went for 'golden hallos', offering up to £2,500 to firms that recruited anybody who had been unemployed for more than six months, giving £1,000 per worker on hiring and a further £1,500 for training. This was sure to swell the precariat, by expanding the number put into temporary jobs and tempting employers to sack existing workers and hire substitutes. South Korea also introduced a hiring subsidy under a policy that required employees to accept a wage freeze, removed bargaining rights and paid the subsidised recruits two-thirds of the wage of existing employees – spreading a multi-tier labour force. In the United States, the Obama administration managed to enact a US$13 billion scheme in 2010 that gave companies a tax credit if they hired unemployed jobseekers. Opportunistic employers would quickly work out how to do beneficial substitutions.

Other countries favoured short-time compensation schemes, mostly directed at manufacturing, by which employers could apply for temporary assistance to supplement wages of regular employees. By 2010, twenty-one EU countries had short-time job schemes covering more than 2.4 million workers; Germany's *Kurzarbeit* scheme alone accounted for 1.5 million workers, involving a wage subsidy stretching over two years. The subsidy offset 60 per cent of the loss of income from being on short time, a formula copied by others, such as the Netherlands. In the United States, seventeen states, including California, introduced a temporary cut in the payroll tax and provision of unemployment benefits for those forced to work part-time.

Subsidised short time operates just like any labour subsidy. It involves moral and immoral hazards, rewarding inefficiency and poor performance. And it distorts markets, hindering the transfer of jobs to higher productivity areas. While subsidies are defended as 'keeping people in jobs, so preserving skills', and reducing the social costs of the recession (Atkins, 2009), they prevent people moving on and acquiring new skills or making better use of those they have.

Coupling short-time labour with government subsidies was one route by which full-time employees were converted into subsidised part-time members of the precariat. And since almost all short-time subsidies have a finite life, many will have only a temporary respite before losing their jobs altogether.

An ultimate irony of subsidies is that they do not fool people for long. While bolstering old jobs and promoting temporary labour, swelling the precariat in unsustainable ways, they leave a nasty taste. One disillusioned South Korean who seemed a recruit to the precariat was quoted as saying, 'Even if I get a job this way, I'll only work for a few months, and during that time I'll always feel like a pathetic extra who exists at the generosity of other workers' (Choe, 2009).

The shadow economy

One other factor has played a role in expanding the precariat. This is variously known as the shadow, grey or black economy. There are many reasons for believing it has grown and is underestimated by available statistics. De-industrialisation has played a part, as has the growth of numerical flexibility, since the shift from large-scale factories and office blocks of employment concentration makes handshake labour easier and harder to detect. The changing character of welfare states has also been relevant, undermining social solidarity and the principles underlying progressive direct tax and social insurance.

Whatever the reasons, the shadow economy is where much of the precariat survives, facing exploitation and oppression. A study by Friedrich Schneider of the University of Linz (*The Economist*, 2010b) estimated that the unofficial economy accounted for over a quarter of Greece's GDP, over 20 per cent of the GDP of Italy, Spain and Portugal, and over 10 per cent of the GDP of Germany, France and the United Kingdom. He attributed much of the tax evasion to 'tax rebellion', arguing that people are more reluctant to pay taxes if they do not think they are obtaining value from the services offered by the state. If so, cuts in public services to reduce budget deficits may encourage more tax rebellion, negating the impact of spending cuts on the deficit.

Given the size of the shadow economy and the existence of a cushion of shadowy labour, in times of relative boom, as before the crash of 2008, a considerable amount of labour goes unrecorded. Poor employment growth records may be misleading. By the same token, a recession may begin with a decline in shadow labour, giving the impression that employment is not falling by much and that unemployment is not rising by much, particularly as those in the shadows would be ineligible for state benefits.

This is consistent with the available data. In the first two years of recession, the fall in employment across Europe was only a third as large as the percentage contraction of the economy. In Spain, by

2010 recorded unemployment had risen to over 4.5 million, well past the level that trade unionists and others had predicted would lead to riots. There were no riots. Some observers attributed that to traditional tolerance of unemployment and family networks that could provide community benefits. Others thought it had more to do with the thriving underground economy. The tax inspectors' union, Gestha, estimated that the underground economy accounted for over 23 per cent of GDP and that it had expanded while recorded GDP was shrinking considerably.

A globalising open market economy characterised by informal contracts, part-time and temporary jobs, project orientation and myriad personal services is surely conducive to shadow labour. It is not an aberration; it is part of the global market system.

The decline of social mobility

Finally, and most revealingly of all, the stratifying character of the globalising labour process has produced a decline in upward social mobility, which is a feature of the precariat. As Daniel Cohen (2009: 19) said of French (and European) workers, today very few rise to middle management, and 'there is now a greater probability of remaining at the bottom of the wage scale for life'. In the United Kingdom, social mobility has declined, which has been linked to the growth of inequality. By 2010, as shown by the Labour government's National Equality Panel (see also Wilkinson and Pickett, 2009), it was harder for a child born into poverty to climb the social ladder than at any time since the 1950s. Those born in 1970 were less likely to have risen in social status than those born in 1958. It is just one sign that class still matters.

Most strikingly, given its self-image of unrivalled opportunity for upward mobility, the United States has long had declining social mobility. Inter-generational mobility is low by international standards (Sawhill and Haskins, 2009). Children born in the lowest and highest quintiles are even more likely to stay there than in the United Kingdom and much more likely to do so than in Sweden or Denmark. With inequality growing to record levels and social mobility declining, the neo-liberal economic and social model has surely failed in its claim to generate merit-based social mobility.

One reason for the slowdown in social mobility is that middle-income jobs have been whittled away. For example, in the United Kingdom, the number of jobs in the top wage decile grew by almost 80 per cent between 1979 and 1999. The second decile grew by 25 per cent, and the bottom two deciles also expanded (Goos and Manning, 2007). But jobs in the middle six deciles shrank. What this trend means, and it is repeated in many countries, is that the 'middle class' is suffering from income insecurity and stress, being pushed into the precariat.

Conclusions

There was a crude social compact in the globalisation era – workers were required to accept flexible labour in return for measures to preserve jobs so that the majority experienced rising living standards. It was a Faustian bargain. Living standards were maintained by allowing consumption to exceed incomes and earnings to exceed what jobs were worth. While the latter fostered inefficiency and market distortions, the former put swathes of the population into bewildering debt. Sooner or later, the devil would have his due, a moment that for many came with the crash of 2008, when their diminished incomes fell below what was needed to pay off debts they had been encouraged to build. A new layer was about to join the precariat.

At the end of the globalisation era, the compact had broken down. On the employers' side, more wished to 'travel light'. On the workers' side, there was more stress, insecurity and psychological detachment. Work-related suicides increased in many countries, including France, Japan and across Scandinavia, the Mecca of social democracy. In the United States, they rose by 28 per cent in one year. Meanwhile, according to the Center for Work-Life Policy, a US consultancy, the proportion of employees professing loyalty to their employers fell from 95 to 39 per cent, and the proportion expressing trust in them fell from 79 to 22 per cent. In the age of the precariat, loyalty and trust are contingent and fragile.

One can see why the precariat is growing. But the greater the size, the more the dysfunctional aspects will grow ominous. Insecurities breed social illness, addictions and anomic angst. Prisons overflow. Robin Hood gangs lose their sense of humour. And dark forces spread in the political arena. We will come to those after considering who is entering the precariat and what is happening to the key assets of the global market society.

3

Who enters the precariat?

One answer is 'everybody, actually'. Falling into the precariat could happen to most of us, if accidents occurred or a shock wiped out the trappings of security many have come to rely on. That said, we must remember that the precariat does not just comprise victims; some enter the precariat because they do not want the available alternatives, some because it suits their particular circumstances at the time. In short, there are varieties of precariat.

Some enter the precariat due to mishaps or failings, some are driven into it, some enter hoping it will be a stepping stone to something else, even if it does not offer a direct route, some choose to be in it instrumentally – including old agers and students simply wishing to obtain a little money or experience – and some combine a precariat activity with something else, as is increasingly common in Japan. Others find that what they have been doing for years, or what they were training to do, becomes part of an insecure precariat existence.

This chapter on demographics, and Chapter 4 on migrants, look at groups that have a relatively high probability of being in the precariat.

The demographics can be summarised in terms of women compared with men and youth compared with old agers. In each group, there are 'grinners', who welcome precariat jobs, and 'groaners', obliged to take them in the absence of alternatives. Among youth, the 'grinners' are students and travelling backpackers, happy to take casual jobs with no long-term future; the 'groaners' are those unable to enter the labour market through apprenticeships or the equivalent, or competing with 'cheaper' old agers with no need for enterprise benefits.

Among old agers, the 'grinners' are those with adequate pension and health care coverage, who can do odd jobs for the pleasure of activity or to earn money for extras; the 'groaners' are those, without a reasonable pension, who face competition from more energetic youth and less needy old agers. Among women, the 'grinners' include those with partners in the salariat, who can treat a job as a sideline; the 'groaners' include single breadwinners and those facing the triple burden of having to care for children and elderly relatives, while needing to take a paid job. Among men, the 'grinners' include those with a partner earning a reasonable income; the groaners include single earners able to obtain only a precariat job.

Women: Feminisation of living?

Early in the globalisation era, it became apparent that women were taking a growing proportion of all jobs, in a global trend towards the feminisation of labour (Standing, 1989, 1999a). This was feminisation in a double sense of more women being in jobs and more jobs being of the flexible type typically taken by women. The trend reflected labour informalisation, the growth of services and use of young women in export processing zones. It did not mean that women everywhere were improving their incomes or working conditions. Indeed, gender-based wage and social income differentials remained inequitable, if modestly improving in some parts of the world.

The jobs that were spreading led to a rising demand for women as well as a shift of men into insecure low-paid jobs long regarded as the norm for women. If flexible labour means more short-term jobs, then there is little premium placed on employment of men perceived – correctly or not – to offer longer term commitment. Fears that women might involve employers in high non-wage costs, because they might become pregnant or withdraw to look after children, are less relevant if jobs are set only to last a few months, if the arrangement is non-binding or contingent on fluctuating demand, or if there is no cost to intermittent labour.

In the globalisation era, export-led industrialisation in developing countries was based quite shamelessly on the organisation of young women as a precariat, mobilised to labour for a pittance and not expected to stay in jobs for long. Many other factors also contributed to the feminisation of labour, in the double sense. One was the demise of the 'family wage', a feature of the industrial age and the compact between capital and the working class. The industrial proletariat developed an expectation that the male worker would receive a wage adequate to maintain a nuclear family, not just the worker himself. This rule of thumb has gone. The 'individualised' wage favoured employment of women; whereas the lower wage induced a lower 'effort bargain' from men, women never expected a family wage.

In addition, more labour was in services, where manual strength was not required and long-term apprenticeship training was not a norm. Political factors also contributed. It was a feature of the loss of momentum of the social democratic agenda in the 1980s that emphasis shifted to social *equity* rather than *equality*. Reducing discrimination and gender-based wage differentials became priority objectives, while reducing structural inequalities was sidelined. Some measures designed to improve social equity even accentuated inequality. The absence of an egalitarian agenda meant that the beneficiaries of anti-discrimination laws were mainly women with positional advantages, not women in disadvantaged segments of society.

Whether cause or effect, women's growing labour market role has coincided with the growth of the precariat. Women have taken a disproportionate share of precarious jobs, being far more likely to have short-term contracts or no contracts at all. This is not just in Europe and North America. In Japan, the shift to non-regular labour coincided with a rising share of women in the labour force. In 2008, over half of Japanese women were in precarious jobs, compared with less than one in five men. In South Korea, 57 per cent of women were in such jobs, compared with 35 per cent of men.

Japan is an extreme case. Gender inequality is a cultural legacy that has fed into a gendered precariat, in which women are concentrated in temporary, low-productivity jobs, resulting in one of the highest male-female wage differentials in the industrialised world. In 2010, 44 per cent of women workers in Japan were receiving less than the minimum wage. The growth of temporary labour also contributed. Women's wages in regular (permanent) jobs are 68 per cent of men's, but in temporary jobs they are less than half of those paid to men. So the trend is having a doubly adverse effect. To add to the inequity, many Japanese women are directed into elder-care jobs, where wages are pitifully low.

This highlights a twenty-first-century challenge. As global feminisation has proceeded, more women have experienced a 'triple burden'. They are expected to do most of the care work for children and 'the home', they are expected to labour in the market in order to afford 'the home', and they are expected to care for the growing number of elderly relatives.

It is because women have always done most of the care work that it has been neglected in economic statistics and social policy. This was brought to its absurd worst in the twentieth century, when doing care work did not count as work at all. One brand of liberal rhetoric did not help. Care work, mostly confined to the family, was depicted as in the private sphere, whereas labour was in the public sphere. Since the public sphere was seen as liberating, it followed that putting more women into jobs, any jobs, would be liberating. So the female labour force participation rate became a measure of liberation (Sen, 1999).

That is fine for middle-class, highly educated women who can anticipate salaried career-oriented employment. But for most women, labouring repetitively on an assembly line, or sewing feverishly in an ill-lit backstreet garment factory, or sitting at a check-out counter for long shifts, jobs are scarcely liberating. They may be part of the triple burden, in which women also have to care for children and elderly relatives 'in their spare time'.

Gains in access to jobs are real. But they have been bought at a price, paid largely by women but also to some extent by men. Most are part-time, temporary or dead-end jobs, with no prospect of occupational development. Yet governments are pushing women to take them.

In the United Kingdom, over 40 per cent of employed women are in part-time jobs, which pay much less per hour than full-time jobs. In 2009, the government proposed to help women in full-time jobs to move into part-time jobs, through subsidies, with an emphasis on flexible working. They also launched a national database on part-time jobs, aimed at so-called 'stay-at-home' mothers seeking 'a return to work', and announced plans to make lone parents of younger children seek 'work'.

In Germany, as in France, women make up 80 per cent of all part-time employees, and they earn a quarter less than men do. School and shop hours, and a shortage of day care, make it difficult for women with children to work full time. The Merkel government introduced 'parents' pay', an earnings-related benefit allowing either parent to take up to 12 months leave from their job. But conservatives in the government insisted that a decision to expand day care be accompanied by a new benefit, *Betreuungsgeld*, given to mothers only if they stay at home with their children. This is unfair, applying a behavioural conditionality that penalises women who wish or have to take jobs as well as look after their children.

As women swell the precariat, while filling the traditional role of child carer and the newer one of caring for elderly relatives, more women are becoming primary 'breadwinners'. This is not just because more are single mothers or living alone. Gender roles are also reversing. In the United States, women's education has risen relative to men's, and in the age group of 30–44 there are more female than male graduates. Whereas in 1970 only 4 per cent of married women earned more than their husbands, now more than one in five does. As more people are marrying within their education bracket, high-earning men are more likely to be married to high-earning women, increasing inter-household inequality. However, despite the publicity given to women high-flyers, women who earn more than their partners are most likely to be found in low-income households, in the precariat.

In the United Kingdom, the rise of female 'breadwinners' has been associated with a rise in the number of men stepping out of a career path, or giving up a fruitless chase for one, to become home-carers. In the 1960s, just 4 per cent of women aged 16–60 earned more than their partners. By 2009, as in the United States, one in five – or 2.7 million – was a 'breadwinner wife' (National Equality Panel, 2010). Some 214,000 men reported that they were not in the labour market because they were looking after their family or home, an 80 per cent jump in 15 years. Meanwhile, the number of women saying that fell from 2.7 million to 2 million, a drop of a quarter. Rob Williams, chief executive of the Fatherhood Institute, a pressure group, commented: 'The idea that men see themselves as bread-winners is collapsing. Since the 1970s, men have become far more egalitarian, and the number who wants to get off the career ladder and spend more time with their children has gone up' (Barrow, 2010).

Involuntary role reversal is more frequent, however. In each successive recession, male unemployment has risen more than female unemployment and the share of women in jobs has grown. Indeed, the post-2008 crash led to a historically unique moment. In 2010, for the first time, women in the United States held half of all jobs.

The Great Recession has been dubbed a 'mancession'. Men have borne the vast majority of job losses, as the core (industrial working class) jobs have disappeared. In the United States, the proportion of men in jobs fell to below 70 per cent in 2009, the lowest since records began in 1948. By 2010, one in five American men aged between 25 and 55 was unemployed. In the 1960s, 95 per cent of that age group were in jobs. In the European Union, three-quarters of the jobs generated since 2000 have been taken by women.

Ironically, women's increased 'public' involvement in the economy has been accompanied by a rising fear of failure due to multiple forms of precariousness. This has gone under a chilling name – 'bag lady syndrome' – a fear of being out in the streets due to job failure. In 2006, a life insurance survey found that 90 per cent of American women felt financially insecure and nearly half said they had 'tremendous fear of becoming a bag lady'. This was even prevalent among women earning over US$100,000 a year. More women reported feeling stressed about money. As one woman put it, 'The inner bag lady, wrinkle-faced and unkempt, is no joke. She's the worst-case-scenario future'. This was taking place in the world's leading economy. And it has grown worse since the crash.

Most mainstream analysis also omits part of the precariat that has been largely the preserve of women – sex services. Millions of women around the world are involved, many forced into it, many driven to it by financial distress, some choosing to be in it for one reason or another. Sex services are riddled with class distinctions and women at the bottom epitomise the precariat existence, renting out their bodies without any control. Criminalising them and denying them rights merely accentuates their plight.

What then of men moving into the precariat? The challenges are not the same. The biggest may be that of adjusting downwards. Insecurity is connected with fear of losing what one has. More men are in that position, by comparison with their own past, previous generations of men, and the expectations and aspirations instilled in them by their families and cultures. As the precariat grows and career jobs evaporate, loss of face compounds the loss of income and the status trappings that go with it. With the world generating precarious labour, men attuned to a self-image of stability and career progression are in danger of being traumatised. Moreover, the dismantling of occupational communities and the disruption to old notions of occupational careers produce status frustration effects as men confront the reality that their careers are truncated.

A 'masculinity' challenge?

While women and men face different challenges around the precariat, the budding precarity movement draws support from groups of diverse sexuality. There are good reasons. Gays and lesbians feel insecure in a society geared to heterosexual mores and standard nuclear families. But there are other tensions too, linked to labour developments. The feminisation of labour affects traditional ideas of masculinity and femininity. One theme that has long preoccupied sociologists is the claim that young men are becoming more alienated and anomic.

Historically, young men had role models to help them into manhood. They were presented with a virilising idea. They would look after their parents, earn enough to be able to support a wife and children, and end their years as respected elders. It was sexist and patriarchal, not a structure to applaud, but ingrained over generations. Now there are few realistic role models for working-class young men to emulate that would gain them self-respect, and their prospects of being a future family 'breadwinner' are dim.

The shortage of aspirational role models could be a second-generation outcome of the flexibilisation of the 1980s and 1990s. The result is a prolonging of adolescence, with young men unable to motivate themselves. As Lucie Russell, director of the UK charity Young Minds, put it, 'How do boys become men in the absence of a role or a job?'

It starts in school where, increasingly, girls are outperforming boys. In England and Wales, 64 per cent of girls achieve five General Certificate of Secondary Education (GCSE) passes (exams at the age of 15 or 16), compared with 54 per cent of boys. Boys not only lack male role models at home but also are taught predominantly by women. About 5,000 schools have no male teachers at all. The gendered disadvantage goes up the educational ladder; half of young women participate in higher education, against 37 per cent of young men. Similar patterns are found in other countries. Overall, at American and European universities, women outnumber men by a third. And after university, among UK graduates, men are 50 per cent more likely to become unemployed.

As a consequence of their precariousness, more young men are continuing to live with or near parents in case of need. In Italy, it is a common phenomenon; young (and not so young) men living with their families, sometimes into their 40s, are called *mammoni*. In the United Kingdom, more than a quarter of men aged 25–29 are living with their parents, double the proportion of women of the same age. One in ten men is still in his parents' home at the age of 35. The image is of the 'boomerang son', returning home after education and drifting into lethargy, part-time jobs, debt, drugs and vague ambitions 'to travel'.

Precariousness discourages marriage and leads to later child-bearing. In 2008, only 232,990 couples married in England and Wales, the lowest number since 1895. The marriage rate, calculated as the number of marriages per capita, fell to its lowest level since records began in 1862. Marriage rates similarly fell in the later stages of the disembedded phase of the Great Transformation at the end of the nineteenth century, at a time of spreading insecurity. The down-ward trend has been similar across Europe, with a rise in cohabitation. It has been estimated that by 2015 a majority of babies in England and Wales will be born to unmarried parents.

Men and women are also marrying later. Between 1998 and 2008, the average age of first marriage in England and Wales rose by three years for both men and women. The provisional mean age at marriage for men marrying for the first time was 32.1 years and for women it was 29.9. The rising age could reflect increased costs – both actual costs and the risk cost of failure. But it surely testifies to a sense of precariousness affecting both men and women, albeit in different ways.

The trend has contributed to a growing number of single-person households in industrialised countries. But, as we have seen, youths have also been trickling back to the parental home, their own precariousness often adding to that of their parents. Among the neologisms coined for this group are 'Kippers' (kids in parents' pockets eroding retirement savings) and 'Ipods' (insecure, pressurised, overtaxed, debt-ridden and saving).

In a polemical book supposedly describing what young men like themselves now face (although their Curricula Vitae (CVs) gave the game away), Ed Howker and Shiv Malik (2010) summed up 'their' existence:

> We work in jobs and live in homes secured on short-term contracts; the steps of our lives are constantly meandering; for many of us our childhood home represents our only fixed point . . . The generation who will bail out Britain can't get started; meanwhile the debts are getting bigger, jobs are getting scarcer, lives are getting tougher.

Youth: Urban nomads

The world's youth, more than 1 billion aged between 15 and 25, comprise the largest youth cohort in history, a majority in developing countries. The world may be ageing but there are a very large number of young people around, with much to be frustrated about. Although many other groups make up the precariat, the most common image is of young people emerging from school and college to enter a precarious existence lasting years, often made all the more frustrating because their parents' generation had seemingly held stable jobs.

Youths have always entered the labour force in precarious positions, expecting to have to prove themselves and learn. But today's youth are not offered a reasonable bargain. Many enter temporary jobs that stretch well beyond what could be required to establish 'employability'. A wheeze of flexibility has been to extend probationary periods, during which firms can legally pay lower wages and provide fewer benefits.

The declining probability of moving into a long-term contract builds up resentment. In France, for example, 75 per cent of all young employees start with temporary contracts and most remain in them; only those with degrees can expect to move into a 'permanent' position. Traditionally, youths could tolerate an initial period of being an outsider since they could look forward to being an insider eventually. Meanwhile, they lived off parents. Family solidarity alleviated the initial precariousness. But today, precariousness has been stretched while family solidarity is weaker; the family is more fragile and the older generation cannot foresee a balancing inter-generational reciprocity.

A feature of the restructuring of social income and wage flexibility has been the fall in wages and incomes of young people relative to their elders. Not only are more youth in precarious jobs, where wages are lower anyhow, but their bargaining position is weakened in accessing all jobs, while the absence of enterprise and state benefits intensifies their vulnerability to poverty.

An example is Japan, where average annual earnings of workers in their 20s fell by 14 per cent between 1997 and 2008. A report by the Ministry of Health, Labour and Welfare in 2010 found that 56 per cent of 16- to 34-year-old employed workers needed a second source of income to help them pay for basic living expenses.

Youths resent the insecurity and mostly want to pursue some sort of career. Yet many with a desire for a fulfilling life are unimpressed by stories of employment drudgery and stress of older generations. They reject the labourism of stable full-time jobs stretching out into the distance. In international polls, nearly two-thirds of young people say they would prefer to be 'self-employed', to work on their own rather than be in a job. But the flexible labour markets forged by the older generation of politicians and commercial interests condemn most youth to spending years in the precariat.

Youth make up the core of the precariat and will have to take the lead in forging a viable future for it. Youth has always been the repository of anger about the present and the harbinger of a better tomorrow. Some commentators, such as Daniel Cohen (2009: 28), see May 1968 as the point at which youth emerged as an 'autonomous social force'. Certainly the 'baby boomers' fractured arrangements created by their parents' generation. But youth has been the change agent throughout history. Rather, 1968 marked the beginning of the precariat, with its rejection of industrial society and its drab labourism. Subsequently, having railed against capitalism, the baby boomers took the pensions and other benefits, including cheap commodities from emerging market economies, and then ushered in flexibility and insecurity for their successors. One embittered jobless graduate (Hankinson, 2010) wrote, 'Baby boomers had free education, affordable houses, fat pensions, early retirement and second homes. We've been left with education on the never-never [student debt] and a property ladder with rotten rungs. And the financial system which made our parents rich has left us choosing between crap job or no job'.

Of course, the tirade against the previous generation presents a false picture; it neglects class. Only a small minority of UK baby boomers went to university, while today half of all school leavers go on to some form of tertiary education. Many in the older generation suffered the ravages of de-industrialisation, as miners, steelworkers, dock workers, printers and so on were shunted into history. And most women had the added burden of economic marginality. The inter-generational interpretation could almost be a diversionary tactic, since it accords with a conservative view that carefully leaves out the role of globalisation (Willetts, 2010). Today's youth is not worse off than earlier generations. The predicament is just different and varies by class. Those former working-class communities had an ethos of social solidarity reproduced from generation to generation. They are now as much zones of the precariat as are the campuses and communities of what Italians call *alternativi*.

Their withering has created three challenges for today's youth. They have seen their parents lose status, income, pride and stability; they have no role models to emulate; and they drift into precarity traps, with low-paying jobs interspersed with spells of unemployment and enforced idleness. Within low-income neighbourhoods the 'work ethic' is passed down from generation to generation (Shildrick, MacDonald, Webster and Garthwaite, 2010). But the experience of a precariatised existence by one generation will also transmit attitudes and behavioural norms to the next. The first generation subject to systemic flexibility came of age in the 1980s. It is their children who are entering the labour market in the early twenty-first century. It cannot help that many expect to earn less and to have weaker careers than their parents. Remarkably, more UK youth say they belong to the working class than think their parents belong to it. There is a sense of downwardness, matched by what they see ahead of them.

Commodification of education

The commodification of education also makes for disappointment and anger. The drive by the education system to improve 'human capital' has not produced better job prospects. An education sold as an investment good that has no economic return for most buyers is, quite simply, a fraud. To give one example, 40 per cent of Spanish university students a year after graduating find themselves in low-skilled jobs that do not require their qualifications. This can only produce a pandemic of status frustration.

At present, the average lifetime monetary gain from going to a college or university is substantial – £200,000 for men in the United Kingdom (Browne, 2010). Imposing high fees may thus seem fair. But fees risk marginalising university subjects that offer no financial return and ignore the fact that the return is a *mean* average. In a market society, winner-takes-all markets proliferate, which is why income differentials have grown way beyond what would be justifiable on productivity grounds. A shrinking number of students gain the high income returns that produce the mean average. More will gain jobs paying well below the mean.

Now factor in what is happening in the labour market. Economies generate new types of job all the time, but we know the direction they are taking. For instance, over the next decade, fewer than half of all new jobs in the United States will be for people with degrees or the equivalent (Florida, 2010). Of those, based on past experience, 40 per cent may be filled by those without college qualifications. After all, Bill Gates was a dropout. So, only a third of all new jobs will be available for young people who complete tertiary education.

A majority will be bumped down into jobs that do not require high-level qualifications. Insult is added to injury. They will be told they should be committed, happy and loyal in jobs that are beneath their qualifications and must repay debts incurred on a promise that their certificates would gain them high-income jobs.

The neo-liberal state has been transforming school systems to make them a consistent part of the market society, pushing education in the direction of 'human capital' formation and job preparation. It has been one of the ugliest aspects of globalisation.

Through the ages education has been regarded as a liberating, questioning, subversive process by which the mind is helped to develop nascent capacities. The essence of the Enlightenment was that the human being could shape the world and refine himself or herself through learning and deliberation. In a market society, that role is pushed into the margins.

The education system is being globalised. It is brashly depicted as an industry, as a source of profits and export earnings, a zone of competitiveness, with countries, universities and schools ranked by performance indicators. It is hard to parody what is happening. Administrators have taken over schools and universities, imposing a 'business model' geared to the market. Although its standards have plunged abysmally, the leader of the global 'industry' is the United States. The idea is to process commodities, called 'certificates' and 'graduates'. Universities tend to compete not by better teaching but by offering a 'luxury model' – nice dormitories, fancy sports and dancing facilities, and the appeal of celebrity academics, celebrated for non-teaching achievements.

Symbolising the loss of Enlightenment values, in the United Kingdom in 2009, responsibility for universities was transferred from the education department to the department for business. The then business minister, Lord Mandelson, justified the transfer as follows: 'I want the universities to focus more on commercialising the fruits of their endeavour . . . business has to be central'.

Commercialisation of schooling at all levels is global. A successful Swedish commercial company is exporting a standardised schooling system that minimises direct contact between teachers and pupils and electronically monitors both. In higher education, teacher-less teaching and 'teacher-less classrooms' are proliferating (Giridharadas, 2009). The Massachusetts Institute of Technology has launched an Open Courseware Consortium, enlisting universities around the world to post courses online free of charge, including professors' notes, videos and exams. The iTunes portal offers lectures from Berkeley, Oxford and elsewhere. The University of the People, founded by an Israeli entrepreneur, provides tuition-free (tuition-less) bachelor degrees, through what it calls 'peer-to-peer teaching' – students learning not from teachers but from fellow students, trading questions and answers online.

Commercialisers claim it is about 'putting the consumers in charge'. Scott McNealy, chairman of Sun Microsystems and an investor in the Western Governors University, which delivers degrees online, argued that teachers should re-position themselves as 'coaches, not content creators', customising materials to students while piping in others' superior teaching. This commodification and standardisation is cheapening education, denuding the profession of its integrity and eroding the passing on of informal knowledge. It is strengthening winner-takes-all markets and accelerating the dismantling of an occupational community. A market in human capital will increase emphasis on celebrity teachers and universities, and favour norms and conventional wisdom. The Philistines are not at the gates; they are inside them.

International financial institutions such as the World Bank demand that 'inappropriate curricula' unrelated to the economy should be removed. A report commissioned by French President Nicolas Sarkozy argued that early schooling should focus on employability and that economics should be taught in all primary schools. The UK's Labour government urged the Financial Services Authority to advise on how 'to embed an entrepreneurial culture' in schools. In Italy, Prime Minister Silvio Berlusconi claimed that all that students needed to learn were the 'three i's' – *inglese, internet, impresa* (English, internet, enterprise). Instead of learning about culture and history, children must be taught how to be efficient consumers and jobholders.

In an experimental scheme in four US cities, students are paid for studying. In Dallas, second-graders are paid US$2 for each book they read; in Chicago, high school students are paid if they attain good grades; in Washington, DC, middle-schoolers are paid for good behaviour and attendance. Some parents have complained that this trend is eroding the intrinsic motivation for learning (Turque, 2010). But the market marches on.

Meanwhile, there are reports of a lost capacity to read, accompanying a collective attention deficit syndrome. The documentary *Waiting for Superman* reported that this is the first generation of Americans that is less literate than its predecessor (Harris, 2010). As English professor Mark Bauerlein told the *New York Times* (Bernstein, 2009), 'We have abysmal rates of civic knowledge and historical knowledge'. One doubts the commercialisers are concerned. Civic knowledge does not buy you a job. It does not even make you 'happy'.

Rote learning and standardised courses go on up the system. French economist Daniel Cohen stated approvingly, 'The university is to the new century what the Fordist firm was to the previous one' (Cohen, 2009: 81). But schooling is producing something historically unprecedented. People are being sold more and more 'credentials' that are worth less and less. Sellers are urged to produce more, buyers urged to buy more, and if they are in debt as a result of buying the last round of 'qualifications', they need to go further into debt to buy the next round, which just might be enough to secure a job that would make the total investment worthwhile. What does this madness mean for the precariat?

Reflect on the impact on capabilities. In his best-selling book *Shop Class as Soulcraft* (2009), Matthew Crawford attacks America for devaluing skilled labour. He argues that, whereas school students were once taught vocational skills that interested them (in 'shop class'), now they must take courses to make them competitive university candidates. Real skills are being sacrificed to the drive to acquire more certificates.

Part of the process of generating the precariat comes from dumbing down the educational system. The game is to maximise profits, by maximising 'throughput'. In the United Kingdom, hundreds of publicly funded university courses provide academic qualifications even though the subjects are non-academic. The Taxpayers' Alliance in 2007 identified 401 such 'non-courses', including a BA Honours Degree in 'outdoor adventure with philosophy', offered at University College Plymouth St Mark and St John, and one in 'lifestyle management' at Leeds Metropolitan University.

Alternative medicine is also doing well. Richard Tomkins (2009) cited forty-two universities offering eighty-four courses in subjects such as reflexology, aromatherapy, acupuncture and herbal medicine, including fifty-one BSc degree courses. They reflect an 'Endarkenment', a drift from rationalist Enlightenment thinking to an emotional way of thinking associated with religion and superstition. In the absence of evidence, advocates of alternative medicine cite patient testimonials. And there is a placebo effect from treatment in which there is faith.

Commodifying higher education legitimises irrationality. Any course is acceptable if there is a demand for it, if it can be sold to consumers willing to pay the price. Anybody can take a pseudo-course giving a credentialist degree 'because you're worth it', which means because you or your parents can pay and because we are here to give you what you want, not what we believe to be scientific or valid based on generations of knowledge. Courses and examinations are made easier, to maximise pass rates and avoid deterring students from enrolling and paying ever-fatter fees.

The cost of going to university has risen faster than incomes, particularly in the United States. Between 1970 and 2010, while median household income rose by 6.5 times, the cost of attending a private college rose by 13 times, and the cost of a state college rose by 15 times for in-state students and 24 times for out-of-state students. Value for money has tumbled. In 1961, full-time students in four-year colleges studied for 24 hours a week on average; in 2010, it was just 14 hours. Dropout and deferment rates are high; only 40 per cent graduate in four years. Both academics and students make short-term gains. Low teaching loads enable academics to sell themselves as researchers for more time, while inflated grades make it easier for students to obtain the commodity of a degree. Absenteeism pays. Senior academics in Ivy League universities, who scarcely do any teaching when they are around, now have sabbaticals every three years; it used to be every seven. They are more like absent teachers, ticking boxes.

Do not blame them. They are acting in accordance with a market society. The system is eating away at the professional ethics of education. A market is based on opportunism. Self-interest is what Adam Smith lauded and is what neo-liberal economists preach. But many academics and teachers who exist in this commodifying space are not cynical or dishonest. Many become depressed and stressed as they try to adjust. The neo-liberal state that fosters commercial behaviour reacts to the reluctance of teachers to do standard teaching by introducing artificial performance and auditing tests and indicators, backed by sanctions and penalties. Youths and teachers share in the loss.

Meanwhile, the international reaction to the financial meltdown of 2008 has included cuts to state education and a further shift of costs onto students and their families. California's former Governor Arnold Schwarzenegger cut US$1 billion from the University of California's budget. Fees were raised by 20 per cent; support staff were laid off; academics had to take unpaid leave. His actions were echoed across the United States. And in the United Kingdom, the government said in 2009 that it planned to cut spending on higher education. The academics' union claimed that thirty universities could close, with a loss of 14,000 jobs. The new government increased the planned cuts and made it clear that higher education was to become even more economically functional. The arts and social sciences were dispensable.

Globally, the squeeze on state spending is facilitating the growth of commercial schooling. The private University of Phoenix, America's largest 'educational service provider', increased its global enrolments in 2009 from 384,000 to 455,000. In England, entrepreneurs and corporations are sponsoring school 'academies', which gives them influence over curricula and specialisms. The scheme, started by the Labour government, is being expanded by the Conservative/Liberal Democrat Coalition. Rupert Murdoch's media group plans to sponsor a school in London, as it is already doing in New York, no doubt bringing its right-wing ideological trappings to bear. Another London school was sponsored by the ill-fated Lehman Brothers before the bank's spectacular bankruptcy in 2008.

This commodification of education is a societal sickness. There is a price to pay. If education is sold as an investment good, if there is an unlimited supply of certificates and if these do not yield the promised return, in terms of access to good jobs and high income with which to pay off debts incurred because they were nudged to buy more of the commodity, more entering the precariat will be angry and bitter. The market for lemons comes to mind. As does the old Soviet joke, in which the workers said, 'They pretend to pay us, we pretend to work'. The education variant would be as follows: 'They pretend to educate us, we pretend to learn'. Infantilising the mind is part of the process, not for the elite but for the majority. Courses are made easier, so that pass rates can be maximised. Academics must conform.

Streaming schooling for the precariat

There are signs that commodified educational systems are being restructured to stream youth into the flexible labour system, based on a privileged elite, a small technical working class and a growing precariat. If the education industry is selling commodities, and many students are not expected to go into a professional career, there is more scope for providing 'plebian' commodities. One surf-loving teenager said he was going to Plymouth University 'to do surf science and technology'; the course would require him to 'surf twice a week and that's compulsory'. These are dumbed-down degrees for dumbed-down workers.

In Germany, the famous apprenticeship system is shrinking, while more youths are being pushed into a 'transitional system', remedial schools that rarely produce sustainable skills. Apprenticeship training is highly specialised and can be provided only by approved schools. Baking bread and making pastries are separate disciplines; if someone wants to manage a McDonald's they must learn *Systemgastronomie*. These narrow specialisms make it hard to obtain a job. In 2005, more than a third of graduates were still unemployed a year after completing their training. The system, suited to an industrial age, is dysfunctional, its rigidity bound to produce misfits in a flexible economy.

There is pressure for general training that would make switching trades easier and give training rights to a wider range of schools. However, the German system is evolving to push more youth into the precariat. Children are streamed as young as 10 into three kinds of secondary school. The lowest tier, the *Hauptschulen*, which traditionally provided apprenticeship recruits, has become a repository for failing children; many who go through it now enter the transitional system. The apprenticeship system now draws recruits from middle-grade schools, *Realschulen*, which used to provide white-collar workers. Even top grammar schools, *Gymnasien*, provide apprenticeship recruits, although they are supposed to steer pupils into university. The educational system is adapting to shape its youth.

Streaming continues into the labour market. Thus the state bureaucracy has four career paths; those selected for one path have little chance of moving into another. One is reserved for people with a *Meisterbrief*, the highest vocational credential. With such a rigid system, those who fail to enter a privileged path in early life must feel hopeless.

The German system is failing its youth; comparative figures compiled by the OECD in 2001 showed 15-year-olds doing worse than in almost all other industrialised countries. More than a fifth could not read or calculate properly, and many teenagers dropped out of school. There has been reform in parts of the country, eroding the caste system between vocational and university training. But progress is slow. Instead, Germany is moving towards three-way streaming, in which a growing part of the system is preparing youth for life in the precariat.

Streaming is also growing in the United States. There, vocational training has long been disdained as blunting opportunity at an early age. Universities have been seen as the route to high salaries and global prowess. By 2005, only a fifth of high school students were taking vocational subjects, compared with a third in 1982. Yet labour demand has been shifting against degree purchasers. Seemingly recognising this, President Obama's Council of Economic Advisers proposed more two-year technical college degrees; some states are trying to revive apprenticeships and 'career academies' are spreading, combining academic and technical curricula with labour experience. President Obama urged every American to commit to at least one year of training. Community colleges are the new great hope. An intermediate streaming process is taking shape, preparing youths for a lower level working life.

On the other side of the world, millions are emerging from second-rung universities to enter the Chinese precariat. The university intake rose from a million in 2000 to 7 million in 2010. The system has produced a familiar path of social immobility (Chan, 2010). Those who go to good primary schools go to good secondary schools; the top universities take students from there. But most are born in poor families, live in poor regions, go to poor primary schools and end up in poor secondary schools from which the top universities do not take students.

Since 2006, more than a million graduates each year have become unemployed on leaving university. They have been called the Ant Tribe (Si, 2009), or the Wandering Tribe, because they rush around in their networks or wander around their old campuses in a desperate effort to retain a network of support and encouragement. Groups of graduates live together on city outskirts in tiny dwellings. Three-quarters are from rural areas, lacking household registration papers. Nearly all are single, living off casual jobs paying low wages, which they share. On those wages, they would have to work for a year to buy a tiny part of their cramped dwellings.

Youth precarity traps

There are two precarity traps for youths emerging from tertiary schooling. One is a debt trap. Assume they want to build occupational identities and careers, which require a long-term strategy. They emerge from college with their certificates and debts, with state-approved bailiffs waiting ominously to collect once they earn (or fail to do so). Many find the jobs they can obtain are temporary and the wages too low to pay off those debts. The jobs are not consistent with their qualifications and aspirations. They see and hear that millions of their peers are stuck in jobs for which their skills are ill-matched. They have had to grab what they can, not what would enable them to build that precious occupational identity. The precarity trap is worsened because potential employers may know of their indebtedness and worry about their reliability.

In Tokyo, students are blacklisted if they have not paid back scholarship loans, their limited access to jobs further weakened by having dubious credit records. That is picked up by recruiting firms doing checks. One thing leads to another. In general, youths are torn between their aspirations, backed by their certificates and years of study, and their need for income. This is the second precarity trap. They may take a temporary job because they need the income to live and pay down debt. They may not because it may dampen their prospects of a career-building alternative. If they turn down the temporary dead-end job, they may be branded as lazy and a scrounger. If they take it, they may be on a losing track.

There has been much discussion on whether today's youths have a different attitude towards work than their predecessors. They are said to want more of what politicians call 'work–life balance', a platitude verging on a tautology, in that one cannot imagine wanting a work-life imbalance. Those in what is variously called Generation Y, the Millennials or the 'iPod generation' (roughly speaking, born since the mid-1970s) are said to be less materially ambitious and less committed to jobs than the baby boomers (born 1946–60) or Generation X (born in between). This may merely reflect the nature of jobs available to the younger generation and the prevalence of the precarity trap. For psychological and economic reasons, many cannot afford to be as committed to jobs that could evaporate at short notice.

Some US studies find that most young employees say they are loyal to their employer (Hewlett et al., 2009). But a survey of college-educated employees in two companies found that 89 per cent of Generation Y and 87 per cent of baby boomers also regarded flexible work as important, and over two-thirds wanted to work remotely some of the time. Only a tiny minority of either generation described themselves as 'work-centric' and most did not see jobs as their route to happiness. The attitudes of the two generations were similar; the difference is in the reality confronting them. These studies focused on those who managed to enter salaried jobs, who would be expected to show more job commitment than those who did not.

A UK study (Centre for Women in Business, 2009) also found young professionals professing loyalty to their firm, but it was contingent loyalty in that most were ready to move on if not promoted. They felt their parents' trust in an 'organisation' had been betrayed and did not want to leave themselves open to such disappointment. While some have claimed that the Great Recession has acted as a needed 'reality check' on Generation Y's 'air of entitlement' (Tulgan, 2009), if anything it will have reinforced young people's feeling that the 'system' is against them.

In the end, the precarity traps reflect a discordance between young people's aspirations and the 'human capital' preparation system that sells credentialist qualifications on a false prospectus. Most jobs on offer do not require all those years of schooling, and to present schooling as preparing people for jobs is to set up tensions and frustrations that will give way to disillusion.

The intern craze

Meanwhile, a new form of precariat work specially designed for youth is spreading. Old-style probationary employment at least led to stable jobs in principle, as did apprenticeships. Internships do not. They are presented as a way of gaining useful experience intended to provide, directly or indirectly, a potential gateway to a regular job. In practice, they are used by many employers as a means of obtaining cheap dispensable labour. Yet youths are competing fiercely for these unpaid or very low-paid internships, in the hope of staying busy, gaining skills and experience, expanding networks and, just perhaps, landing that elusive job.

Internships are becoming a *rite de passage* for middle-class youth in some countries. The United States even has 'virtual interns', who work remotely for one or more companies, doing research, sales talks, marketing, graphic design or social media development. While students are exposed to potential spheres of future work and can work when it suits, potential drawbacks include isolation and a lack of networking.

In the United States, interns can collect unemployment benefits of about US$400 a month, as long as they can claim to be seeking employment. Being an intern disguises unemployment, gives artificial employment and improves resumés. Federal law prohibits the use of interns as substitutes for regular employees. But it is hard to check. To avoid legal complications, some firms limit internships to students receiving school credits. So some young workers enlist in schools just to allow themselves to do internships. Youths who become unemployed are also joining the market for internships. These intern applicants are advised to say they are looking for a career change or to learn something, and not to say that they lost their job and have nothing to do (Needleman, 2009). It is all rather sad and desperate.

Internships have crept into labour market policy. The Administrative Internship Scheme in South Korea, set up in 2008, offers temporary labour for graduates, who are placed as interns in government departments or public agencies for up to 11 months. The interns are not recognised as civil servants, are not covered by the Labour Standards Act or the Government Official Act, are banned from being employed as public officials after being in the programme, cannot be converted into full-time employees and are paid below the minimum wage. They can receive employee training, notably remote training, but as most are on internships lasting five months, not the 11 stipulated as the upper limit, this is limited. In a survey, only 8 per cent said the internship gave them any chance to develop professional skills.

In the United Kingdom, interns come mainly from middle-class families, which can afford to support their offspring in seeking a little extra on their CVs and a route into a real job. There have even been auctions for internships in the media and other privileging sectors, since unpaid or paid 'work experience' is increasingly required for access to 'decent jobs'. Though it is against the law to employ somebody without paying them anything, this is what happens with interns. A court case in 2009 (*Nicola Vetta vs London Dreams*) established that an intern had the right to the national minimum wage, even though she had agreed to work for the film company on an 'expenses only' basis. The legal point was that nobody could 'agree' to an unlawful arrangement. But it is happening all the time.

Internships are a threat to youth in and around the precariat. Even if a payment is made, the interns are doing cheap dead-end labour, exerting downward pressure on the wages and opportunities of others who might otherwise be employed. An internship may give positional advantage to a few young people, but it is more like buying a lottery ticket, in this case involving a private subsidy, usually paid by the intern's family.

Finally, it would be a mistake to think interns are just a feature of rich countries and middle-class youths. Apart from South Korea, they are also widespread in China. A strike at Honda's large transmission plant in Foshan revealed that interns comprised one-third of all employees, reflecting a widespread use of students and temporaries in Chinese manufacturing (Mitchell, 2010). Like everywhere else, interns are a precariat substitute for regular labour.

The generational tension

Youth in industrialised countries enter a labour market in which they will have to make increasing contributions from their low wages to finance the retirement income of the rising number of pensioners. The demographics are dispiriting. In Japan, where the ageing trend is most advanced, the number of workers to support each pensioner fell from ten in 1950 to four in 2000 and is expected to fall to two by 2025. No less than 70 per cent of the country's social security budget goes to the elderly and only 4 per cent to child care (Kingston, 2010). We will consider what is happening to old agers later. How it affects youth concerns us here.

Not only must youth of the twenty-first century pursue ever more qualifications, at high cost, in order to have a low probability of attaining a career entry point – a receding mirage for many – but even if they succeed, they will pay contributions, as today's workers, for the pensions of yesterday's employees. Since the cost of doing that is rising, mainly because of ageing, the state is raising the contributions that today's employees must pay and is pushing back the age at which today's employees can obtain a pension. To make the deal even less attractive to today's employees, the state is cutting the real value of tomorrow's state pension. And today's workers are told they must bear more of the risk, by having more of their contributions put in defined-contribution schemes (i.e. instead of having a guaranteed level of pension, contributions are put into investment funds that may go up or down in value). Often workers are required to put contributions into pension funds that make investments on their behalf, whether or not those funds are competent to do so.

Lack of Voice and the post-2008 recession

Youth are entering labour markets in some disarray, many experiencing status frustration, feeling economically insecure and unable to see how to build a career. Their predicament in many countries is compounded by unemployment. The financial meltdown hit youth hard. Millions lost jobs, millions more could not enter the labour market, and those who did found they had lower wages than their predecessors. By 2010, youth unemployment (aged 16–24) in Spain was over 40 per cent, in Ireland 28 per cent, in Italy 27 per cent, in Greece 25 per cent. The unemployment rate among US teenagers was a staggering 52 per cent. Across the world, youths dropped out of the labour force at three times the rate of adults. Many went back or tried to go back into further education, exacerbating the spiral of 'qualifications' exceeding requirements for the jobs available.

In Japan, the crisis accelerated the shift of youth into the precariat as companies froze initial entry to executive-track salariat positions. Traditionally, university graduates emerged in March each year to begin a salaryman job that would set them up for lifetime employment. There was a partial freeze during the slump in the early 1990s but after 2008 the freeze spread. In 2010, more than one in five graduates did not have any job offer. The salaryman model had crumbled. Almost half of all large and medium-sized firms said they did not intend to hire any regular employees at all. Graduates must adjust to new lifetime prospects, as employers grow more comfortable with abandoning lifetime salaryman norms.

Youth's disarray in the labour market has been compounded by its alienation from the main mechanism for venting frustration and for exercising Voice in bargaining for a less precariatised future. The strengthening of entitlements for regular employees, a twentieth-century achievement of unions and social democratic movements, has led to hostility towards unions by the young precariat. They see unions as protecting privileges of older employees, privileges they cannot anticipate for themselves. In former bastions of unionism, such as Spain and Italy, youth bitterly reject unions. To be fair, unions have wanted benefits extended to temporary employees. But they cannot achieve it. They see wages declining and jobs going elsewhere, further eroding their legitimacy – so much so that social democratic politicians find it expedient to distance themselves from them. Even union leaders are at a loss. Richard Trumka, on being elected head of the AFL-CIO in 2010, admitted that when young people 'look at unions, too often what they see is a remnant of their parents' economy'.

Today's youth find it difficult to form collective associations in the production process, partly because they are part of the flexible labour force, in temporary jobs, working remotely and so on. Youth comprise the bulk of the world's urban nomads, hurrying from one public place to another, from internet cafés to wherever else doubles as workplace and play-place. Thus Alessandro Delfanti, of the San Precario Connection, said, 'Our generation has lost the right to exert conflict within the productive sphere' (Johal, 2010). This is true, but youth need collective voice of some sort.

Dismal prospects

Youth have a combination of challenges. For many, a precarity trap beckons. For many, exposure to a commodifying education system leads to a period of status frustration. While for some, a short period of playing in the precariat may be an interlude between education and entering the rich salariat or even the elite, for the majority, the future promises a stream of temporary jobs with no prospect of developing an occupational career. For an increasing number, it is about being trained in 'employability', to be made presentable and flexible in any number of ways, none corresponding to what they really want.

For some it is just too much. One reaction to the clash between education and the prospect of precariat jobs has been to opt out of the pursuit of jobs altogether, becoming what Italian observers have dubbed *alternativi* or '*cognitariat*', who live a bohemian existence that trades security for a life of creativity and autonomy (Florida, 2003: 35). This is only feasible for a few and is a Faustian bargain, in which freedom and excitement are paid for later, in lack of a pension or other material comforts. But it tugs the sentiments of many more.

Warren Buffett had a snowball theory. The earlier someone can define their skills and ambitions, the longer they have to let them roll, accumulating size and power. If early precious years are spent groping around in precarious jobs, the capacity to develop will be permanently impaired. It is this that may make the young most angry. The prospect of persistent insecurity sits uncomfortably with a feeling that it is contrived, not necessary.

This is the sum of it. The youth part of the precariat is railing against the dimming of the light of education and against the commodification of life, in which there is a clash between a commercial educational process and alienating jobs that appear to be beneath the qualifications they are supposed to possess. They share a vision of life as an unfolding drama of status frustration yet reject the drabness of the labourism that was the lot of their parents' generation. There is some rethinking to be done.

Old agers: Groaners and grinners

The world is 'ageing', a sobering idea that has become part of our vocabulary. One could describe the same process as 'younging', for although people are living longer and the share of the population in older age groups is rising, more 'old agers' are active and energetic for longer. It is common to hear that today's 70-year-old is yesterday's 50-year-old. This may be wishful thinking by some, but it is roughly right.

While youths are having trouble beginning a viable life, old agers are confused, some in a pleasant way, some in a wretched one. After decades of being told they were not wanted, eased into early retirement in recessions, now they are being told they must work longer.

In the first recession of the neo-liberal era, in the early 1980s, rich country governments rushed old agers into the economic shadows, easing them onto incapacity benefits, even though many were not incapacitated, or onto special unemployment benefits or into early retirement. The objective was to free up jobs for youth. But although it looked clever to politicians at the time, the policy was a costly failure. The main result was that the effective retirement age plunged below the official one. By 2004, in OECD countries, only 60 per cent of those aged 50–64 were in jobs, compared with 76 per cent of those aged 24–49.

Meanwhile, in rich countries, young women stopped having babies; the fertility rate fell to below the reproduction rate. Suddenly, governments became alarmed at the 'pension time bomb', as the number approaching pension age exceeded the number of young workers entering the labour force who could contribute to pension schemes. A crisis was building up.

The slow death of pensions

The era of pensions was a wonder of the modern world, even though it lasted for only a tiny fraction of history. It was part of the delusion of globalisation. For a few years in industrialised countries, net of taxes and social security contributions, mandatory pensions averaged 70 per cent of previous net earnings and over 80 per cent for the low paid. In the Netherlands in 2005, the average net pension exceeded net median earnings; in Spain, it was over 80 per cent; in Italy, Sweden, Canada and France, over 60 per cent; in Germany and the United States, nearly 60 per cent. Only in the United Kingdom and Japan, among major OECD countries, did it remain below 50 per cent. The UK state pension has fallen to such a low level that the link with earnings severed by the Thatcher government is being restored as from 2012.

What scares the politicians and pension fund analysts is simple arithmetic. The share of the world's population aged 65 and over will double between 2010 and 2040, to 14 per cent. In Western Europe, unless the migration floodgates are opened, the share will rise from 18 per cent to over 28 per cent. By 2050, one-fifth of the world's 9 billion people will be over age 60, and in today's rich countries it will be one-third. Nearly one in ten will be over 80. Developing countries already have 490 million people aged over 60; that will rise to 1,500 million by 2050. The United Nations estimates that life expectancy at birth globally will rise from 68 in 2010 to 76 by 2050 and in rich countries from 77 to 83. And there will be far more elderly women, since on average they live over five years longer than men.

Others are even more optimistic about longevity. They estimate that the long-term trend upwards has been about three months a year, so that by 2050 life expectancy in the high-longevity countries will be well over 90. That is coming with increased capability to be active. Disability among those aged over 65 has declined, and there has been a compression of morbidity into the final year of life. So there will be a lot more active old agers around.

The trouble is that pensions were not designed for what is unfolding in the twenty-first century. When the United States introduced its Social Security (state pension) scheme in 1935 to prevent old-age poverty, the retirement age was 65 while average life expectancy was 62. Since then, life expectancy has risen to 78. In 1983, the United States legislated to raise the retirement age to 67, in small steps, by 2027. But this means the pension promise will continue to cover many more years of retirement than in the 1930s, unless there are further changes. There will be. Similar developments will take place in all rich countries.

The main fact for our analysis is that on average people can spend a very long time in nominal retirement. The OECD estimated in 2007 that, in its member countries, men could anticipate between 14 and 24 years in retirement, women between 21 and 28. This was

50 per cent more than in 1970 and was an underestimate in using life expectancy in 2007 rather than in the future. The situation is fiscally unsustainable.

According to the IMF, the cost of the financial shock will be dwarfed by the cost of the 'ageing crisis'. Its calculation is based on current pension fund pressures, a continuation of the current pattern of labour force participation and a rising 'old-age dependency' ratio – the number aged 15–64 divided by the number aged 65 and over. In the European Union, this ratio will fall from four to two in 2040. So, whereas today the contributions of four workers are required to support one pensioner, that will fall to just two. The challenge is even greater, since not everybody aged 15–64 is in the labour force. Taking that into account, the old-age dependency ratio is set to fall from just under 3 to just under 1.5. Roughly speaking, every three people in the labour force will be expected to support two people over the age of 65, if they were all in pensioned retirement.

That will not happen. It is the idea of retirement that will fade, along with the pension, which was suited to an industrial age. The reaction to the fiscal crisis has been to roll back early retirement schemes and age-related incapacity benefits, to lower state pensions, to push back the age at which people can claim a state pension and the age at which they can claim a full state pension. Contribution rates have been climbing and the age at which people can receive a pension has gone up, more for women than for men to approach equality. The number of years of contributions to gain entitlement to a state pension has gone up, with the number required to receive a full pension increasing even more. In some countries, notably in Scandinavia, the legal retirement age for eligibility for a state pension is now pegged to life expectancy, so that access to a pension will recede as people on average live longer and will recede with each medical breakthrough.

This amounts to tearing up the old social compact. But the picture is even more complex, for while governments are convinced they are in a fiscal hole with pensions, they are worried about the effect of ageing on labour supply. Bizarre though it may seem in the midst of recession, governments are looking for ways of keeping older workers in the labour force rather than relying on a pension because they think there will be a shortage of workers. What better way to overcome this than to make it easier for old agers to be in the precariat?

From early retirement to retirement labour

Here policy makers have an open door. Because more jobs are precariat in character, old agers are better placed to take them, and because there are more old agers around, more jobs are put into the precariat. This is reversing a long trend.

The United Kingdom is a good example. Les Mayhew (2009) has observed that the share of people in the labour force drops sharply after the age of 50 – roughly when private pension eligibility begins. By age 64 fewer than half of men and less than a third of women are doing labour activity. Most are healthy and the health of people aged 50–70 is rising all the time. The healthier and the more educated the person, the more likely an old ager is to be economically active. Mayhew estimated that, already on average, people are healthy enough to go on working for 11 years beyond the existing state retirement age of 65. The pool of old agers able to work is huge.

Many are already doing so, often unrecorded. Many are firmly within the precariat. Indeed, old agers have become a driving force in its growth. Old agers have become a source of cheap labour, paid low wages, given few benefits, easily sacked. In some respects, they play roles similar to migrants, who are considered later. In one respect, they do not, which is that more people positively welcome a precariat existence, in the narrow sense of the term. They are often grateful just to be wanted. They already work in vast numbers as volunteers. The activist organisation for the elderly, Age Concern, has estimated that in this guise they contribute £30 billion a year to the UK economy, which does not take account of their grand-parenting (and, in a growing number of cases, parenting) work.

Old agers are attracted to part-time, temporary and self-employment activities. Opinion polls in the United States and Europe have found that, except in France and Germany, while most baby boomers are in favour of working longer for a bigger pension, most want part-time jobs. And a 2007 Eurobarometer survey found that 61 per cent of Americans would rather be self-employed than in a job. Although Europeans under the age of 24 were almost as enthusiastic for this relative freedom and risk-taking, older Europeans were slightly more inclined to prefer employment. However, age differences overlaid national differences. Some 57 per cent of Portuguese would prefer self-employment, compared with 30 per cent of Belgians.

There is growing support for policies to make it easier for old agers to be in the labour market after retirement age. Both young and old regard this positively, although attitudes vary by country. Almost nine out of every ten people in the United Kingdom, Denmark, Finland and the Netherlands told Eurobarometer that older people should be helped to find work if they wished. By contrast, 55 per cent of Greeks were opposed, and in Greece, Cyprus, Hungary, Italy and Portugal, a majority felt that old agers would take jobs from the young.

In the post-2008 recession, governments did the reverse of what they had done in the 1980s, encouraging old agers to stay in the labour market by restricting disability benefits and making it harder to take early retirement. Many old agers postponed thoughts of retirement because their pension savings were hit by the financial meltdown.

Revealingly, old-ager employment did not decline in the post-2008 recession by anything like as much as youth employment. In the United States, partly due to the erosion of pensions, the supply of elderly labour increased. One survey found that 44 per cent of respondents aged over 50 planned to postpone retirement, half of them planning to remain in the labour force for three years longer than previously expected. Over a quarter of the US labour force are aged over 55, so that implies a substantial rise in the old-ager labour force. According to annual surveys by the Employment Benefit Research Institute, the change has been dramatic. In 2007, 17 per cent planned to retire before the age of 60; in 2009, only 9 per cent did so. Those planning to retire between 60 and 65 also fell. Those planning to retire after 65 rose from 24 to 31 per cent, and those expecting not to retire at all jumped from 11 to 20 per cent. What a change in mental perspective this represents! It is not the classic 'secondary worker' effect, as was the norm of every recession in the twentieth century. It is something new.

Ageing is producing awkward challenges for inter-generational relations. In industrial society, youths and prime-age adults were responsible for the needs of their children and were not concerned about parents because they were dead or were not expected to be around for very long or did not make many demands if they were. Nowadays, more youths, seeing a life in the precariat, cannot contemplate supporting parents, especially since this might need to continue for many years. And, because of later childbearing, the prospect is made more daunting by the thought that they would be supporting children and elderly parents at the same time.

So old agers are losing the prospect of support from their children. That is driving more into the labour pool, to be willingly part of the precariat. But the state is not neutral. An older generation cut off from family support could become a fiscal burden. Some governments are refusing to tolerate this prospect. Chindia is taking the lead. In China, as in India, a law, passed in 1996, makes it a legal obligation for adults to care for their parents. In formalising a Confucian tradition, the state revealed the tradition was under stress. The fear is that a '4–2–1' rule will spread, with one offspring having responsibility for supporting two parents and four grandparents. And people are finding it harder to live in a three-generational unit because of geographical mobility.

In other countries, the state places more hope on 'workable' old agers looking after the frail elderly and on more women accepting the triple burden of child care, elder care and paid employment, with social workers and care homes picking up the slack.

The subsidised generation

The precariat is being boosted by old agers uninterested in career building or long-term employment security. This makes them a threat to youth and others in the precariat, since they can take low-wage dead-end jobs lightly. They are not frustrated by the career-lessness, in the way youths would be. But old agers too may be grinners or groaners.

The grinners just want something to do. They have a pension to fall back on, their mortgages are paid off, their health insurance is covered and their children are off their hands, perhaps even available to lend a hand or give them financial support, or that is what they hope. Many seek and find that elusive 'work–life balance'.

The balance is usually seen as something of concern to young couples with children. But other factors among old agers are as powerful. Lucy Kellaway (2009) was puzzled when a 56-year-old former marketing director told her he had become a postman:

> But then he said something that made more sense. His new job had allowed him to reclaim his mind. When he goes home at 1 p.m. every day he does not have to give work another thought till 7.30 a.m. the next day. In his old job, worries from the office took up permanent residence in his head, making his synapses too ragged to allow him to focus properly on anything else. And then I started to realise why he loves this job so much. It has nothing to do with how nice it is to be a postman in absolute terms but how nice it is relative to being a senior manager. He enjoys lugging his big bag because he knows what the alternative is. He knows how wretched it is spending your working life trying to get people to do things they don't want to do and bearing responsibility for things that you can't change.

Many old agers could relate to that, even to feeling content to do something that has no career. They take temporary jobs in which they deliberately underuse their technical capabilities and experience. As such, they can be unprecedented competitors for younger workers trying to climb onto an occupational ladder.

Meanwhile, the groaners have no pension to write home about, have a residual mortgage or have nothing to write home about because they have no home. They need the money; they fear being out in the street, as a 'bag lady' or 'bag man'. Their desperation makes them a threat to others in the precariat, since they will take anything going. And, whether groaners or grinners, old agers are being helped to compete with youth in the precariat, as governments react to the combination of the pension crisis and the perception that in the longer term there will be a labour shortage.

First, governments are offering subsidies for private (and some public) pension investments. Fearing spiralling pension costs, governments have introduced tax incentives for private pension savings. These are inegalitarian, as are most subsidies. They are a bribe to those who can afford to do what is in their long-term interest. From an equity viewpoint, they are hard to justify. The subsidy enables old agers to compete more effectively with younger workers. Those in their 50s and 60s gain pension income from their subsidised schemes and so can take jobs with lower wages, without pension contributions from employers. And they will be more inclined to work 'off the books'.

Second, governments are encouraging firms to retain older employees and even to recruit them. Some are offering subsidies here too. In Japan, working for income well beyond retirement age is becoming a norm. But firms such as Hitachi are rehiring many who reach the age of 60 on lower pay (in Hitachi's case, 80 per cent of regular pay), with low status and without seniority, aided by a government subsidy.

Third, old agers are one of the last frontiers for protective regulation. Because of images formed in industrial society, age discrimination remains rife. Policy makers are combating this. It started with the US Age Discrimination in Employment Act of 1967, which was designed to provide equal opportunities to the over-40s. It was later amended so that firms could set mandatory retirement ages for most jobs. In France, the government imposes a tax – the Delalande contribution, worth up to a year's pay – on any firm that sacks older workers. The tax has acted as a deterrent to the hiring of old agers and in 2010 was in the process of being scrapped. But in many countries, led by an EU directive, there is a charge to ban age discrimination.

If one accepts that productivity declines with age, then anti-age discrimination laws may lead employers to use other tactics to rid themselves of lower productivity workers. If governments try to compensate for the perception of lower productivity by providing subsidies for old agers, they may equalise opportunities. But, in a tertiary system, productivity differences may not be great; policies intended to equalise opportunities may thus actually strengthen old agers' advantages. Vegard Skirbekk of the International Institute for Applied Systems Analysis has shown that in many jobs productivity does indeed decline in middle age. While 3D jobs (dirty, dangerous and demanding) may have shrunk, more jobs require cognitive skills, which decline among those in their 50s. 'Fluid intelligence' drops, including numerical skills and ability to adjust to novelty. But, fortunately for old agers, 'crystallised intelligence' – general knowledge, experience and verbal ability – does not decline until people are elderly. It could also be that those with more career-oriented experience acquire capabilities that those with long exposure to a precariat existence do not, giving them an advantage in many service jobs.

More decisively, old agers are subsidised by not needing various enterprise benefits that younger workers want. They do not need the promise of maternity leave, crèches, medical insurance, housing subsidies, sports club memberships and so on. So, because they cost less, old agers are eroding the bargaining position of youths.

In the United States, corporations are reaching out to pre-retirement baby boomers, offering incentives to induce more work from them or taking advantage of tax breaks. For instance, Cisco Systems, the communications equipment maker, has connected its elegantly named 'legacy leaders network' (pre-retirement employees) with its 'new hire network' (a less impressive euphemism) to encourage knowledge transfer. This is inducing more work-for-labour by old agers and intensifying labour input. The fancy name is 'mentoring'; the un-fancy name is low-cost training.

As pensioners become more numerous, resentment by today's workers at paying for yesterday's will intensify, especially as they are not being promised the same deal. Multi-pillar pension systems are one outcome, with private plans being a subsidised addition to shrinking public schemes. They open up moves to lifetime savings schemes, which in theory would suit the precariat and proficians, adding a source of income security through accessible grants in times of need. In practice, the changes may leave more people insecure because they cannot contribute regularly or enough. People are unable to save enough to cover pension risks, and there is limited cross-subsidisation of the sort found in social insurance schemes.

Pension risks are compounded by the possibility of pension funds going bankrupt or making bad investments, as occurred after the financial crash. It is old agers who bear these risks, which is one reason why in each recession they will expand the labour pool, pushing up unemployment and lowering wages.

Encouraging old agers to labour may have other costs for the state. More labour may mean less unpaid work done by old agers. Many retirees undertake voluntary and care work, looking after grandchildren, frail elderly parents and so on. Pushing more into the precariat would have costs there too. But the biggest problem will be that old agers are subsidised relative to younger workers and are relatively amenable to accepting a precariat status. Resolving the tensions will require further reforms, along the lines proposed in Chapter 7.

Ethnic minorities

It is not clear that ethnic minorities will always have a high propensity to enter the precariat. We mention them here because they face high labour market barriers. But there is evidence that ethnic minorities try to reproduce their occupational niches over generations, often doing so through family businesses and ethnic contacts and networks.

This is by no means true for all minorities. Thus, while the post-2008 US recession has been a 'mancession', the hardest hit were black men. Half of all young black men were unemployed by late 2009, and this startling statistic was based on a labour force figure that excluded all those in prison, at a time when there were nearly five times as many blacks behind bars as whites.

American black men suffer from a cruel combination of circumstances – prison records, concentration in high-unemployment
regions and lack of contacts in small-scale businesses, as well as
below-average schooling. By 2010, only about half of all adult blacks
were in employment, and the proportion was close to 40 per cent
among young black men. For adult whites it was 59 per cent. Blacks
who became unemployed were unemployed on average five weeks
longer than others, accentuating loss of skills, positive attitudes,
contacts and so on. The chances of building a career and avoiding a
life in the precariat were slim.

The 'disabled': A concept under reconstruction?

The notion of 'the disabled' is unfortunate. We all have impairments
or disabilities of some kind. Most of us go through life without many
people knowing or caring about our impairments – physical, mental,
psychological or whatever. But many suffer because their particular
impairment is noticed and taken into account in how they are
treated.

In today's electronically charged world of instant diagnosis and
communication, it is easier to identify and categorise an individual's
impairment and to tag that person for eternity. This means many more
are sized up for classification, for treatment or for neglect. Among
that is a looming wall of discrimination.

This is how disability and the precariat come together. Those
identified as different are not only more likely to find life opportunities
restricted to precarious options but they are also more likely to be

pushed that way. And one aspect of ageing societies is that more people are moving into old age marked by disabilities, and their longer lives are giving more people longer to notice them.

The state has reacted to the growing recognition of disability by constructing an armoury of policies. In labour market terms, they have institutionalised quota systems, specialised workplaces, anti-discrimination laws, equal opportunity workplace amendments and so on. And they have increasingly tried to sift out the deserving poor. In the 1980s, many countries resorted to incapacity benefits, often doing so on a loose basis, to move people from unemployment to being out of the labour force altogether. By the beginning of the twenty-first century, governments were looking at the mounting benefit bills with sceptical fiscal eyes and set out to reduce them by re-medicalising disability, by seeking to make more of the disabled 'employable' and by pushing them into jobs. Many joined the precariat by the side door.

Reflect on an aspect little discussed in public debates, 'episodic disability'. This is causing a growing connection between disability and the precariat. Millions suffer from conditions that hit from time to time, ranging from migraine and depression to diabetes and epilepsy. They are likely to be casualties of the world's flexible labour markets, with employers reluctant to recruit and eager to dispense with the 'performance impaired'. Many will drift into precarious jobs and a precarious cycle of disadvantage and insecurity. That may intensify their medical difficulties and bring on others. Those with episodic disabilities may face barriers in the welfare system as well. They may be told they are capable of labouring, which they are, and be denied benefits. Probably the majority would wish for paid employment. But who is going to employ them when others are seen as more 'reliable'?

The criminalised: Precariat from behind bars

The precariat is being fed by an extraordinary number of people who have been criminalised in one way or another. There are more of them than ever. A feature of globalisation has been the growth of incarceration. Increasing numbers are arrested, charged and imprisoned, becoming denizens, without vital rights, mostly limited to a precariat existence. This has had much to do with the revival of utilitarianism and a zeal for penalising offenders, coupled with the technical capacity of the surveillance state and the privatisation of security services, prisons and related activities.

Contrary to predictions in the 1970s by Michel Foucault, David Rothman and Michael Ignatieff, who thought the prison was in terminal decline, the prison has become an extensive institution and policy instrument. Since the 1970s prison numbers have doubled in Belgium, France and the United Kingdom; tripled in Greece, the Netherlands and Spain; and quintupled in the United States (Wacquant, 2008). Every day 700 more are added to the Italian prison population. The prison is an incubator of the precariat, a laboratory for precariat living.

The United States, China and Russia have become the greatest criminalisers, each incarcerating millions of their own citizens and many foreigners. More than one in every fifty Americans has a criminal record, diminishing their rights in society. Countries such as the United Kingdom and France, having increased their criminalisation rates, are maintaining people as criminalised denizens. About 40 per cent of all inmates in UK prisons were once in the 'care system'.

They keep re-offending because they have no 'job' and cannot get a job because they have been in prison.

Criminalisation condemns people to a precariat existence of insecure and career-less jobs, and a degraded ability to hold to a long-term course of stable living. There is double jeopardy at almost every point, since beyond being punished for whatever crime they have committed, they will find that punishment is accentuated by barriers to their normal involvement in society.

However, there is also growth of a precariat *inside* prisons. We consider how China has resorted to prison labour in Chapter 4. But countries as dissimilar as the United States, United Kingdom and India are moving in similar directions. India's largest prison complex outside Delhi, privatised, of course, is using prisoners to produce a wide range of products, many sold online, with the cheapest labour to be found, working eight-hour shifts for six days a week. Prisoners with degrees earn about US$1 a day, others a little less. In 2010 the new UK justice minister announced that prison labour would be extended, saying he wanted prisoners to work a 40-hour week. Prison work for a pittance has long been common in the United States. The precariat outside will no doubt welcome the competition.

Concluding points

The precariat does not consist of people with identical backgrounds and is not made up just of those groups we have highlighted. It makes sense to think there are varieties of precariat, with different degrees of insecurity and attitudes to having a precariat existence.

The growth of the global precariat has coincided with four remarkable shifts. Women have been displacing men, to the point where there is talk of 'mancessions' and feminisation of labour markets. Men have been dragged into the precariat, while women have been confronted by the prospect of the triple burden. More remarkably, old agers have been marching back into labour markets, subsidised in taking precariat jobs and pushing down wages and opportunities for youths. For their part, youth are faced with status frustration, career-less prospects and subsidised competition from home and abroad. If they hold out for better, they risk being demonised as lazy, as we shall see. It is an impasse.

Also remarkably, proportionately more adults seem to suffer from some socially recognised disability, making them more likely to be relegated to insecure career-less labour, perhaps subsidised by the state. And finally, for all sorts of reasons, more of our fellow human beings are being criminalised and left little option beyond the lower rungs of the precariat. It remains to consider those perhaps best described as the light infantry of the whole process, migrants.

4

Migrants: Victims, villains or heroes?

Migrants make up a large share of the world's precariat. They are a cause of its growth and in danger of becoming its primary victims, demonised and made the scapegoat of problems not of their making. Yet, with few exceptions, all they are doing is trying to improve their lives.

The term 'migrant' comes with historical baggage and covers a multitude of types of experience and behaviour. Some resemble nomads, moving around with no fixed home, driven or acclimatised to roam, always expecting to settle 'one day'. The authentic nomad did know where he or she was going and why. The modern nomad is more opportunistic. Then there are 'circulants', leaving their home in search of earnings or experience but planning to return sooner rather than later. And there are settler migrants, those who move with the intention of remaining if they can, as well as refugees and asylum seekers.

Having dipped in the mid-twentieth century, when economies were more closed, the mobility of people around the world has soared with globalisation. One billion people cross national borders every year, and the number is rising. According to the International Organisation for Migration, there were 214 million international migrants in the world in 2010, three per cent of the global population. That is probably an underestimate, as undocumented migrants are obviously hard to count. In addition, perhaps 740 million are 'internal' migrants, including the 200 million rural migrants to China's industrial cities who share many of the characteristics of international migrants (House, 2009).

Although documented migration into industrialised countries slowed down after the 2008 financial crisis, until then it had been growing by 11 per cent a year (OECD, 2010a). One in four Australian workers is a migrant, as is one in five Irish workers. In Europe, 12 million European citizens live in an EU country other than their own.

The United States remains the major recipient of migrants. In the first decade of the twenty-first century, over a million 'legal' migrants and perhaps a further half a million 'illegal' migrants entered each year. Today, one in eight people is a migrant, and nearly one in six workers is foreign born, the highest proportion since the 1920s. Carefully erected barriers saw the migrant share of the US workforce dip from a high of 21 per cent in 1910 to 5 per cent in 1970. But, by 2010, it was back to 16 per cent. In California, immigrants account for over one in three workers, and in New York, New Jersey and Nevada, over one in four. Although migrants are mainly in agriculture, construction, catering, transport and health care, a quarter of highly educated workers with doctorates are foreign born.

Other countries have also become big recipients. By 2000, migrants accounted for over 10 per cent of the population in 70 countries, compared with only 48 countries in 1970. In Germany, 16 million of the country's population of 82 million are of migrant origin. In some cities, more than a third of the residents are immigrants and more than half of them are children. In other European countries too, migrants make up a rising share of the population, partly because of the low fertility rates of nationals. In the United Kingdom, one in every ten people is a migrant and the first decade of the twenty-first century saw the largest in-migration ever experienced. On current trends, the 'white' British could be in a minority in the second half of this century (Coleman, 2010).

Modern migration is not just about moving from poor to rich countries. Roughly a third of the world's migrants have moved from a poor to a rich country, a third have moved from one rich country to another and a third have moved from one poor country to another. Many countries, such as South Africa, experience large flows of out-migration and in-migration simultaneously. Moreover, while the image of migration is still one of settlement, today's migration has seven features that mark out the Global Transformation and fuel the growth of the precariat.

First, a historically high share is undocumented. Many governments have connived in this, claiming they are limiting migration while facilitating the growth of a low-wage disposable labour supply. The United States has the most undocumented migrants, with an estimated 12 million in 2008, up 42 per cent since 2000; over half come from Mexico. The political response has been incoherent. In 2006, the House of Representatives passed a bill making 'illegal migration' a felony, but it failed to pass in the Senate, which tried unsuccessfully to pass a similar bill in 2007. In 2009, two trade unions produced a plan to regularise the situation and launched a campaign for legalisation.

This too has run into the ground. Advocates of reform argue that bringing immigrants' shadow economy into the open would raise tax revenue, end abuse of illegal migrants, raise wages all around and boost growth. But the political will to legalise has remained feeble. Too many interests benefit from an army of illegal migrants, and too many populists depict attempts at legalisation as eroding the security of the citizenry.

Undocumented migration has been growing elsewhere as well, with similar posturing and conflicts of interest. Undocumented workers provide cheap labour and can be fired and deported if necessary or if they prove recalcitrant. They do not appear on the payrolls of firms and households, and fade into the nooks and crannies of society when recession hits. Productivity appears to rise wonderfully in a boom, as more are recruited without appearing in the statistics, and employment mysteriously drops less than the drop in output and demand in recessions. They are truly a shadow reserve army.

Second, a rising share of migration consists of 'circulation', in contrast to the last peak in migration early in the twentieth century when most migrants were settlers. The modern circulants see themselves as itinerants, moving to take temporary jobs, often with the hope of remitting money to relatives.

A *third* distinctive feature is the feminisation of migration (OECD, 2010b). Women, often moving on their own, make up a greater share of international migrants than at any time in history. They have long comprised a high share of internal migrants, in some countries a majority. There are well-documented sinister trends, with trafficking and prostitution the most conspicuous, and there is the sadness of 'household care chains', where women go from villages to towns to abroad, leaving children to be cared for by others. Often in bonded contracts, in debt, they are vulnerable, abused, given no protection and often live a shadowy existence. There has also been an unedifying flow of dubious marriage transfers, with young women given no choice by their families or cultures. However, much of the migration has been like that of men, undertaken in the search for a better life.

A *fourth* feature of the migration induced by globalisation is student mobility. While not new, the mobile student population has grown dramatically and, partly due to counter-terrorism measures, a larger proportion are now going to countries other than the United States. Between 2001 and 2008, the US share of foreign students fell from 28 to 21 per cent, while the number of globally mobile students rose by 50 per cent.

A *fifth* feature is movement within multinational corporations. This too has been practised throughout the ages; it was a feature of the great merchant banks of the Middle Ages, for example. But today it is systemic. It involves most levels, from executives to junior staff. It creates fragmented careers and a heady mix of experience.

A *sixth* feature is more ominous. There have never been anything like as many refugees and asylum seekers as there are today. The modern legal treatment stems from the response to the mass displacement before and during the Second World War, which led to the 1951 UN *Convention Relating to the Status of Refugees*. The problem was regarded as one of short-run adjustment as people were helped back to their countries or enabled to resettle elsewhere. Now, increasing numbers seeking to escape from degradation, oppression and conflict are running up against rising barriers to entry. Many fall into chronic social and economic insecurity.

According to the UN refugee agency, in 2009 there were over 15 million refugees, a majority in Asia and Africa, with another million asylum seekers awaiting decision. And some 27 million people were displaced within their countries as a result of conflict (Internal Displacement Monitoring Centre, 2010). Globally, a tragedy has been unfolding. Millions of people are spending years in squalid hostels, detention centres, camps or pieces of wasteland losing their dignity, skills and humanity.

The lofty principle of *non-refoulement* – that no country may send a person back to their homeland if they would face danger – is increasingly abused. In some countries, the average time for processing applications has risen to over 15 years. The plight of those trapped in transit countries, hoping to reach somewhere else where the doors are closed, has worsened. In many countries, where a majority of citizens favour more stringent restrictions on immigration, hostility to refugees and asylum seekers is greater than to more favourably placed economic migrants.

Finally, there is a new migrant group – 'environmental refugees'. Environmental degradation, including rising sea levels and other manifestations of climate change, could drive 200 million people from their homes by 2050 (Environmental Justice Foundation, 2009). Hurricane Katrina in 2005 induced the largest movement of people in the history of the United States. In two weeks, 1.5 million fled the Gulf coast, three times as many as moved in the Dust Bowl migration of the 1930s. Half the population of New Orleans had not returned five years later. It may be a harbinger of many such events.

In sum, migration is growing and changing character in ways that are intensifying insecurities and putting many more into precarious circumstances. As if that were not enough, there is also a 'de-territorialisation' of migration. This is an ungainly term for an ungainly trend. More and more people who 'look like migrants' are subject to intrusive scrutiny within national borders, stopped by police and vigilante groups demanding they prove their identity and legality.

The US state of Arizona's law SB1070 of 2010 has mandated 'de-territorialisation'; people stopped on suspicion of doing something illegal are required to prove the legality of their migrant status. Defenders of SB1070 claim this is not 'racial profiling', but it certainly gives police licence to target people who look like migrants. What is happening in Arizona is happening in much of the world.

The new denizens

Considering the varieties of migrant – nomadic, circulatory, illegal, refugee, settler and so on – leads to a neglected concept with deep historical roots. This is the *denizen*, as distinct from the *citizen*. In the Middle Ages, in England and other European countries, a denizen was an alien who was discretionarily granted by the monarch or ruler some – but not all – rights that were automatically bestowed on natives or citizens. Thus, in return for payment, an alien would be granted 'letters patent', enabling him to buy land or practise a trade.

In common law, a denizen was not a full citizen but had a status similar to that of a 'resident alien' today; the law followed the ancient Roman idea of granting someone a right to live in a place but not to participate in its political life. Later, the word was to take another connotation, as indicating someone who frequented a type of place, as with 'nightclub denizens'; it was also used to refer to non-slave blacks in the United States before the abolition of slavery.

All international migrants are denizens, with different groups having some rights – civil, social, political, economic and cultural – but not others. The ongoing construction of an international rights structure means there are varieties of denizen. Beginning with the least secure, asylum seekers and undocumented migrants have civil rights (such as protection against assault) – usually based on the territoriality principle, covering everybody when they are in the country's territory – but no economic or political rights. Slightly more secure are legalised temporary residents, but they too do not have full economic or political rights. Most secure are those who have acquired full citizenship rights by due process. This layered system has emerged in an *ad hoc* way and varies even within a regional bloc such as the European Union.

Denizenship is complicated by dual citizenship and multiple statuses. Migrants may be reluctant to opt for citizenship of the country where they reside or work for fear of losing citizenship of their country of origin. A person may have the right to live in one country but not to take a job there, while having a right to work for wages in another country without a right to take up residence there if not employed. Some jurists refer to this as 'cosmopolitan denizenship' (Zolberg, 1995).

However, the denizen concept is useful in delineating what people can and cannot do in society. The spectrum begins with asylum seekers, who have practically no rights at all. As their numbers rise, governments are making their lives harder. Often, they are humiliated and treated as if they were criminals. Those who can may try to survive by living a precariat existence. Many simply languish, seeing their lives wasting away.

Next are the undocumented migrants, who have civil rights as human beings but lack economic, social or political rights. They usually have no alternative to eking out an existence in the precariat, with many in the shadow economy. In the United States, the millions of undocumented migrants have no right to work for pay but are hired anyway. They live with the threat of deportation and without rights to social protection, such as unemployment benefits. In Spain, millions of undocumented migrants are thought to account for the country's huge shadow economy. The story is probably similar in most countries.

Then there are those granted temporary residence but restricted by their visa status in what they can do legally. They may have some social rights, such as entitlement to enterprise and state benefits, and perhaps entitlement to belong to economic organisations such as trade unions or business associations. But they have limited or no rights to socio-economic mobility and no political rights, giving them little opportunity to integrate into local society. They are classic denizens.

Further along the spectrum are denizens who are granted long-term residence and formally allowed to pursue jobs of their choice. They may be relatively secure but face structural limitations on economic and social rights, for example, if they possess qualifications that are not recognised in the country. Thus an engineer, an architect or a dentist who qualifies in one country may not be allowed to practise in another, simply because there is no mutual recognition of standards. By such means, millions of qualified migrants are blocked from their occupation and obliged to scramble for lower level 'brain-wasting' jobs in the precariat.

This is due mainly to the way occupational licensing has developed (Standing, 2009). In Germany alone more than half a million immigrants are unable to do jobs for which they are qualified because the state does not recognise their qualifications. But the phenomenon is global. Occupational licensing has been a way of limiting and shaping migration. Anybody going to New York will find migrant lawyers and PhDs driving taxis. In federal countries, such as the United States, Australia and Canada, even people who move from one state or province to another can find themselves as denizens, denied the right to practise their profession or trade. But the denial across national borders is much more systematic. Licensing has been a part of the global labour process, and so far it has been a powerful way of denying economic rights to a growing number of people around the world.

Usually, these same denizens are also statutorily excluded from the civil service and political office, and are more likely to have legal access to self-employment than to jobs. They are susceptible to expulsion for public security reasons, if they do not behave as 'good citizens'. This limits integration, reinforcing their position as 'outsider-inhabitants'. In France and Germany, there is a three-layer system, with full political rights for citizens, partial political rights for citizens of other EU countries and no political rights for third-country (non-EU) nationals. In the United Kingdom, some third-country nationals – from the Commonwealth and Ireland – are included in the first or second groups.

Governments have been increasing the number of conditions necessary to be a legal migrant, in the process putting more people in more precarious denizen statuses. And denizens may have *de jure* rights but be excluded from them *de facto*. Some of the most egregious instances arise in developing countries.

In India, although every Indian is supposed to have equal rights, this is not true in law, policy or practice. For example, urban slum dwellers may after many years obtain a voter's identity and a ration card but may not obtain a right to be linked to the city's water and sewerage system. There are also no rules about how long it will take someone to obtain rights connected to local residency. Migrants within the country do have a right to labour and live elsewhere in India but may be unable to send their children to school or obtain ration cards, since states have different rules on eligibility. Denizenship also maps with informal workers. For example, a home-based worker in an urban slum will not have a right to electricity. A street vendor is treated as a criminal. And 'non-citizens', such as Bangladeshi or Nepali domestic workers, have no rights at all.

Denizenship has grown most in China, where 200 million rural migrants have lost rights in moving to the cities and industrial workshops that serve the world. They are denied the *hukou*, the residence passbook that would give them residence rights and the right to receive benefits and be employed legally in their own country.

Unlike in the early twentieth century, much of today's migration is not assimilation to new citizenship but is more of a *de-citizenship* process. Instead of being settlers, many migrants are denied several forms of citizenship – rights held by local nationals, rights of citizenship from where they come and rights that come with legal status. Many also lack occupational citizenship, with the right to practise their occupation denied. They are also not on a trajectory to gain the rights initially denied to them, making them super-exploitable. And they are not becoming part of a proletariat, a working class of stabilised labourers. They are disposable, with no access to state or enterprise benefits, and can be discarded with impunity, for if they protest the police will be mobilised to penalise, criminalise and deport them.

This highlights the fragmented labour process in which varieties of the precariat have different entitlements and a different structure of social income. It feeds through into the issue of identity. Natives can display multiple identities, legal migrants can focus on the identity that gives them most security and illegals must not display any identity, for fear of being exposed.

Bearing in mind the idea of denizens, we consider how distinctive groups of migrants are being treated and how they figure in the growth of the global precariat.

Refugees and asylum seekers

Let us start with refugees and asylum seekers. An example may bring home their misery. According to a report by the Parliamentary and Health Service Ombudsman (2010), the UK Border Agency (UKBA), in charge of refugees, had a backlog of a quarter of a million asylum cases. Cases remained unresolved for years on end; a Somali granted indefinite leave to remain in 2000 did not receive his documents until 2008. Such people live in the economic shadows, their lives on hold. While languishing in this denizen status, they are granted a miserly £42 a week and not allowed to take jobs, following moves by the Labour government to restrict help for asylum seekers. It is a recipe for a shadow-economy precariat.

Undocumented and illegal migrants

Demonising 'illegal migrants' has become part of the populist reaction to the insecurities visited on the precariat in general. They, rather than labour flexibility policies and shrinking social assistance, are blamed for the tribulations of local workers. On re-election as Italy's prime minister in 2008, Silvio Berlusconi's first statement was a pledge to defeat 'the army of evil', his term for undocumented migrants. He promptly issued a decree authorising private vigilante groups, which made no pretence about their intended targets. And he expelled Roma from their camps across Italy.

After African migrants in Calabria, in the toe of Italy, went on the rampage in January 2010 in protest at unpaid wages, their makeshift encampments were bulldozed and many were summarily deported. They had been recruited as cheap labour on agricultural estates, controlled by the local mafia, which had simply stopped paying wages after the financial crisis hit. When the Africans protested, possibly instigated by the mafia itself in the expectation of what would follow, they were shot at and beaten by vigilantes, applauded by local residents. The riots followed years of harassment and attacks by local youth. Yet Roberto Maroni, Italy's interior minister, said in an interview that they were the fruit of 'too much tolerance'. Similar attacks on immigrants have been happening all over Italy.

In France, President Nicolas Sarkozy, ironically himself of migrant origin, took up the populist mantra, issuing orders to destroy 'illegal' Roma camps and expel their residents. They were duly sent to Bulgaria and Romania, many swearing to return since they had a legal right to move around the European Union. A leaked memorandum from the interior minister made it clear that Roma were a priority target, in likely violation of the French constitution (Willsher, 2010). The immigration minister, Eric Bosson, told a press conference, 'Free movement in the European area doesn't mean free settlement'. Apparently, migrants were to be kept on the move. What sort of society is this?

Meanwhile, on the other side of the Atlantic, zealous groups with religious tattoos and T-shirts were arming themselves and manning the Arizona-Mexico border, peering through binoculars to identify scurrying ill-clad desperados, most merely seeking a better life. Some migrants do carry drugs, often forced to do so by people traffickers. Some are 'criminals'; every population group has its share. But demonisation is pervasive. The growth of the migrant precariat in the United States was matched by official commando-style raids on factories suspected of employing 'illegals'. Although President Obama ordered an end to such raids, they could easily return.

The Arizona law of 2010, which made illegal immigration a state misdemeanour as well as a federal civil violation, intensified the tension between migrants and 'native citizens' fearful of joining the precariat. It requires local police, after making 'lawful contact', to check the immigration status of those who cause 'reasonable suspicion' and to arrest them if they lack documents, opening the door to random stopping of Hispanic-looking drivers on minor pretexts. The law led to national protests by Hispanics and sympathisers. But it tapped into a populist nerve, linked to what some have called a 'cultural generation gap', which is thinly veiled racism. In Arizona, 83 per cent of older people are white, but only 43 per cent of children are. Older whites believe they are paying taxes for children whom they do not recognise as their own. This is fuelling the anti-tax populism of the Tea Party, in which male baby boomers figure prominently. Something similar is happening in Germany, where in many cities migrants already account for a majority of children.

Most Americans appear to support the Arizona law. One national poll produced the following results, showing the percentages in favour of each proposition:

- increasing fines for employers of illegal immigrants   80%

- criminalising employment of illegal immigrants   75%

- requiring police to report illegals to federal government 70%

- National Guard patrols of the Mexican border   68%

- building more border fences   60%

- allowing police to demand proof of migrant status   50%

- excluding illegal immigrant children from school   42%

- requiring churches to report illegal immigrants   37%

In South Africa, an even more ugly development typifies what is happening in many parts of the world. Millions of migrants slip across the borders and make their way to the townships, particularly around Johannesburg. They come from Zimbabwe, Malawi, Mozambique and elsewhere on the African continent, as well as from Pakistan and other parts of Asia. There may be over 4 million of them. Most have no work visas but have to work. The government makes it hard for them to obtain visas, and thousands travel long distances every day to queue in the hope of acquiring one.

Many young South Africans cannot obtain legal jobs paying legal wages because desperate migrants are obliged to take illegal jobs paying illegal wages without benefits. Their presence lowers the bargaining position of workers in general, swells the precariat, and allows politicians and economists to claim there is massive unemployment and that real wages and labour protections must be lowered. In reality, much of the employment is simply not being measured. Claims that the unemployment rate in South Africa ranges up to 40 per cent are nonsense. However, in May 2008, tensions became explosive and migrants in the townships were savagely attacked. Scores were killed and thousands fled. They were victims in a society that has grown even more unequal since the end of apartheid.

Temporary and seasonal migrants

Many other migrants, despite being legal, are left vulnerable to such an extent that any dispassionate observer would be led to wonder whether it is not deliberate, to please some local interests, to placate local workers or because they have no political rights and cannot vote. Some recent examples are indicative.

After a number of incidents, notably the deaths of 23 Chinese cockle pickers caught by the tide at Morecambe Bay in February 2004, the UK government set up a Gangmasters Licensing Authority to regulate agency labour. But an enquiry by the Equality and Human Rights Commission (EHRC, 2010) on meat and poultry processing factories, which employ 90,000 people, showed that the authority was too under-funded to do its job.

In what is by some measures the largest manufacturing sector left in the United Kingdom, the enquiry found appalling working conditions, with workers forced to stand for hours on fast-operating production lines, unable to go for toilet breaks and subject to abuse. Pregnant women were shockingly affected; some had miscarriages and many faced open discrimination. Workers had to put in 16- to 17-hour shifts, with only a few hours sleep in between. In some cases, the agencies entered their homes to wake them early in the morning because supermarkets operating just-in-time ordering practices were leaving orders to the last minute, putting pressure on the factories to have staff on standby.

A third of the labour force comprised agency employees; 70 per cent were migrants from Eastern Europe, with a few from Portugal. Most said employers treated agency workers worse, while British workers were reluctant to work in the sector, deterred by the low wages and poor working conditions. Some British workers told the EHRC that agencies only hired migrants, a practice unlawful under the Race Relations Act. Abuse of agency workers was associated with deliberately lax inspection.

Disappointingly, the EHRC recommended that the industry should improve its practices voluntarily, a bit of wishful thinking; it did not intend to litigate. In other words, the precariat was to be left exposed to abuse. And the Gangmasters (Licensing) Act 2004 does not cover the care and hospitality sectors, where migrants are concentrated in the greatest numbers.

Also in the United Kingdom, in the harsh winter of 2009–10, when many East European migrants were jobless and made homeless by debt, local authorities started to send them home. In Boston in Lincolnshire, migrant agricultural labourers made up a quarter of the population in 2008. When the farm jobs dried up, many returned to their countries but others remained, hoping to find new jobs. They did not qualify for state benefits, notably Jobseeker's Allowance (unemployment benefit), which requires a person to have been employed continuously for at least a year. In the mid-winter, some, homeless and moneyless, resorted to living in makeshift tents. Seeing them as a social sore, with rising morbidity and petty criminality, the government opted to rid the local community of the nomadic labour force. The Boston authorities hired a Pied Piper, in the form of Crime Reduction Initiatives (CRI), an organisation funded by government and local councils to address the causes of disorder in communities.

The job description for CRI's contract was benign enough – to ascertain if the homeless were eligible for benefits and, if not, to offer them a one-way ticket home. One might ask why the government would use a firm with a crime-fighting title to do such a job. It looked like a step towards privatised policing. The CRI's John Rossington told the press, 'Boston has a problem with rough sleepers, most of whom are from eastern Europe. Almost all these people are unable to receive benefits either because they are not entitled to them or they have lost their papers and cannot verify this. We are encouraging them to come forward so we can establish their situation' (Barber, 2010). CRI made the commercial objective clear, saying repatriation would save money. 'These are people who have no money and are extremely vulnerable, especially if they are living outside in the cold weather. If they end up offending or become ill, they are likely to cost the taxpayer more than a cheap one-way flight to eastern Europe'.

Long-term migrants

In many countries, legally settled migrants have been demonised for cultural reasons. This can easily lead to discriminatory policy and xenophobic violence. We will content ourselves with two poignant examples, albeit indicating wider trends.

In the 1950s and 1960s, Germany welcomed hundreds of thousands of guest workers from Turkey and other parts of southern Europe, needed to provide cheap labour in building the German miracle, as the country's regeneration was dubbed. It was assumed they would go home when their contracts expired. So the state ensured that they did not integrate socially, politically or economically. They were given a special status outside society. But they stayed. This created a basis for animosity; as the German population started to shrink due to its low fertility, populists were able to depict a future of alien population dominance, with images of an Islamic underclass refusing to integrate in German society. First, the state prevented the migrants from integrating; then it blamed them for not being integrated.

In 2000, their children were given the option of taking German citizenship, as long as they did so before they reached the age of 23. This reflected the denizen-citizenship situation, since German nationality law was traditionally based on a person's blood, not place of birth. But the guest-worker system had laid the seeds for tension.

The predicament will be one faced by other European nations. The native German population is shrinking, the total is shrinking, a labour shortage is feared. But only a minority of German voters wish to see 'managed immigration' as a partial solution to the problem (Peel, 2010). An attempt by the pro-business Free Democrats to introduce a points system for bringing in skilled migrants was blocked by the Christian Democrats, who claimed it was an attempt to bring in cheap labour rather than train local workers. Nevertheless, in 2011, the German borders will be opened freely to workers from Eastern Europe for the first time. Germany already has 2.5 million EU migrants, more than any other EU country.

A 'national integration plan' has expanded language training and teaching Islam is now possible in state schools. But racism is rampant. In 2010, Thilo Sarrazin, a prominent Social Democrat politician, said that Berlin's Turks and Arabs were 'neither willing to integrate nor capable of it'. Opinion polls found that a majority of Germans agreed. Sacked as a member of the Bundesbank board, Sarrazin published an instant bestseller claiming he did not wish his grandchildren to live in a society overrun by an alien culture. To talk of shadows of the past is scarcely an exaggeration.

Now consider what has happened in France. For decades after the Second World War, labour migration was left to private firms, which recruited workers from abroad to plug shortages at home. The period coincided with decolonisation of France's North African possessions, and Maghrebians from Morocco, Tunisia and Algeria accounted for a rising share of migrants, reaching 30 per cent by 2005 (Tavan, 2005). For decades, tensions between French citizens and North African migrants were muted. As most of the migrants were young and employed, they were net contributors to the social security system, while French citizens were net beneficiaries. But the state was building a precariat. Migrants' wages are lower than those of French workers and they are more vulnerable to unemployment, partly because they are in low-skilled jobs, such as construction, and more affected by economic fluctuations, partly because of discrimination. Unemployed Maghrebians often do not have the contribution record needed to claim unemployment benefit and are obliged to rely on the means-tested RMI (*Revenu minimum d'insertion*). However, to be eligible for the RMI, housing benefit and health protection, non-French nationals must possess a residence permit and must have lived in France for five years. Many Maghrebians have simply been locked out.

The state had allowed undocumented migration to build up but after 1996 put many immigrants from the Maghreb and sub-Saharan Africa in the awkward status of what they came to call themselves, *sans-papiers* (without papers). Even though they had worked for years in France, suddenly their status was made uncertain if not illegal. The *sans-papiers* organised to contest their outsider status, demanding to have their temporary labour contracts converted into regular contracts. But by this time the state was hostile. While some had their situations 'regularised', thousands were sent back – 29,000 in 2009. In April 2010, the immigration minister announced that *sans-papiers* who asked for regularisation would still be expelled.

Even when they are French citizens, Maghrebians are denizens, having equal rights in law but not in practice. For example, the Labour Code asserts the principle of equal treatment during employment but does not cover discrimination in recruitment. A study for the Equal Opportunities and Anti-Discrimination Commission reported that in Paris people with Maghrebian names were five times less likely to be called for a job interview, and Maghrebian university graduates were three times less likely to be interviewed than their French counterparts (Fauroux, 2005). It was no surprise that the riots in the *banlieues* (high-rise housing estates in the suburbs) in late 2005 were led by second-generation Maghrebians let down by a system that proclaimed their equality but engendered their precarity.

These examples – both involving Muslims, in the heart of Europe – show how once-welcomed migrants can become demonised outsiders even after they have put down deep roots. They are being re-marginalised.

The precariat as a floating reserve

The Great Recession following the shock of 2008 could have been expected to alter migrant flows, but in a global economy what happens is not easy to predict. For instance, return migration from the United Kingdom was considerable in 2009; the number of registered workers from the new EU member nations in Eastern Europe dropped by over 50 per cent. It was forecast that 200,000 skilled workers would return from industrialised countries to India and China over the next five years. But at the same time a remarkable shift was taking place.

As the recession deepened, the share of total employment taken by migrants *rose* sharply. Businesses continued to hire foreigners even as unemployment rose. The number of people in employment born in the United Kingdom fell by 654,000 between late 2008 and late 2010 while the number of migrants in employment rose by 139,000. This may have partly reflected the sectoral nature of job cuts, since old industries where the local working class and lower level salariat were concentrated were badly hit. It also reflected a tendency for firms to use recessions to rid themselves of older and more costly long-term employees. And it reflected a rise in labour churning and the greater ease in shifting to lower cost temporaries and those paid 'off the books'. With a global flexible labour process, old queuing mechanisms and the LIFO ('last-in, first-out') system have broken down. Recessions now accelerate the trend towards precariat labour, favouring employment of those most resigned to accept lower wages and fewer benefits.

The substitution of migrants has happened even though many have been sent or transported home, often at a cost borne by governments. Spain and Japan have offered cash incentives for immigrants to leave. The United Kingdom has paid for one-way tickets home. But governments trying to curb migration have run up against resistance from business interests.

While politicians may posture as favouring limits on migration and sending migrants 'back', business wants them for their cheap labour. In Australia, a survey found that companies were refusing to retrench visa-holding skilled migrants rather than local workers. They were paying migrants less than half what they were paying, or would have had to pay, local workers. In the end, the Labour government sided with business in accepting that firms no longer had to give preference to Australian workers (Knox, 2010).

In European countries such as France and Italy, with their low fertility rates and ageing populations, business organisations have been equally opposed to migration curbs, especially on skilled labour. In the United Kingdom, multinational companies have lobbied the Coalition government to retract its plans to cap the numbers of skilled migrants from outside the European Union coming into the country. Unedifying ideas of auctioning limited work permits were mooted.

In Japan, while some politicians have become more stridently anti-migrant and nationalistic, businesses have welcomed South Koreans, Brazilians of Japanese stock and Chinese bonded labourers. In the United States, where, in 2005, undocumented migrants were estimated to comprise half of all farm labourers, a quarter of workers in the meat and poultry industry and a quarter of dishwashers, business has favoured legalisation and opposed expulsions (Bloomberg Businessweek, 2005).

Capital welcomes migration because it brings low-cost malleable labour. The groups most vehemently opposed to migration are the old (white) working class and lower middle class, squeezed by globalisation and falling into the precariat.

From queuing to hurdles?

Traditionally, migrants were seen as entering a queue for vacant jobs. That was a reasonably accurate image in the pre-globalisation era. But queuing no longer operates, mainly due to labour market and social protection reforms.

In flexible labour markets with porous borders, wages are driven down to levels only migrants will willingly accept, below what residents habituated to a higher standard of living could tolerate. In the United Kingdom, falling wages and worsening conditions in the care, hospitality and agricultural sectors where migrants are concentrated have intensified downward pressure in other sectors. Prime Minister Gordon Brown's jingoistic rhetoric in 2007 – 'British jobs for British workers' – changed nothing; indeed, in-migration increased. A more inegalitarian society, combined with a cheap migrant labour regime, enabled the affluent to benefit from low-cost nannies, cleaners and plumbers. And access to skilled migrants lessened pressure on firms to train the unemployed in manual skills, leaving locals at a further disadvantage.

Another reason for the breakdown of queuing was the dismantling of the labourist social security system. As governments rushed to replace social insurance by social assistance, long-term citizens found themselves disadvantaged in accessing benefits and social services. This has probably done more than anything to fan resentment of migrants and ethnic minorities, particularly in decaying urban areas that had been strongholds of the working class. While some of its own members blamed the Labour Party's loss in the United Kingdom's 2010 General Election to its failure to reach out to the white working class over immigration, they failed to see, or did not wish to acknowledge, that the means-testing system they themselves had built was the main problem.

Means testing destroyed a pillar of the welfare state. A social insurance-type system based on entitlements gained through labour-based contributions rewards those who have been in the system for a long time. If benefits and access to social services are determined by proof of financial need, then those who have contributed will lose out to those, such as migrants, who are demonstrably worse off. For the withering 'working class', this is perceived as unfair. So it is ironic that in the United Kingdom and elsewhere social democratic governments were the ones moving policy in that direction.

In the United Kingdom, the shift to means testing helped accelerate the break-up of working-class extended families, as the pioneering study of the East End of London by Dench, Gavron and Young (2006) demonstrated. Incoming Bangladeshi migrants, being the poorest, went to the front of the queue for council housing, while old working-class families were bumped down the list and were obliged to move away to find cheaper housing.

Migrants also inadvertently contribute to other social problems. They are under-recorded in censuses, which leads to a significant population under-count in areas where they are concentrated, resulting in under-funding from central government for schools, housing and so on. In 2010, on some estimates, there may have been over 1 million people living in the United Kingdom 'illegally'.

As queuing mechanisms have ceased to function, countries are seeking other ways to manage migration. Some operate complex schemes to select occupations deemed to have shortages. Until 2010, Australia had 106 'occupations in demand'. This was changed to a 'more targeted' list, designed to focus on health care, engineering and mining. Such measures do not work well. In the United Kingdom, Tier 1 visas are granted to migrants deemed to possess 'high skills' in short supply. Yet, in 2010, at least 29 per cent of Tier 1 visa holders were identified as doing unskilled jobs (UKBA, 2010), part of a 'brain-wasting' process.

It has also become harder to gain UK citizenship. In 2009, modelled on an Australian scheme, the United Kingdom outlined plans to make immigrants 'earn' a passport by accumulating points, through voluntary work, speaking English, paying taxes, having useful skills and being prepared to live in parts of the country where there is a perceived shortage of skills. Moving to a points-based system, rather than giving an automatic right to citizenship for anyone who had lived in the country for five years without a criminal record, meant the government could alter the hurdles as it chose. A Home Office source said, 'We are going to be tougher about people becoming citizens. There won't be an automatic right any longer, and the link between work and citizenship is effectively broken' (Hinsliff, 2009).

This is converting migrants into permanent denizens, more primed for the precariat. The UK Labour government was also planning a points-based system for temporary migrants, restricting work permits for those from outside the European Union and taking some occupations off the list of those deemed to have shortages. In 2010, the new Coalition government tightened the process even further.

In sum, because the old queuing system has dissolved, and because governments cannot or do not wish to reverse the labour market reforms they have instituted, they have increasingly sought to raise barriers to entry, make the denizen status of migrants more precarious and encourage or oblige them to leave when no longer needed. This opens up some ugly possibilities.

Migrants as cheap labour in developing countries

Your labour is glorious and deserves respect from all society.

WEN JIABAO, Chinese Prime Minister, June 2010

To die is the only way to testify that we ever lived. Perhaps for the Foxconn employees and employees like us – we who are called *nongmingong*, rural migrant workers, in China – the use of death is simply to testify that we were ever alive at all, and that while we lived, we had only despair.

Chinese worker blog, after the twelfth suicide leap at Foxconn

National capitalism was built on rural-urban migration, led by the exodus from the English countryside into the mills and factories but repeated across the world in slightly different forms. In today's industrialising economies, governments have facilitated the movement by setting up export processing zones in which labour regulations are loosened, union bargaining restricted, temporary contracts are the norm and subsidies are thrown at firms. That story is well known. What is less appreciated is how the greatest migration in history is being organised to accelerate and restructure *global* capitalism.

Global capitalism has been built on migrant labour, first in what used to be called the NICs (newly industrialising countries). In the 1980s, I recall many visits to the export processing zones of Malaysia to factories run by some of the great names of global capital, such as Motorola, Honda and Hewlett Packard. It was not a proletariat being formed but a temporary precarious labour force. Thousands of young women from the *kampongs* (villages) were housed in shabby hostels, labouring for incredibly long workweeks and then expected to leave after several years, once their health and capacities had deteriorated. Many left with poor eyesight and chronic back problems. Global capitalism was built on their backs.

That system still operates in the latest batch of emerging market economies, such as Bangladesh, Cambodia and Thailand. It embraces international migrants as well. Thus, in Thailand, in 2010, there were 3 million migrants, mostly undocumented, many from Myanmar (Burma). Following tensions, the government launched a registration scheme, ordering migrants to apply to their country of origin for special passports so that they could labour legally and, in principle, have access to state benefits and services. Those from Myanmar did not wish to return there, fearing they would be unable to leave again. So most who did register were from Laos and Cambodia. Failure to register by the deadline meant arrest and deportation. In practice, this was not systematic since Thai companies depended on migrant labour to do low-paid jobs and did not want millions kicked out. But, according to Human Rights Watch (2010), even legal migrants suffer terrible abuses, being at the mercy of employers, not allowed to form or join unions, not allowed to travel freely, often not paid their wages, subject to summary dismissal and abused by officials supposedly protecting them.

These are labour market realities in emerging market economies. Although campaigns and international agencies could do more to rectify them, they will continue. However, most relevant for understanding the shaping of the global precariat are developments in the economy that is rapidly becoming the world's largest.

The Chinese state has shaped a denizen labour force unlike anything else ever created. It has a working-age population of 977 million, which will rise to 993 million by 2015. Some 200 million are rural migrants lured to the new industrial workshops where Chinese and foreign contractors act as intermediaries of household-name multinational corporations from all over the world. These migrants are the engine of the global precariat, denizens in their own country. Because they are unable to obtain the *hukou* residence permit, they are forced to live and work precariously, denied the rights of urban natives. The state is riding a tiger. For two decades it fashioned this flexible labour force of young migrants, treating them as disposable, subsidised by their rural families and expected to slink back after their most productive years have passed. There have been historical parallels, but they are minor compared with the vastness of what has been done in China.

After the shock of 2008, which hit Chinese exports, 25 million migrants were retrenched, although they did not appear in the unemployment statistics because, being 'illegal' in their own country, they had no access to unemployment benefits. Many returned to their villages. Others took wage cuts and lost factory benefits. Resentment built up; thousands of local protests and strikes – over 120,000 in one year – were kept out of public knowledge; stress deepened.

As the economy rebounded, the state tried to let out some of the pressure. It stood by while some very public strikes occurred in foreign-owned factories, a change of stance interpreted by many foreign observers as a turning point. This may be wishful thinking. The rural areas still contain 40 per cent of China's labour force – 400 million languishing in dismal conditions, many waiting to be drawn into the precariat. Even if there were no rapid rise in productivity in those industrial workshops, which is most unlikely, a supply of labour will be there for many years. By the time the surplus dries up and wages rise in China and in other emerging market economies in Asia, the downward effects on wages and labour conditions in today's rich tertiary societies, mainly in Europe and North America, will have been completed.

Some commentators believe that what we may call the 'precariat phase' of Chinese development is coming to an end because the number of young workers, the main group of temporary denizens, is declining. To put such claims in perspective, there will still be over 200 million Chinese aged 15 to 29 in 2020, and five out of every six rural workers under the age of 40 still say they would be prepared to migrate for those temporary jobs.

China's migrant labour conditions are not accidental. International brands adopted unethical purchasing practices, resulting in substandard conditions in their supply chains. Walmart, the world's largest retailer, sources US$30 billion of cheap goods from these supply chains annually, which helped Americans to live beyond their means. Other companies were able to flood the world market with their artificially cheap gadgets. Local contractors have used abusive illegal methods to raise short-term efficiency, generating workplace grievances and resistance. Local Chinese officials, in collusion with enterprise management, have systematically neglected workers' rights, resulting in misery and deeper inequalities.

Despite the growing tensions, the *hukou* registration system has been maintained. Millions of urban residents remain denizens, lacking entitlement to schooling, health care, housing and state benefits. Although the first nine years of schooling are supposed to be free for all, migrants are forced to send their children to private schools or send them home. Because annual school payments can be equivalent to several weeks' wages, millions of children of migrants stay in the countryside, rarely seeing their parents.

Reform of the *hukou* rules is slow in coming. In 2009, the city of Shanghai declared that henceforth seven years of employment in the city would entitle someone to a *hukou*, as long as they had paid tax and social security contributions. However, migrants lacking a *hukou* mostly have inadequate contracts and do not pay tax or contribute to welfare funds. Only 3,000 of Shanghai's millions of migrants were expected to qualify for a *hukou* under the new rule.

Meanwhile, migrants maintain a link to the countryside because it provides some security, including rights to a homestead and to farm a small plot. This is why millions flock out of cities around Chinese

New Year, returning to their villages to be with relatives, to renew connections and to tend land. The tension of being a floating worker was epitomised by a survey by Renmin University in 2009, which showed that a third of young migrants aspired to build a house in their village rather than buy one in a city. Only 7 per cent identified themselves as city people.

The migrants' denizen status is strengthened by the fact that they cannot sell their land or homes. Their rural anchor blocks them from acquiring roots in urban areas and prevents rural productivity and incomes from rising through land consolidation. The rural areas provide a subsidy for industrial labour, making it possible to keep money wages below subsistence level, so making those fancy commodities even cheaper for the world's consumers. Land reform has been under consideration. But the Communist Party has been fearful of the consequences. After all, when the global crisis hit, the rural system acted as a safety valve, with millions returning to the land.

The Chinese precariat is easily the largest such group in the world. Earlier generations of social scientists would have called them semi-proletarian. But there is no reason to think they are becoming proletarians. First, stable jobs would have to come and stay. That is unlikely and surely will not come before social tensions turn ugly.

Already, while the authorities are organising mass migration, the floating labour force has posed a threat to locals, creating ethnic tensions. An example was the government-organised transportation of Turkic-speaking Muslim Uighurs 3,000 miles to labour for the Xuri toy factory in Guangdong. The Uighurs, housed near the Han majority, were paid much less than the Hans they displaced. In June 2009, in riots over the alleged rape of a local woman, a Han mob killed two Uighurs. When news was relayed to the north-western province of Xinjiang, the Uighurs' home, street protests erupted in Urumqi, its capital, resulting in many deaths.

The toy-factory incident was a spark. For years, the government has moved people from low-income areas to the wealthy eastern provinces buoyed by export-led growth. Over 200,000 from Xinjiang moved in just one year, signing one- to three-year contracts before travelling to live in cramped humid factory dormitories. They were participating in an extraordinarily rapid process. Industrial estates sprouted almost overnight. That toy factory had been an orchard just three years before. The migrants were an instant community. Symbolically, situated at the base of an electricity pylon outside the factory gate was a giant TV screen, sponsored by Pepsi, where hundreds gathered every night to watch *kung fu* films after their shifts.

Placating an itinerant labour force is hard enough. But the scale of the movement was bound to raise tensions. As one Han worker told a journalist, 'The more of them there were, the worse relations became'. In those riots, the Uighurs claimed their death toll was understated and that the police did not protect them. Whatever the truth, the violence was an almost inevitable outcome of mass migration of temporary workers across unfamiliar cultures.

The internal migration in China is the largest migratory process the world has ever known. It is part of the development of a global labour market system. Those migrants are having an effect on how labour is being organised and compensated in every part of the world.

The emerging labour export regimes

An early feature of globalisation was that a few emerging market economies, notably in the Middle East, became magnets for migration from other parts of the world. In 2010, 90 per cent of the labour force of the United Arab Emirates was foreign; in Qatar and Kuwait, over 80 per cent; and in Saudi Arabia, 50 per cent. In downturns, the authorities instruct firms to fire foreigners first. In Bahrain, where foreigners hold 80 per cent of private sector jobs, the government charges 200 Bahraini dinars (US$530) for a work visa and 10 dinars a month for each foreign employee. Since 2009, it has allowed foreigners to quit their sponsoring employer, giving them four weeks to find a new job before they must leave Bahrain.

This form of migration has spread, so that groups from the poorest countries can be found labouring in discomfort and oppression in countries higher up the income spectrum. In the process, millions of migrants labouring as anything from nannies and dishwashers to plumbers and dockworkers are sending more money to low-income countries than is going in official aid. The World Bank estimated that foreign workers sent US$328 billion from richer to poorer countries in 2008, three times what all OECD countries sent in aid. India alone received US$52 billion from its diaspora.

However, a new phenomenon has emerged, in the form of the organised mass transfer of workers from China, India and other Asian market economies. Historically, this sort of practice was a trickle, with governments and companies sending a few people to work abroad for a short time. In the early globalisation era, much was made of the organised export of Filipina maids and related workers, usually with personal bonds to ensure their return. Today, 9 million Filipinos work abroad, about a tenth of the Philippines population; their remittances make up 10 per cent of the country's gross national product (GNP). Other countries took note.

Led by China, governments and their major enterprises are organising the systematic export of temporary workers in their hundreds of thousands. This 'labour export regime' is helping to transform the global labour market. India is doing it in different ways. The result is that armies of labourers are being mobilised and moved around the world.

China has taken advantage of its combination of large state corporations with access to financial capital and a huge supply of workers resigned to labour for a pittance. In Africa, China is operating a variant of the Marshall Plan, adopted by the United States to assist Western Europe recover from the devastation of the Second World War. Beijing provides low-cost loans to African governments to build infrastructure needed for Chinese factories. It then imports Chinese workers to do much of the labour.

China has been winning contracts elsewhere too, using its own workers to do construction jobs building power plants, factories, railroads, roads, subway lines, convention centres and stadia. By the end of 2008, according to the Chinese Ministry of Commerce, 740,000 Chinese were employed abroad officially, in countries as diverse as Angola, Indonesia, Iran and Uzbekistan. The number is growing. Chinese project managers report they prefer Chinese workers because they are easier to manage, according to Diao Chunhe, director of the China International Contractors' Association. Perhaps frighten is a better word than manage.

Chinese labour brokers are also thriving. Following a 2007 deal between the Chinese and Japanese governments, large numbers of young Chinese workers have been induced to pay brokers large fees and, once transported to Japan, are obliged to guarantee further payments when they start earning. Lured by the promise of 'learning' skills on a scheme approved by their government, the bonded migrants are labouring in virtual slavery in the food processing, construction, and garment and electrical manufacturing firms in which they are concentrated (Tabuchi, 2010). They are forced to work long workweeks for sub-minimum wages in a country where their presence is resented and where they can expect no institutional support in the face of a disregard for regulations.

Many are isolated, ending up in distant regions, living in company dormitories, forbidden from going far from their workplaces, unable to speak Japanese. The bonded labour trap means they fear being sent back before they earn enough to pay off their debts to the brokers, equivalent to over a year's salary. Unless they can repay, they risk losing their one possession, their home in China, often advanced as security when they took the bait. Although some may gain skills, most are in the global precariat, a source of insecure labour that acts as a lever to lower standards for others.

Japan is not a solitary case. Of all places, given its iconic status for social democrats, Sweden found itself the centre of critical attention in mid-2010 when it was revealed that thousands of Chinese, Vietnamese and Bangladeshi migrants had been brought in, many on tourist visas, to labour in the forests of northern Sweden picking wild cloudberries, blueberries and lingonberries for use in cosmetics, pharmaceutical syrups and nutritional supplements. Wages and working conditions for pickers are notoriously bad, and firms were using contractors to bring in Asians *en masse*. It emerged that they were being crowded into squalid dwellings lacking basic sanitation, without warm clothes or blankets for freezing night conditions. When some were not even paid their wages, they resorted to locking up bosses, bringing attention to their plight.

The Swedish Migration Board admitted it had issued work permits to 4,000 Asians but said it could not follow up on abuses because it had no authority to do so. The Municipal Workers' Union, *Kommunal*, won entitlement to organise the pickers but admitted that it could not reach agreement with the companies because the staffing agencies were in Asia. The government took a similar view (Saltmarsh, 2010). A spokesman for the migration ministry claimed, 'It is difficult for the government to act on contracts signed abroad'. Or was it a case of middle-class Swedes wanting their berries?

These are skirmishes in a bigger picture. The labour export regime could be a harbinger of the global labour system to come. It is leading to protests and violence against Chinese workers and efforts by countries such as Vietnam and India to reform labour laws to restrict the number of Chinese workers. And it is hard to deny that the Chinese are taking jobs from locals, staying after their contractual period and sequestering themselves in enclaves, similar to US military communities around the world.

Although Vietnam bans the import of unskilled workers and requires foreign contractors to hire Vietnamese for civil works projects, 35,000 Chinese workers are in the country. Many are cloistered in dingy dormitories where Chinese firms have won government contracts (Wong, 2009), bypassing the regulations by paying bribes. There are entire villages occupied by Chinese migrants. In a construction site at the port of Haiphong, a Chinatown has sprung up, with dormitory compounds, restaurants, massage parlours and so on. One installation manager summed it up, 'I was sent here, and I'm fulfilling my patriotic duty'. Chinese workers are segregated by occupational groups, such as welders, electricians and crane operators. A poem on a door of one of the dormitories reads, 'We are all people floating around in the world. We meet each other, but we never really get to know each other'. One could scarcely imagine a more poignant message from the global precariat.

Anger erupted in 2009 when the Vietnamese government gave a contract to China's Aluminum Corp to mine bauxite, using Chinese workers. General Vo Nguyen Giap, the 98-year-old icon of the Vietnam War, sent three public letters to party leaders in protest at the growing Chinese presence. In response to unrest, the government detained dissidents, shut down critical blogs and ordered newspapers to stop reporting on the use of Chinese labour. It also made a show of tightening visa and work permit requirements and, in a populist gesture, deported 182 Chinese workers from a cement plant. However, it could not be too strident, for it too has been building a labour export regime. With 86 million people, its potential to do so is large. Already half a million Vietnamese are working abroad in fourteen countries, according to the Vietnamese General Confederation of Labour.

When Laos won its bid to host the South-East Asian Games, China offered to build a 'natatorium' outside the capital Vientiane in return for a 50-year lease on 1,600 hectares of prime land, where China's Suzhou Industrial Park Overseas Investment Company wished to build factories. Protests erupted when it became known that the company was bringing in 3,000 Chinese labourers to do the building work. The land leased out was subsequently cut to 200 hectares. But the wedge had been inserted.

There is a more sinister element in this labour export regime. China has the world's largest prison population, estimated at around 1.6 million in 2009. The government allows firms to use prisoners as labour on infrastructure projects across Africa and Asia, as exemplified by the use of thousands of convicts in Sri Lanka (Chellaney, 2010). China has established itself as the world's leading dam builder, and its special precariat workforce has been part of that endeavour. Convicts are freed on parole for such projects and used as short-term labourers, without any prospect of 'career'. While they reduce the chances of jobs coming the way of locals, no doubt they are 'easier to manage'.

China is moving its export labour regime into Europe. In the aftermath of the financial crisis, it has taken advantage of its huge foreign exchange reserves to buy up depressed assets on the fringes of Europe, focusing on ports in Greece, Italy and elsewhere, and providing billions of dollars to finance public infrastructure projects using Chinese firms and workers. In 2009, China outbid European firms to build a highway in Poland using Chinese workers and European subsidies.

India is also moving into the pool. More than 5 million Indians are working abroad, 90 per cent of them in the Persian Gulf. In 2010, the Indian government announced plans for a contribution-based 'return and resettlement fund' for overseas workers that would provide benefits on their return. It has also set up an Indian Community Welfare Fund to provide emergency aid to 'distressed' workers in seventeen countries. This is a parallel social protection system, a dangerous precedent. The fund supports welfare measures, including food, shelter, repatriation assistance and relief. These workers are not among India's poorest, even if they are exploited and oppressed. The scheme is a subsidy to risk-taking workers and to countries employing them. It reduces pressure on governments to provide migrants with social protection while making it cheaper for firms to use Indian labour. What would be the consequences if many countries followed the Indian example?

India has negotiated social security agreements with Switzerland, Luxembourg and the Netherlands, and is in negotiations with other nations with a large immigrant Indian workforce. Agreements covering recruitment practices, terms of employment and welfare have been reached with Malaysia, Bahrain and Qatar. This is part of the global labour process. It seems fraught with moral and immoral hazards.

The millions of migrants drawn into labour export regimes are part of foreign and trade policy. They lower costs of production and facilitate a flow of capital into the sending countries in the form of remittances. They are an extraordinarily cheap labour source, which operates like a colossal precariat and drives host-country labour markets in similar directions. If it is found in Vietnam, Uganda, Laos, Sweden and elsewhere, we should recognise we are seeing a global phenomenon that is growing very rapidly indeed. Labour export regimes are leveraging labour conditions in recipient countries. Migrants are being used to accentuate the growth of the global precariat.

Concluding reflections

Migrants are the light infantry of global capitalism. Vast numbers vie with each other for jobs. Most have to put up with short-term contracts, with low wages and few benefits. The process is systemic, not accidental. The world is becoming full of denizens.

The spread of the nation state made 'belonging to the community into which one is born no longer a matter of course and not belonging no longer a matter of choice' (Arendt, [1951] 1986: 286). Today's migrants are rarely stateless in a *de jure* sense; they are not expelled from humanity. But they lack security and opportunity for membership of countries to where they move. More are 'de-citizenised', *de facto* denizens, even in their own country, as in China.

Many migrants are 'barely tolerated guests' (Gibney, 2009: 3). Some observers (such as Soysal, 1994) believe that differences in the rights of citizens and non-citizens have waned, due to post-national human rights norms. But more see a growing gap between formal legal entitlements and societal practices (e.g. Zolberg, 1995). What we can say is that in a flexible open system, two meta-securities are needed for the realisation of rights – basic income security and Voice security. Denizens lack Voice. Except when desperate, they keep their heads down, hoping not to be noticed as they go about their daily business of survival. Citizens have the priceless security of not being subject to deportation or exile, although there have been worrying slips even there. They may enter and leave their country; denizens are never sure.

The combination of a precariat made up of migrants, a tax-based social assistance system and a taxation system that places most emphasis on income tax levied mainly on those around the median income accentuates hostility towards migrants and 'foreigners'. The structure that leaves taxpayers feeling they are paying the bills for poor migrants means tensions cannot be dismissed as racial prejudice. They reflect abandonment of universalism and social solidarity.

Tensions are growing. According to a 2009 poll in six European countries and the United States, the United Kingdom was most hostile to migrants, with nearly 60 per cent believing they took jobs from natives. This compared with 42 per cent of Americans, 38 per cent of Spaniards, 23 per cent of Italians and 18 per cent of French. In the Netherlands a majority believed migrants increased crime. The United Kingdom had the highest share (44 per cent) of people saying that *legal* immigrants should not have an equal right to benefits, followed by Germany, the United States, Canada, the Netherlands and France. Polls in 2010 showed a worsening set of attitudes everywhere.

In rich OECD countries, migration involves a special precarity trap. Real wages and jobs with career potential are declining, creating a status frustration effect. Those becoming unemployed face the prospect of jobs offering lower wages and less occupational content. It is unfair to criticise them for resenting this or being reluctant to give up on long-acquired skills and expectations. Meanwhile, migrants come in from places where they had lower income and expectations, making them more prepared to accept part-time, short-term and occupationally restrictive jobs. Politicians play the populist card, blaming the outcome on the laziness of locals, thereby justifying both tighter controls on migration and bigger benefit cuts for the unemployed. This demonises two groups that will please the middle class, displaying the modern utilitarians at their most opportunistic. It is not 'laziness' or migration that is at fault; it is the nature of the flexible labour market.

Instead, migrants in public discourse are increasingly displayed as 'dirty, dangerous and damned'. They 'bring in' diseases and alien habits, are a threat to 'our jobs and way of life', are trafficked 'ruined victims', prostitutes or sad spectacles of humanity. The outcome of these crude attitudes is more border guards and harder conditions for entry. We see the latter in points systems and puerile citizenship tests being adopted in some countries. Rogue traits of a few are displayed as normal tendencies against which the state must take the utmost precautions. Increasingly, migrants are guilty until they can prove innocence.

In the background, what has been happening is a sharpening of hostility fanned by populist politicians and fears that the Great Recession is turning into long-term decline. We shall come back to that once we have considered one other aspect of the precariat, its loss of control of time.

5

Labour, work and the time squeeze

We cannot grasp the Global Transformation crisis, and the pressure building up on the precariat, without appreciating what the global market society is doing to our sense of time.

Historically, every system of production has operated with a particular conception of time as its guiding structure. In agrarian society, labour and work were adapted to the rhythm of the seasons and weather conditions. Any idea of a regular 10- or 8-hour working day would have been absurd. There was little point in trying to plough or harvest in the pouring rain. Time may have waited for no man, but man respected its rhythms and spasmodic variations. That is still the case in much of the world.

However, with industrialisation came time regimentation. The nascent proletariat was disciplined by the clock, as the historian E. P. Thompson (1967) so elegantly chronicled. A national industrial market society emerged, based on enforced respect for the time, the calendar and the clock. In literature, the wonder of it was caught by Jules Verne's *Around the World in 80 Days*. The timing of that book, and the excitement it aroused among Victorians in the 1870s, was no coincidence. Fifty years earlier, it would have seemed absurd; 50 years later, it would have been insufficiently fanciful to excite the imagination.

With the transition from rural societies to national markets based on industry, and from that to a global market system geared to services, two changes in time occurred. The first was the growing disrespect for the 24-hour body clock. In the fourteenth century, for instance, different parts of England operated with local variants of time, adapted to traditional ideas of local agriculture. It took many generations before the state could impose a national standard. Lack of standardisation is still with us, in that we have a global society and economy but multiple time zones. Mao forced the whole of China onto Beijing's time, as a form of state building. Others are moving in the same direction in the name of business efficiency. In Russia, the government is planning to reduce the number of time zones from eleven to five.

Time zones operate because we are naturally habituated to daylight and socially habituated to the concept of the working day. The body rhythms accord with daylight and darkness, when the human sleeps and relaxes, recovering from the exertions of the day. But the global economy has no respect for human physiology. The global market is a 24/7 machine; it never sleeps or relaxes; it has no respect for your daylight and darkness, your night and day. Traditions of time are nuisances, rigidities, barriers to trading and to the totem of the age, competitiveness, and contrary to the dictate of flexibility. If a country, firm or individual does not adapt to the 24/7 time culture, there will be a price to pay. It is no longer a case of 'the early bird catches the worm'; it is the sleepless bird that does so.

The second change relates to how we treat time itself. Industrial society ushered in a unique period in human history, which lasted no more than a hundred years, of life ordered in time blocs. The norms were accepted as legitimate by the majority living in industrialising societies and were exported all over the world. They were a mark of civilisation.

Society and production operated around blocs of time, alongside ideas of fixed workplaces and homeplaces. In life, people went to school for a short time, then spent most of their life in labour or work and then, if lucky, had a short period of retirement. During their 'working years', they rose in the morning, went to their jobs for 10 or 12 hours, or whatever was set in their loosely defined contracts, and then went 'home'. There were 'holidays', but these shrank during industrialisation, to be replaced gradually by short blocs of vacation. Although patterns varied by class and gender, the point is that time was divided into blocs. For most people, it made sense to think they were at home for, say, 10 hours a day, 'at work' for 10 hours, the remainder being for socialising. Separation of 'workplace' and 'homeplace' made sense.

Work, labour and play were distinct activities, in terms of when they were undertaken and where the boundaries of each began and ended. When a man – and it was typically a man – left his workplace, where he was usually subject to direct controls, he felt himself to be his own boss, even if he was too exhausted to take advantage of it, apart from inflicting arbitrary demands on his family.

Economics, statistics and social policy took shape against the backdrop of industrial society and the way of thinking it induced. We have come a long way from there, but we have yet to adjust policies and institutions. What has emerged in the globalisation era is a set of informal norms that are in tension with the industrial time norms that still permeate social analysis, legislation and policymaking. For instance, standard labour statistics produce neatly impressive figures indicating that the average adult 'works 8.2 hours a day' (or whatever the figure might be) for five days a week, or that the labour force participation rate is 75 per cent, implying that three-quarters of the adult population are working eight-hour days on average.

In considering how the precariat – and others – allocate time, such figures are useless and misleading. Underlying what follows is a plea: We must develop a concept of 'tertiary time', a way of looking at how we allocate time that is suitable for a tertiary society, not an industrial or an agrarian one.

What is work?

Every age has had its peculiarities about what is and what is not work. The twentieth century was as silly as any before it. For the ancient Greeks, labour was done by slaves and *banausoi*, the outsiders, not by citizens. Those who did labour had 'employment security' but, as Hannah Arendt (1958) understood, in the Greek vision that was deplorable since only the insecure man was free, a sentiment the modern precariat understands.

To recall points made in Chapter 1, in ancient Greece, work, as *praxis*, was done for its use value, with relatives and friends around the home, in caring for others – reproducing them as capable of being citizens themselves. Work was about building civic friendship (*philia*). Play was needed for relaxation but, distinguished from that, the Greeks had a concept of *schole*, which has a double meaning, signifying leisure and learning, built around participation in the life of the city (*polis*). Knowledge came from deliberation, from stillness as well as involvement. Aristotle believed some laziness (*aergia*) was necessary for proper leisure.

The denizens, the *banausoi* and *metics*, were denied citizenship because they were deemed not to have time to participate in the life of the *polis*. One does not want to defend a flawed social model – such as their treatment of slaves and women and the distinction of types of work suitable for citizens – but their division of time into labour, work, play and leisure is a useful one.

After the Greeks, the mercantilists and classical political economists like Adam Smith made a mess of deciding what was productive labour, as discussed elsewhere (Standing, 2009). But the foolishness of deciding what was work and what was not came to a head in the early twentieth century, when care work was relegated to economic irrelevance. Arthur Pigou, the Cambridge economist ([1952] 2002: 33), admitted the absurdity when he quipped, 'Thus, if a man marries his housekeeper or his cook, the national dividend is diminished'. In other words, what was labour depended not on *what* was done but *for whom* it was done. It was a triumph for market society over common sense.

Throughout the twentieth century, labour – work having exchange value – was put on a pedestal, while all work that was not labour was disregarded. So work done for its intrinsic usefulness does not appear in labour statistics or in political rhetoric. Beyond its sexism, this is indefensible for other reasons as well. It degrades and devalues some of the most valuable and necessary activities – the reproduction of our own capacities as well as those of the future generation and activities preserving our social existence. We need to escape from the labourist trap. No group needs that to happen more than the precariat.

The tertiary workplace

Before going further into work, we may highlight a related historical change. The classic distinction between the workplace and the home was forged in the industrial age. In industrial society, when today's labour market regulations, labour law and social security system were constructed, the norm was a fixed workplace. It was where the proletariat went early in the morning or on shifts – the factories, mines, estates and shipyards – and where the salariat went, slightly later in the day. That model has crumbled.

As noted in Chapter 2, some observers have referred to today's productive system as a 'social factory', to indicate that labour is done everywhere and that the discipline or control over labour is exercised everywhere. But policies are still based on a presumption that it makes sense to draw sharp distinctions between the workplace and home, and between the workplace and public spaces. In a tertiary market society, that makes no sense.

Discussions about 'work–life balance' are similarly artificial. Home is not even where the heart is anymore, given that more and more people, particularly those in the precariat, are living alone, with parents or with a series of short-term housemates or partners.

A growing proportion of the world regards their home as part of their workplace. Although less noticed, more of what was once the preserve of the home is done in or around workplaces.

In many modern offices, employees turn up early in the morning in casual or sports clothes, take a shower and groom themselves over the first hour 'at work'. It is a hidden perk of the salariat. They keep clothes in the office, have mementoes from home life scattered around and in some cases allow young children to play, 'as long as they don't disturb daddy or mummy', which, of course, they do. In the afternoon, after lunch, the salariat may take a 'power nap', long regarded as a home activity. Listening to music on the iPod is not unknown to while away those hours at work.

Meanwhile, more work or labour is done outside the notional workplace, in cafés, in cars and at home. Management techniques have evolved in parallel, shrinking the sphere of privacy, altering remuneration systems and so on. The old model of occupational health and safety regulation sits oddly in this blurred tertiary work scene. The privileged salariat and the proficians, with their gadgets and specialist knowledge with which they can disguise how much 'work' they do, are able to take advantage of this blurring.

Those nearer the precariat are induced to intensify their effort and the hours they spend in their labour, for fear of falling short of expectations. In effect, the tertiary workplace intensifies a form of inequality, resulting in more exploitation of the precariat and a gentle easing of the schedules of the privileged, as they take their long lunches and coffee breaks or interact in bonding sessions in hotels constructed for the purpose. Workplaces and play places blur in a haze of alcohol and stewed coffee.

Tertiary time

In an open tertiary society, the industrial model of time, coupled with bureaucratic time management in large factories and office blocks, breaks down. One should not lament its passing but should understand that the breakdown has left us without a stable time structure. With personal services being commodified, including most forms of care, we are losing a sense of distinction between the various activities most people undertake.

In this, the precariat is at the risk of being in a permanent spin, forced to juggle demands on limited time. It is not alone. But its difficulty is particularly stressful. It may be summed up as a loss of *control* over knowledge, ethics and time.

So far, we have not managed to crystallise an idea of 'tertiary time'. But it is coming. An aspect is the indivisibility of time uses. The idea of doing a certain activity in a certain definable space of time is less and less applicable. This is matched by the erosion of the fixed workplace and the division of activities by where they are done. Much of what is regarded as home activity is done by some people in offices and vice versa.

Consider time from the perspective of the demands placed on it. The standard presentation in economics textbooks, government reports, mass media and legislation is dualistic, dividing time between 'work' and 'leisure'. When they say work they mean labour, that part of work that is contracted or directly remunerated. This is misleading as a means of measuring the time devoted to work, even the work required to earn income, let alone the forms that have no direct connection to labour. The other side of the dualism, leisure, is equally misleading. Our Greek ancestors would have scoffed.

Labour intensification

A feature of tertiary society and the precariat existence is the pressure to labour excessively. The precariat may take on several jobs at the same time, partly because wages are falling, partly for insurance or risk management.

Women, faced by a triple burden, are being drawn into a quadruple one, of having to care for children, care for elderly relatives and do perhaps not one but two jobs. Recall how more women in the United States are doing more than one part-time job. In Japan too, women as well as men are increasingly immersed in multiple jobholding, combining what appear to be full-time jobs with informal side-jobs that can be done outside office hours or at home. These may add up to eight or ten hours a day on top of an eight-hour day. One woman in that position told the *New York Times* it was an insurance policy as much as anything else (Reidy, 2010): 'It is not that I hate my main job. But I want to have a stable income without being completely dependent on the company'.

One 2010 Japanese survey found that 17 per cent of employed men and women aged 20–50 had some form of side-job, and another found that almost half the employed said they were interested in having a side-job. The main reasons were a desire to smooth income and to moderate risks – jobholding for risk management rather than for career building, in the absence of state benefits. People are labouring more because the returns to any one job are low and risky.

Excessive labour is bad for health. A long-term study of 10,000 UK civil servants estimated that those who worked three or more hours of overtime a day were 60 per cent more likely to develop heart trouble than those who worked a seven-hour day (Virtanen et al., 2010). Long hours also increase the risk of stress, depression and diabetes; stress leads to social isolation, marital and sexual problems, and a cycle of despair.

Another study referred to 'binge working' (Working Families, 2005). The European Working Time Directive specifies a maximum working week of 48 hours. But in the United Kingdom, besides those who do so occasionally, more than a million people frequently work in their job for more than 48 hours, with 600,000 doing so for more than 60 hours, according to the Office of National Statistics. Another 15 per cent work 'antisocial' hours.

Labour intensification through insecurity may not be required by employers, merely encouraged by them. More likely, it will be due to insecurities and pressures inherent in a flexible tertiary society. Policymakers should be asking whether this labour intensification is societally healthy, necessary or unavoidable. That is not a call for regulations; it is to consider incentives to gain greater control of time.

Work-for-labour

It is not as if labour is all the work that people do. To function well in a tertiary flexible-labour society, much time must be used in 'work-for-labour', work that does not have exchange value but which is necessary or advisable.

One form of work-for-labour done by the precariat to a greater extent than others is in the labour market. Someone who exists through temporary jobs must spend a lot of time searching for jobs and dealing with the state bureaucracy or, increasingly, its private commercial surrogates. As welfare systems are restructured in ways that force claimants to go through ever more complex procedures to gain and to retain entitlement to modest benefits, the demands on the time of the precariat are large and fraught with tension. Queuing, commuting to queue, form filling, answering questions, answering more questions, obtaining certificates to prove something or other, all these are painfully time consuming yet are usually ignored. A flexible labour market that makes labour mobility the mainstream way of life, and that creates a web of moral and immoral hazards in the flurry of rules to determine benefit entitlement, forces the precariat into using time in ways that are bound to leave people enervated and less able to undertake other activities.

Some other work-for-labour is complementary to the labour a person does in a job, such as networking outside office hours, commuting or reading company or organisational reports 'at home', 'in the evening' or 'over the weekend'. This is all too familiar; yet we have no idea of its extent through national statistics or indicators of 'work' or 'labour' regurgitated in the media. But much more is connected with trying to function in a market society. For instance, some work-for-labour is 'work-for-insurance', which will rise with the spread of social, economic and occupational insecurity. Some is covered by the idea of 'keeping options open'. Some is strategic, cultivating goodwill and trying to pre-empt bad will.

Some is what might be called 'training-for-labour'. One management consultant told the *Financial Times* (Rigby, 2010) that, because skills have a shorter and shorter lifespan, people should devote 15 per cent of their time to training every year. Presumably the amount will depend on a person's age, experience and labour market position. Someone in the precariat, particularly if young, would be advised to spend more time in such training, if only to extend or retain options.

Tertiary skill

In societies where most economic activity consists of the manipulation of ideas, symbols and services done for people, mechanical processes and tasks shrink into secondary significance. This puts technical notions of 'skill' in disarray. In a tertiary society, skill is as much about 'body language' and 'emotional labour' as about formal skills learned through years of schooling, formal qualifications or apprenticeship schemes.

Typically, the precariat has a lower expected return to investment in any specific sphere of training, while the cost of acquiring it is a higher share of actual or potential income or savings. Someone in the salariat or a profician will have a clearer trajectory of a career – and thus could expect an economic return to such training – and a greater appreciation of what not to bother with. A perverse outcome of labour being more flexible and insecure is to lower the *average* return to self-determined training.

One growing form of training-for-labour is ethical training. Doctors, architects, accountants and some other occupations have to devote time to learning what is regarded as correct ethical behaviour in their professional circles. This will spread to other occupations and may even become mandatory, or part of a global accreditation system, which would be a desirable development.

More relevant for the precariat is the increasing need for forms of training-*for*-labour (rather than training-*in*-labour), such as personality refinement, employability, networking and the skill of information gathering to maintain familiarity with current thinking on a range of subjects. That management consultant who recommended, 'Spend up to 15 per cent of your time learning about fields adjacent to yours', also added, 'Rewrite your CV every year'. Working on those manufactured CVs, in the dispiriting effort to impress, to sell oneself and to cover as many bases as possible, takes up a huge amount of time. It is dehumanising, trying to demonstrate individuality while conforming to a standardised routine and way of behaving. When will the precariat protest?

The erosion of the industrial-era workplace as the locus of the 'standard employment relationship' opens up sensitive questions of discipline, control, privacy, health and safety insurance, and the appropriateness of bargaining institutions. But a key point about the dissolving industrial model is the increased fuzziness of the notion of 'skill'. Many commentators use the term with abandon, often to say there is a 'skills shortage'. In a tertiary society such statements are unhelpful. There is always a shortage, insofar as one cannot see a limit to potential human competencies. However, no country in the world has a measure of the stock of the skills of its population, and standard indicators such as years of schooling should be regarded as woefully inadequate. Is a gardener or plumber unskilled because he/she has no secondary or tertiary schooling? The skills required to survive in a precariat world are not captured by years of formal schooling.

One might claim rather the reverse – that modern market society has a 'skills excess', in that millions of people have bundles of skills that they have no opportunity to exercise or refine. A British survey found that nearly 2 million workers were 'mismatched', having skills that did not match their jobs. But that must be the tip of the proverbial iceberg; huge numbers have qualifications and diplomas that they do not use and that rust away in their mental lockers.

For years there was a debate in economics and development journals about 'voluntary unemployment'. Much unemployment was said to be voluntary because many of the unemployed had more schooling than those in jobs. Schooling was supposed to produce human capital, which was supposed to make people more employable. If those with human capital were unemployed, it had to be because they were choosing to be idle, waiting for a high-level job. Although a few may have corresponded to this stereotype, the simplification was misleading. Indeed, schooling may act to block the development of skills needed to survive in a precarious economic system. To be 'streetwise' is a skill, as is the capacity to network, the ability to earn trust and build up favours, and so on. These are precariat skills.

The skills required in a tertiary society also include the ability to limit self-exploitation to an optimal and sustainable level. For instance, the online gathering and analysis of information (for whatever purpose), such as searching, downloading, comparing and emailing, can be infinitely time consuming. The process is addictive but induces weariness and burnout. The skill arises in self-discipline, the ability to limit diligence to sustainable involvement. Focusing on the screen for hours on end is a recipe for attention deficit, an inability to concentrate and wrestle with complex problems and tasks.

Another range of skills in a tertiary society are personal deportment skills, covered by what some sociologists call 'emotional labour'.

The ability to look good, produce a winning smile, a well-timed witticism, a cheery 'good day' greeting, all become skills in a system of personal services. There may be a correlation between them, schooling and income, in that those from affluent families tend to develop more refined personable skills and also obtain more schooling. But it is not the schooling that provides the skills. In many countries, women's relative earnings have risen, which is usually attributed to their improved schooling, anti-discrimination measures and changes in the type of jobs they do. But reverse sexism has surely played a part. Customers like pretty faces; bosses love them. One may deplore it, but it is hard to deny. And good-looking youths will have an advantage over less attractive middle agers.

It is no wonder that 'beautification' treatment is booming. Those in the precariat, or fearful of being in it, learn that 'a nose job', breast enlargement, Botox or liposuction is potentially an income-earning investment as well as lifestyle enhancing. The borderline between personal 'consumption' and 'investment' is blurred. Youthfulness and beauty are partly acquired or re-acquired. One should not dismiss this as pure narcissism or vanity. If commodifying interests favour a climate of 'competition', behavioural and cosmetic adaptation is rational. Yet such 'skill' is insecure. Good looks fade and are harder to recreate. Attractive mannerisms can become tiresome and stale.

If a youth learned a trade in the industrial age, he or she could have been reasonably confident that the skills would have yielded a return over decades, perhaps for an entire income-earning life. In the absence of such stability, making decisions on time use outside a job involves a much more risky set of decisions. For the precariat, it is more like a lottery that produces losers as well as a few winners. Someone who takes a training course or a university degree does not know whether it will yield anything, unlike someone already in the salariat who takes a course as part of a well-mapped career. The problem is compounded by the likely increase in the status frustration effect, due to having more skills without the opportunity to use them.

Should I allocate time to learning about this? Is it useful? As I spent a lot of time and money on doing that last year, and nothing came of it, should I bother again? As what I learned last year is now obsolescent, is it worth repeating the same cost and stressful experience of taking another course? Such questions are part of the jobholding tertiary society.

Insecurity is greater with certain occupational skills. One may spend years acquiring qualifications and then find they have become obsolescent or insufficient. An acceleration of occupational obsolescence affects many in the precariat. There is a paradox. The more skilled the work, the more likely it is that refinements will take place, requiring 'retraining'. Another way of putting it is as follows: The more trained you are, the more likely you are to become unskilled in your sphere of competence. Perhaps deskilled would be a way to describe what happens. This gives a strange time dimension to the idea of skill. It is not just a case of being as good as you were yesterday but of being as good as you should be tomorrow. The behavioural reaction to skill insecurity may be a frenzy of time-using investment in upgrading or it may be a paralysis of the will, inactivity due to a belief that any course would have a very uncertain return. Commentators who endlessly call for more training and bewail a lack of skills merely contribute to an existential crisis. This is not a social climate conducive to capability development; it is one of constant dissatisfaction and stress.

Work-for-reproduction

There are many other forms of work-for-labour, some complementary to contracted labour, some obligatory as part of the labour relationship. There is also growth in 'work-for-reproduction'. The idea has a double connotation. The main one is a loosely defined range of activities that people must undertake, or feel they should, in order to maintain their capacities to function and live as best they can, given their circumstances. These should be separated from 'work-for-labour'. Among the more challenging is financial management work. The salariat and proficians can afford accountants and rely on banking services for advice and assistance. If there is a cost, it will be modest relative to their earnings and the benefit gained from professional help.

The fluctuating earnings of the precariat may create more serious difficulties; yet the availability of financial advice is more limited and costs more of their earnings. Many will be on their own, unable or reluctant to buy the services they need. Some will be obliged to spend more time worrying about and dealing with managing their income and financial affairs. Others will respond by avoiding the work altogether. One UK survey suggested that 9 million adults were 'financially phobic', scared by the perceived complexity of making rational decisions about money management. In a tertiary society, financial phobia can make the difference between modest comfort and misery, particularly in moments of financial stress. The cost is not randomly borne by all segments of the population. It is a hidden form of inequality, one felt adversely by the precariat.

The precariat is also disadvantaged in the increasingly significant sphere of legal knowledge. A society of strangers relies on contracts; binding regulations creep into every crevice of life. To function as a citizen in a society governed by complex laws and regulations, we need to know the laws and be able to access reliable sources of knowledge and advice. While few these days can know every aspect of the law that might apply to them, the precariat is especially disadvantaged in this respect. The salariat and proficians have positional advantages that translate into economic advantages. The precariat is not just likely to be more ignorant but is also likely to be more constrained by ignorance, for example, in setting up a small business.

Another form of work-for-reproduction is connected with consumption. Self-service is booming. Jobs are being outsourced to customers, with people urged to use websites rather than hotlines and automated checkouts rather than manned registers. Retailing, hospitality and health care firms have been spending billions of dollars on self-service technology and investment is growing by 15 per cent a year. Firms claim this is about 'joys of customer empowerment'. In reality, it is a shift of labour into work. Pigou would have seen the irony: National income and jobs decline, work goes up!

The time for work-for-reproduction, or care, is hard to measure because it embraces so many activities and tends to expand to fill the time available. It is a sphere of time use subject to conflicting pressures. In many societies, child care has become more time intensive and more commercialised through paid care. According to a 2009 survey by the United Kingdom's National Children's Bureau, more than half of all parents found the pace of life too hectic to devote enough time to playing with their children (Asthana and Slater, 2010). Long working hours, lengthy commutes and 'unavoidable commitments', along with excessive homework, left millions frustrated. A US survey revealed that three-quarters of American parents felt they had insufficient time to spend with their children. This may reflect societal pressure on people always to feel they must do *more*. But if children are deprived of care due to the demands of labour and other work, the long-term costs may include children growing up deprived of socialisation values that come from the inter-generational transfer of knowledge, experience and simple closeness.

At the other end of the age spectrum, with more living into their 70s, 80s and 90s, elder care has become a major time use. To some extent it is being commodified through commercialised services, care homes and so on, alongside a weakening of inter-generational reciprocities and responsibilities. Nevertheless, many people have to devote considerable time to the care of others in their lives. Many would like to do more than they can afford because of other calls on their time.

While women continue to bear most of the burden, often pressured to be available at short notice, men are also being drawn to do more care work. Although some commentators would deny this is work, for most people it is an obligation with economic value in terms of opportunity cost, in terms of reproducing the recipient's capabilities and in terms of lowering the cost to the economy that would arise if responsibility fell entirely on the state or if neglect led to longer-term health care costs.

Members of the precariat may be pressured to do more care work than they would wish, because of a perception that they have more 'time on their hands' and because they may need to retain the goodwill of those around them in case they need financial or other assistance. Once again, they are not in control of their time. They must adapt in an atmosphere of personalised insecurity.

There is another sphere of work-for-reproduction, which expanded in the late nineteenth century at a time of transformative crisis and again in the globalisation era. People are being encouraged to seek out counselling to combat their anxieties and ailments, and to resort to therapy, particularly cognitive behavioural therapy, to handle the stresses and strains of their insecure lives.

Those in the precariat face a quandary. If they are uncertain about what they should do, they will soon find themselves under pressure to receive counselling, including 'employability training'. They can be depicted as abnormal in not knowing what to do or not being able to 'settle down' in a steady job, or they may be labelled 'virtually unemployable'. The epithets are all too familiar, churned out by the media, by soap operas on television and by politicians. They are consistent with a model in which the emphasis is placed on changing people's personalities and behaviour rather than facilitating diversity of lifestyle.

All these demands on time – labour, work-for-labour, work-for-reproduction – are stressful in themselves. They require diligence and effort without a particular end in sight. Much of this labour and work is done in insecure circumstances, with an uncertain economic return and a high perceived opportunity cost, simply because the need for money is great.

Among the reactions may be a frenzy of activities that take up all available hours almost every day, potentially leading to burnout and anxiety as well as superficiality. Or the uncertainties may prove overwhelming, inducing mental paralysis and self-destructive stupor. Probably, the most typical outcome is a feeling of being under pressure and devoting more time to work in its several forms than one would wish.

A result is a crowding out of activities that have social or personal value, such as time spent with family. There is nothing new in this multiple time use. What is new is that it has become the norm. It is a reflection of technological developments, affluence, commercialisation of life and crumbling of a life in fixed spaces for specific functions.

There is much talk about 'multitasking', the ability to do several activities in the same period. According to folk wisdom, women are better at multitasking than men, although this is said more tongue-in-cheek, in that women are obliged to undertake several work and labour activities at the same time and so may have learned better how to 'muddle through' or make 'satisficing' (good enough) decisions more readily. The latest neologism is 'multi-multitasking'. The backup phrase is as follows: How to do more with less! Research shows that heavy multitaskers have more difficulty in focusing and shutting out distracting information. Moreover, when people are forced to think hard about something, they remember it better. With multitasking it is impossible to think hard about anything. The precariat have an additional problem: They are not in control of their time and they know it.

Youth and 'connectivity'

For some activists, the 'connectivity' of the internet and social media is a defining feature of the precariat. Today's youth is wired in ways that previous generations could not have imagined and it has a lifestyle to match. Wired up, wired in, always on, youth in particular, but the rest of us too, are using up more and more time in making and maintaining more and more connections. Stillness and silence are endangered. Connectivity fills every space in time.

Already, in 2010, there were over half a billion Facebook users. Over half were logging on every day; 700 billion minutes a month were being spent on Facebook globally. Twitter had 175 million registered users, with 95 million tweets each day. There were over 5 billion mobile phone subscribers globally, in some countries exceeding 100 per cent of the population. In the United States, about a third of teenagers send over 100 text messages a day.

The debate on the balance of good and bad consequences will rage for years, probably inconclusively. However, it is worth noting several concerns. The most discussed is a 'collective attention deficit syndrome'. Constant connectivity strengthens weak ties and weakens strong ties. A signal of an incoming call or message disrupts personal conversations or other activities. Checking and responding to emails break into periods of concentration. Facebook and other social media linking people to 'friends' they have never met are an incursion into real life. Restlessness is fostered while traits of patience and determination are eroded.

Spending a vast amount of time online has become part of the precariat existence, and research shows it can have a depressing effect, as social networking is replacing actual interaction with people. Twice as many people in the United Kingdom are addicted to the internet as to the conventional forms of gambling. Youth is most vulnerable, the average age of addiction being 21, according to a survey by Catriona

Morrison (2010). As she concluded, 'The internet is like a drug for some people: it soothes them, it keeps them calm. If people are addicted it can affect a person's ability to perform at work or they may be failing to do chores so they can go online'.

Constant connectivity may not only produce the precariatised mind but, because the precariat has no control of time or a regular schedule, it is more vulnerable to the distractions and addictions of the online world. There is nothing wrong with connectivity; it is the context that matters.

The leisure squeeze

The growth of labour, work-for-labour and work-for-reproduction also eats into 'leisure'. The loss of respect for leisure, and for reproductive and productive 'idleness', is one of the worst outcomes of the commodifying market society. Those who experience intensive work and labour find their minds and bodies 'spent' and have little energy or inclination to do anything other than to indulge in passive 'play'. People who are spent want to relax in 'play', often by watching a screen or conducting a dialogue with a series of screens. Of course, we all need 'play' in some form. But if labour and work are so intense, we may have no energy or inclination to participate in more active leisure activities.

Mark Aguiar and Erik Hurst (2009) estimated that, despite the rise in women's involvement in the labour force, Americans have four hours more leisure a week than in 1965, men six hours more. But leisure is not the same as time not participating in paid labour.

Although other social groups face pressures, the precariat must do a lot of work-for-labour and other work to survive or function in the lower rungs of the market.

Real leisure faces a triple squeeze. One form of leisure is participating in demanding cultural and artistic activity. To appreciate fine music, theatre, art and great literature, and to learn about our history and that of the community in which we are living, all take what in popular parlance is called 'quality time', that is, time in which we are not distracted, nervous from insecurity or spent from labour and work, or by the sleeplessness induced by it. A result is a leisure deficit. The time is perceived as unavailable. Or those in the precariat feel guilty about devoting time to such activities, thinking they should be using their time in networking or in constantly upgrading their 'human capital', as all those commentators are urging.

Where are the incentives to allocate time to leisure? The message even goes deep into the universities. When governments make universities and colleges more 'business-like' and require them to make profits, they typically look at cultural zones where there is no prospect for profit. In 2010, the United Kingdom's University of Middlesex announced it would close its philosophy department. A university without a philosophy department would have struck all the great educationalists as a contradiction in terms.

Even more dispiriting is the crowding out of what the ancient Greeks regarded as true leisure, *schole*, participation in public life, the sphere of the citizen. Those in the precariat – and they are not alone – are detached from political life. They may turn out occasionally to join a spectacle or vote for a charismatic candidate, but that is different from participating in a sustained way. This vital form of leisure is squeezed by the labour-work-play colonisation of time. Too many people feel they do not have enough quality time to come to grips with what they are told are complex topics 'best left to experts'. This is easily converted into a rationalisation for detachment and may lead from education to reliance on emotions and prejudices. Be that as it may. The precariat is induced to devote less time to that most human of activities, political leisure. Where are the incentives to do otherwise?

Another aspect of the time squeeze is a profound inequality in the control over time. It is part of the overall inequality in a tertiary market society, partly because time is a productive asset. The precariat must be at the beck and call of potential users of their labour. Those floating around internet cafés or drifting around at home, in pubs or on street corners may appear to have 'time on their hands'. However, they are often unable to develop or sustain a strategy on how to allocate time differently. They do not have a clear narrative to tell, and as a result their time is dissipated when they are not in jobs. The use of time in apparent idleness is a reflection of the flexible jobs market. It wants the precariat to be on standby. The structuring of time is taken away from them.

The devaluation of leisure, particularly working-class leisure, is among the worst legacies of labourism. The erosion of values-reproducing education results in the divorce of youth from their culture and a loss of social memory of their communities. The notion of 'street corner society' has become one of the great urban images. 'Hanging around' becomes a dominant form of using time; filling time becomes a challenge. Some call this 'leisure poverty'. Material poverty limits the leisure lives of the young precariat, with neither the money nor the occupational community nor the sense of stability to generate the control over time that is needed. This feeds into an anomic attitude to all activity, including work and labour. This is a precarity trap. Merely to survive requires an adequate set of public spaces, and even those are being eroded by austerity measures. After all, the neo-liberal mentality sees them as a 'luxury', in that they do not contribute directly to output or economic growth. Only if the precariat becomes a threat to stability will that arithmetic be reassessed.

As quality public spaces shrink for the precariat, aggressive behaviour will be fostered. Globalisation and electronic technology may shift identity away from purely local forms (Forrest and Kearns, 2001). But this cannot replace the need for physical space in which to move and interact. A sense of territoriality is a human trait that is part of our genes. Cramp it and empty it of developmental meaning, and the result will be ugly.

Working-class 'leisure careers' have been lost (MacDonald and Shildrick, 2007), due not simply to lack of money but to an erosion of social institutions. In the United Kingdom, these included working men's clubs and public spaces, which fell victim to the neo-liberal radicalism of Thatcherism. In France, the bistros, which Honoré de Balzac described as 'the parliament of the people', are disappearing.

Impoverished working-class education and leisure careers create an environment for criminality and drug use, to fill time and gain status in some form. Petty crime may provide a thrill that feels better than simply hanging around. The neo-liberal mantra that success is measured by consumption is conducive to shoplifting and theft, a tiny surge of achievement in a long spell of deprivation, of failure. This is part of the wider precarity trap for young men. Faced with the insecurities of being male, they may gain momentary low-level 'respect' that way (Collison, 1996). But, of course, there are longer term consequences.

Part of class is one's 'habitus', the zone and the way of living that defines 'things to do or not to do' (Bourdieu, 1990: 53), what one aspires to do and what one does not do. The precariat lifestyle matches its workstyle in being fleeting and flexible, opportunistic rather than progressively constructed. People may shrink into a closer space out of fear and anxiety bred of insecurity, but it will be a surly anomic shrinking. In a society based on flexibility and insecurity, people dissipate time more than use it to construct a developmental model of behaviour.

This leads us back to the crumbling of the workplace concept, which disrupts the life chances of the precariat. The norm for the precariat involves a workplace in every place, at any time, almost all the time. Working and labouring outside a workplace is not indicative of *autonomy* or being in control of the self. And the statistics lie. 'Hours at work' are not the same as 'hours of work'. It is misleading to think that, because of the fuzziness of place and time, there is free labour. Just as employers can induce workers to do unpaid work-for-labour, so can they induce more to labour and to work away from the formal workplace.

A relationship of power exists. It is free labour in that it is unpaid; it is unfree in that it is not done autonomously. An influential analysis by Hardt and Negri (2000) claimed service labour is free, 'immaterial' and 'outside measure'. However, the amount of labour can be measured and the boundary of measured labour can be affected by the bargaining capacities of those involved in negotiating labour relationships. The precariat is currently weak, due to its insecurity and the flexible labour culture. Most of the benefits of work-for-labour go to those who hire labour. We are in uncharted territory. But there is a difference between saying that service work is 'outside measure' and saying that work-for-labour is hard to measure.

Concluding points

The precariat is under time stress. It must devote a growing amount of time to work-for-labour, without it offering a reliable road to economic security or an occupational career worthy of the name. Labour intensification and growing demands on time put the precariat at constant risk of being spent or, as one woman put it, in a mental state of being foggy and fuzzy.

The tertiary lifestyle involves multitasking without control over a narrative of time use, of seeing the future and building on the past. To be precariatised is to be wired into job-performing lifestyles without a sense of occupational development. We respond to signals, which redirect attention hither and thither. Multitasking lowers productivity in each and every activity. Fractured thinking becomes habitual. It makes it harder to do creative work or to indulge in leisure that requires concentration, deliberation and sustained effort. It crowds out leisure, leaving people relieved just to play, passively in the mental sense. Non-stop interactivity is the opium of the precariat, just as beer and gin drinking was for the first generation of the industrial proletariat.

The workplace is every place, diffuse, unfamiliar, a zone of insecurity. And if the precariat does have occupational skills, those may vanish or cease to be a reliable ticket to a secure identity or long-term sustainable life of dignity. This is an unhealthy combination that is conducive to opportunism and cynicism. It creates a lottery ticket society, with downside risks that the precariat bears disproportionately.

Meanwhile, the time squeeze turns leisure into a jeopardised part of life and leads to 'thin democracy', in which people are disengaged from political activity except when motivated for a short while, enraptured by a new charismatic face or energised by a shocking event. It is to this that we will now turn.

6

A politics of inferno

The neo-liberal state is neo-Darwinist, in that it reveres competitiveness and celebrates unrestrained individual responsibility, with an antipathy to anything collective that might impede market forces. The state's role is seen primarily as setting and strengthening the rule of law. But the rule of law has never been minimalist, as some neo-liberals depict it. It is intrusive and oriented to curbing nonconformity and collective action. This extends to what Wacquant (2008: 14) called 'the public anathematization of deviant categories', notably 'street thugs', the 'unemployed', 'scroungers', the failures, losers with character flaws and behavioural deficiencies.

The market is the embodiment of the Darwinian metaphor, 'the survival of the fittest'. But it has a disquieting tendency to turn strugglers into misfits and villains, to be penalised, locked up or locked out. Policies and institutions are constructed that treat everyone as potential misfits and villains. For example, those who are 'poor' must prove they are not 'lazy' or that they are sending their children to school regularly to obtain entitlement to state benefits.

The precariat hovers on the borderline, exposed to circumstances that could turn them from strugglers into deviants and loose cannons

prone to listen to populist politicians and demagogues. This is the
primary issue underlying this chapter.

The panopticon society

While the 'social factory' is not right as an image of how life for the
precariat is being constructed, a better image is a 'panopticon society',
in which all social spheres are taking the shape envisaged by Jeremy
Bentham's panopticon papers of 1787 (Bentham, 1995). It is not just
what is *done* by government but what is *allowed* by the state in an
ostensibly 'free market' society.

Let us recall Bentham's vision. He is known as the father of
utilitarianism, the view that government should promote 'the greatest
happiness of the greatest number'. This conveniently allows some to
rationalise making the minority thoroughly miserable, in the interests
of preserving the happiness of the majority. Bentham took this in a
scary direction, in a design for an ideal prison. An all-seeing guard
would be in a central watchtower overlooking prisoners in their cells
in a circular building. The guard could see them, but they could not
see him. The guard's power lay in the fact that the prisoners could
not know whether or not he was watching, and so acted as if he was
watching, out of fear. Bentham used the term 'an architecture of choice',
by which he meant that the authorities could induce the prisoners to
behave in desired ways.

The key point for Bentham was that the prisoner was given an
appearance of choice. But if he did not make the *right* choice, which
was to labour hard, he would be left to 'languish on bad bread and

drink his water, without a soul to speak to'. And prisoners were to be isolated, to prevent them forming 'a concert of minds'. He realised, just as neo-liberals were to realise, that collective agency would jeopardise the panopticon project.

It was an idea Michel Foucault took up in the 1970s as a metaphor for producing 'docile bodies'. Bentham believed his panopticon design could be used for hospitals, mental asylums, schools, factories, the workhouse and all social institutions. Around the world his design has been adopted and has been extended inadvertently by twenty-first-century company towns. The worst case so far is Shenzhen, where 6 million workers are watched by closed circuit television (CCTV) cameras everywhere they go and where a comprehensive databank monitors their behaviour and character, modelled on technology developed by the US military. One could talk of 'Shenzhenism' in the way social scientists talk of 'Fordism' and 'Toyotism' as systems of production and employment control. 'Shenzhenism' combines visual monitoring with 'dataveillance' and behavioural incentives and penalties to sift out undesirables, identify suitably conformist workers and induce workers to think and behave in ways the authorities want.

The invasion of privacy

Panopticon techniques are on the march. Let us start with a vital aspect of life, privacy or the space for intimacy, where we live with our secrets and most precious emotions and spaces. It is an endangered species.

What is legitimised as privacy is subject to legal interpretation, and legal rulings have tended to shrink it. But the panopticon trend is remorseless. CCTV is ubiquitous, used not only by the police but also by private security companies, businesses and individuals. Nor is the footage simply for private use. Consider one little example. A resident in a tough neighbourhood of San Francisco, concerned about street security, set up Adam's Block as an open-access site webcasting a video feed from a street intersection. That site was obliged to shut after threats and complaints to the webcam owner that privacy was being abused. But others secretly installed cameras in the same area, live-casting under a new name, claiming to 'empower citizens to fight crime and save lives'. There are said to be many similar neighbourhood webcams throughout the United States.

Google Street View, launched in 2007, has already attracted the attention of data protection regulators in North America and Europe for illegally (apparently inadvertently) obtaining personal information from unsecured wireless networks along routes travelled by Google's cameras. Street View puts people's houses, cars and activities on display for all the world to see, and there is no way to object apart from politely requesting that images be blurred. This is something few people will know how to undertake, assuming they have checked what Street View has captured in the first place.

Social media, such as Facebook, are also shrinking the zone of privacy, as users, predominantly young people, reveal, wittingly or unwittingly, their most intimate details to 'friends' and many others besides. Location-based services take this a step further, letting users alert 'friends' to where they are (and enabling businesses, the police, criminals and others to know too). Mark Zuckerberg, Facebook founder and chief executive, told Silicon Valley entrepreneurs: 'People have really gotten comfortable not only sharing more information and different kinds, but more openly and with more people . . . That social norm is just something that has evolved'.

Surveillance prompts images of a 'police state', and certainly it starts with the police, strengthening a divide between the police and the watched. Surveillance also induces 'sousveillance', watching the watchers. During demonstrations against a Group of 20 meeting in London in 2009, an amateur video taken on a mobile phone showed a policeman beating a man who had been innocently walking in the street; the man died. It was a reminder that guards are not necessarily protectors. And as sousveillance grows, police surveillance will become more pre-emptive. Watchers of the police will be transformed into categories to be dealt with because they are a threat to the police.

The invasion of privacy and the technological capacity to peer deep into our lives are a base for extending the panopticon and its objectives into every aspect of them. There is even monitoring from inside the body. New pills produced by US drug companies will provide doctors with data from inside the body. Some might regard this as beneficial and a matter of free choice. But the situation could arise where, if we did not agree to internal monitoring, health (or other) insurance premiums could be raised or we could be denied coverage. Such technology could become mandatory or be enforced by insurance firms.

On the internet, surveillance is business. Information from people's web searches, social media pages and other internet activities is routinely fed to commercial companies. Social networking may have started as 'friendly encounters of a voyeuristic kind'. But it is becoming 'complicit surveillance', co-opted for commercial or more sinister motives. A net-watch society is being built.

As the US *National Broadband Plan* (Federal Communications Commission, 2010) points out, it is now possible for a single firm to build up individual 'digital identity' profiles, 'including web searches, sites visited, clickstream, email contacts and content, map searches, geographic location and movements, calendar appointments, mobile phone book, health records, educational records, energy usage, pictures and videos, social networks, locations visited, eating, reading, entertainment preferences, and purchasing history'. Most people do not know what information is being collected about them and who has access to it.

When Facebook launched Facebook Beacon in 2007, automatically sending 'friends' details of members' online purchases, a sousveillance campaign by MoveOn.org forced it to switch the application to an 'opt-in' programme. In 2009 Beacon was shut down following a class action privacy lawsuit. But Facebook is still collecting information on members from other sources, such as newspapers, messaging services and blogs, 'to provide you with more useful information and a more personalised experience'. Most users, from inertia or ignorance, accept Facebook's default privacy settings, which share information widely. According to one US survey, 45 per cent of employers checked social network profiles of prospective employees. Non-US users also consent, without realising it, to having personal data transferred and processed in the United States. Users are not notified when or how the data are used.

Website privacy controls have not worked well. Electronic systems have eroded privacy and given the state enormously powerful tools with which to construct a panopticon system. Those in the precariat are most vulnerable because they indulge in activities that are open to monitoring and judgement calls and because they are more exposed to the consequences.

Warrantless wiretapping is spreading too, monitoring us all. The 'war on terror' has brought the panopticon society closer. The US National Security Agency has advanced digital identification and monitoring techniques as a global system (Bamford, 2009). It can now indulge in non-legalised access to everything we do electronically or over phone lines. The surveillance-industrial complex is global. The Chinese are matching the United States. When the National People's Congress was held in Beijing in 2010, 700,000 security personnel were posted across the city. Inside the Great Hall of the People, proposals reportedly put forward by delegates included calls for all internet cafés to be taken over by the government and for all cell phones to be equipped with surveillance cameras. Soon it will be impossible to tell.

Panopticon schooling

It starts early. Schools and universities are using electronic methods to teach, monitor, discipline and assess. A Swedish businessman has created a largely automatic schooling model, used for thousands of Swedish schoolchildren, which is being exported with commercial success. The children are closely monitored, but they see their teachers for only 15 minutes a week. Former UK Prime Minister Tony Blair was attracted by the system for academy schools in London.

Some schools in the United States have provided students with laptops equipped with security software allowing remote activation of the computer's webcam, enabling them to view the students at any time without their knowledge. A class action suit was brought by students in February 2010 against a school district in suburban Philadelphia after a school accused a student of indulging in 'improper behaviour in his home'. This was surely a violation of his civil rights. And apart from opening up blackmail possibilities, such technology also provides the panopticon capacity to create docile minds and bodies. A middle school in South Bronx, New York, installed software in laptops so that officials could view whatever was displayed on the screen. The school's assistant principal spent part of each day checking what students were doing, often observing them using Photo Booth, a programme that uses the webcam to turn the screen into a virtual mirror. 'I always like to mess with them and take their picture', he told a documentary programme.

Most of us do not know if we are subject to such practices. Those Philadelphia children certainly did not. The fact is that the techniques exist to monitor behaviour, and the data can be accessed and used as people move into their adult lives. That is what is happening.

Hiring, firing and workplace discipline

The encroachment of panopticon apparatus into hiring, discipline, promotion and dismissal strategies of companies and organisations has been largely unchecked. It particularly jeopardises the life chances of the precariat, in subtle and diverse ways.

The neo-liberal state claims to favour non-discriminatory labour practices, trumpeting equal opportunity as the essence of 'meritocracy'. But it has largely turned a blind eye to discriminatory techniques and practices based on electronic surveillance, insurance markets and subsidised research in behavioural psychology. The resultant discrimination is more refined but works in the same way as crude forms based on gender, race, age or schooling. The latest twist is genetic profiling. It is appropriate that crucial research has been done in authoritarian Singapore. A study there showed how people with a particular variant of a gene (called HTR2A) are less moody and more likely to make docile workers. What is the message of this path-breaking research? Give temporary workers some variant HTR2A or weed out those without it?

Hormones also play their part. Research in Japan suggests that those with low levels of the stress hormone cortisol were more prepared than those with higher levels to accept low current income in the hope of receiving more later. If you were hiring someone for a temporary job, which person would you recruit if you knew their hormone levels? Then there is testosterone. High levels go with a desire to dominate and take risks. For most jobs, particularly precarious jobs, employers do not want workers frustrated by low status and high control. The Singapore research indicated that high testosterone diminishes a person's capacity to be a conforming team worker. It is not hard to identify the level of someone's testosterone – a mouth swab will do. Or firms can devise 'aptitude tests' that applicants must complete.

The precariat must be careful, since the way one lives affects testosterone level. If you live an exciting life, it goes up; if you live a docile one, it goes down. Job access could depend on keeping it low! Some will dismiss such scenarios as scaremongering. But what is the purpose of this genetic research? Unless there are checks on its use, behavioural sifting will only grow stronger. The Economist (2010c) enthused that it would make 'management science into a real science'. On the contrary, it is more likely to lead to social engineering.

Besides those developments, a growing number of US firms weed out job applicants with bad credit records, believing they would make risky employees. So past behaviour outside your work is used against you. Companies are doing this systematically, also drawing on social networking sites to assess character traits as well as past misdemeanours, relationships and so on. But this is unfair discrimination. There are many reasons for a spell of 'bad credit', including illness or a family tragedy. Secret screening by crude proxies for possible behaviour is unfair.

We mentioned earlier how firms are demanding that job applicants produce time-consuming CVs and that at some stage there will be resistance. Will that be anomic protest, through sullen refusals to comply? Or will be it a 'primitive rebel' action, such as saturating agencies with phoney applications? Or will it be a political protest, through organised resistance, by a campaign to limit the boundaries of personality vetting, by setting codes for what companies should and should not do? The last could become a badge of honour, respected by those with empathy for the condition of the precariat, as an assertion of a right of privacy, a rejection of the intrusion.

Beyond recruitment, the panopticon is in its element in tertiary workplaces. National industrial capitalism spawned company towns. There were over 2,500 in the United States (Green, 2010). In modified forms, this paternalistic concept has persisted, some evolving into vast corporate creations. Thus IBM and PepsiCo have town-sized campuses in the middle of nowhere. The Chinese have gone further with Shenzhen; Foxconn is the global leader. But they are all exhibits of a panopticon market society.

In early 2010, it was revealed that Wall Street firms were hiring 'moonlighting' active Central Intelligence Agency (CIA) agents to train managers in 'tactical behaviour assessment' techniques. These are ways of checking on employee honesty by reading verbal and behavioural clues, such as fidgeting or use of qualifying statements like 'honestly' and 'frankly'.

Privacy in jobs is evaporating. Most US firms now require recruits to sign electronic communications policies stating they have no rights to privacy or to ownership over any content on company computers. Whatever is put on a computer belongs to the company. All notes, photographs and drafts are alienated. Moreover, firms now prefer to remove an employee immediately rather than have them serve a notice period, during which they could download information, contact lists and so on.

Two-thirds of American employers electronically monitor employees' internet use, according to a 2010 survey by the American Management Association and the ePolicy Institute. It is distance control, since employees do not know if they are being watched. They are monitored for sexual harassment, boss disparagement, spilling trade secrets and so on.

Managements can now view computer screens, capture computer keystrokes, identify websites frequented and track workers' where-abouts through GPS-enabled mobile phones, webcams and minuscule video cameras. Lewis Maltby, author of *Can They Do That?* (2009), attributed the growing monitoring to financial pressure, which has made firms want to tighten control and lower costs, and to the increased ease of doing it. Companies can buy machine-monitoring software and worker-tracking cameras at a local shop or through internet retailers. It is that easy.

Smarsh, one of many firms providing monitoring systems, services over 10,000 US companies. Its Chief Executive Officer (CEO) boasted, 'Employees should assume that they are going to be watched'. A national survey found that one in two employees knew of someone who had been fired for email or internet misuse; many also said they knew of someone fired for inappropriate cell phone use, instant messaging misuse or inappropriate text messaging. Monitoring for dismissal has grown as much as for hiring and ordinary discipline. Surveillance is direct, personal and intrusive. It will become more so.

A form of employee monitoring favoured by the United Kingdom's Labour government was the online grading of service providers by 'clients'. This is like naming and shaming, a shabby way of seeking to control by stigmatisation. The health minister introduced a scheme by which patients could rate doctors. A society demanding constant feedback does not trust its professionals to be professional. The doctors' ratings website followed similar monitoring of teachers. Should they be hounded by children who take grim pleasure in denigrating them, without any sense of accountability? It risks turning professionals into walking wounded and tipping them in a precariat direction. Why risk being humiliated online by being rigorous? Give them what they want! This is an illusion of empowerment that degrades responsibility and professionalism. Soon, everybody will be rating everybody else.

The state as libertarian paternalist

A new perspective on social and economic policy is behavioural economics, which has produced libertarian paternalism. *Nudge*, an influential book by Cass Sunstein and Richard Thaler (2008), two Chicago-based advisers and friends of Barack Obama, was premised on the idea that people have too much information and so make irrational decisions. People must be steered, or nudged, to make the decisions that are in their best interest. The authors do not attribute the idea to Bentham but say the state should create 'an architecture of choice'.

On becoming US President, Obama appointed Sunstein to head the Office of Information and Regulatory Affairs, based in the White House. Meanwhile, in the United Kingdom, Conservative Party leader David Cameron told members of parliament to read the book; on becoming Prime Minister in 2010 he set up the Behavioural Insight Team, quickly dubbed 'the Nudge Unit', in Downing Street, advised by Thaler. The mandate was to induce people to make 'better' decisions, in the interest of 'society'.

Steering people is always questionable. How do we know that the nudgers know what is best for any individual? Today's conventional wisdom becomes yesterday's error. Again and again, policies or practices that seem unwise turn out later to become norms and vice versa. Who is liable if the guided decision proves to be wrong or if it leads to a mishap?

As an example of how nudging is proceeding, in 2010 the UK National Health Service sent a letter offering people a 'summary care record', giving their medical history, that would be made available to any health worker. Those receiving the letter faced a designed 'choice environment', requiring a decision to opt out or be automatically covered. But there was no opt-out form included, so people wishing to do so had to go to a website, find a form to download, print it, sign it, send it as a letter to their general practitioner (GP) and hope it would be acted upon. Bureaucratic hurdles were deliberately raised, increasing the cost of opting out and giving a bias to 'presumed consent'.

Those least likely to opt out are the uneducated, the poor and the 'digitally excluded', mostly elderly without access to online facilities. As of 2010, 63 per cent of all those over the age of 65 in the United Kingdom lived in a household without internet access. There is government pressure, led by its 'digital inclusion champion', for more people to have access. And the cost of not having it is being raised. In effect, people are being penalised for not having access.

Old-fashioned state paternalism is popular with governments. It can infantilise citizens and demonise parts of the precariat. In 2009, the United Kingdom's Department of Business, Innovation and Skills issued a guide called *Parent Motivators* directed at parents of dependent unemployed graduates. It was condescending, clearly presuming that graduates could not work out basic decisions for themselves. One commentator concluded it was the first time educated adults in their 20s were 'being officially infantilized, a move that is unlikely, moreover, to dispel growing suspicion about the value of many modern degrees' (Bennett, 2010). Other guides of the same genre included *Preparing for Emergencies*, *Break Out* on how to avoid paedophiles, *Heat Wave*, the *Dad Card* on how to be a good father, and a *Breakfast4Life* toolkit.

Parent Motivators, written by consultant psychologists at public expense, suggested parents were partially to blame for their offspring's unemployment and urged them to show 'tough love'. One of its authors said, 'If you are making life too comfortable at home, why would they get a job?' At least that recognised that jobs were not attractive in themselves. But here was the state indulging in paternalistic steering while contributing to the demonisation of part of the precariat. They cannot work out how to behave themselves!

One could give many examples of the use of behavioural economics and libertarian paternalism to bear on the lives of the precariat, notably through clever use of 'opt-out' rules, making it hard to opt out and almost obligatory to 'opt in'. The new buzz word is 'conditionality'. There has been a remarkable growth of conditional cash transfer schemes or CCTs. The leading examples have been in Latin America, led by the *Progresa* scheme (now *Oportunidades*) in Mexico and Brazil's *Bolsa Familia*, which by 2010 was reaching over 50 million people. Seventeen Latin American countries have CCTs. The essence of these schemes is that people are given small state benefits, in the form of cash, only if they behave in predetermined ways.

Conditionality has been imported into rich countries, including the United States, and CCTs have been widely used in Central and Eastern Europe. One of the most detailed was *Opportunity New York – Family Rewards*, an experimental scheme with incredibly intricate financial incentives and penalties for doing and not doing certain things. The premise of all CCTs is that people need to be persuaded to behave in ways that are best for them and for 'society'. Thus the World Bank (Fiszbein and Schady, 2009) believes they can overcome 'persistent misguidedness'; it attributes poverty to an inter-generational reproduction of deprivation, such that CCTs will break the cycle by persuading people to behave responsibly.

The morality of this approach is dubious. It epitomises the Bentham project of creating an 'architecture of choice', chipping away at not just freedom but also personal responsibility. The relevance for the precariat is that there is talk about 'second-generation CCTs' to be targeted at young adults. Already there are conditionalities in many benefit schemes and these are being tightened. Thus in the United Kingdom, doctors are now required to report on their patient's degree of employability if they are receiving disability benefits, turning a confidential doctor-patient relationship into social policing.

One should worry where such trends could lead. In India, following the libertarian paternalists, a cash transfer scheme targeted at economically insecure women promises them cash when their first child reaches adulthood, on condition that they are sterilised after the birth of a second child. This too creates an 'architecture of choice'.

Making the precariat 'happy'

Meanwhile, the paternalists who have dominated social policy since the 1990s have refined a utilitarian mentality built around the desire to make people 'happy', to the extent that provision of happiness has become quasi-religious and dignified by being called 'the science of happiness'. In some countries, including France and the United Kingdom, official statistics are being collected to measure people's happiness.

Let us suppose we have a society in which politicians and their advisers want to make people 'happy'. The utilitarian rationalisation for inducing labour has grown in sophistication. Calvin sanctified capitalism by saying that salvation came to those who did good works. But ours is the first society where policy makers and commentators purport to believe that jobs make us happy.

By saying jobs should make us happy and that jobs define us and give us satisfaction, we are setting up a source of tension because the jobs most of us have to perform will fall short of those expectations. The precariat will suffer from stress. We should be happy; why are we not happy? The sane response should be that jobs are not there to make us happy, and so we should treat them as mainly instrumental, to obtain an income. Our happiness comes primarily from the work, leisure and play we undertake outside our labour, and from the income security we obtain from a job, not from the job itself.

If this were accepted as the premise for social policy, we could pursue a balance between how we use our time. Intuitively, many in the precariat may understand that. They cannot move to a stable and satisfying way of life because social and economic policies do not provide the basic security and sense of being in control of time that are indispensable.

Hedonistic happiness based on jobs and play is dangerous. Endless play would be tedious. The pleasure is transient and self-limiting. We stop when we think we have had enough. As pleasure from play is ephemeral, people who depend on it are doomed to fail. Hedonism is self-defeating – the hedonistic treadmill. Hedonists fear boredom. The great philosopher Bertrand Russell understood the need for boredom, expressed best in his wonderful essay *In Praise of Idleness*. Hedonistic happiness through play and 'pleasure' eventually induces addiction and intolerance of anything other than pleasure, a point brought out by behavioural biologist Paul Martin in his book *Sex, Drugs and Chocolate: The Science of Pleasure* (2009).

Satisfaction is contentment with life in general and with one's relationships. However, making a fetish of happiness is not a prescription for civilised society. The precariat must beware of the modern equivalent of a bread-and-circuses existence being offered by the state through pseudo-science and nudging.

The therapy state

While they set out to make people happy, libertarian paternalism and the utilitarianism underlying it have unleashed a cult of therapy, mirroring what happened in the period of mass insecurity at the end of the nineteenth century (Standing, 2009: 235–8). The hegemonic instrument in today's equivalent is cognitive behavioural therapy (CBT), which originated in the United States but which is globalising with indecent commercial speed.

In the United Kingdom, after the shock of 2008, instead of dealing with the structural causes of stress and depression, the government mobilised CBT to treat the outcomes. It claimed that millions were suffering from anxiety or depression, as if those were the same. Cognitive behavioural therapists were expected to teach people how to live, how to react and how to change their behaviour. The government launched the Improving Access to Psychological Therapies programme, by which anybody could be referred by their doctor to the National Health Service for CBT. This was buttressed by a 'talking treatment' programme, in which mental health coordinators were stationed in Jobcentres. The claim was that CBT would raise employment, as a result of Jobcentres sending the unemployed to therapy centres around the country. The need for a doctor's referral was dispensed with. Why bother with diagnosis when the cure has been identified?

The government put aside funds to pay for initial treatments of eight sessions, planning that within five years anyone would be allowed to 'refer themselves in' for treatment. How eight CBT sessions would 'get Britain working', as was claimed, was unclear. Instead of recognising the causes of difficulties, the intention was to treat the victims of economic mismanagement and encourage them to think they needed therapy.

It is normal to be anxious if you are living a precariat existence, in and out of unemployment, worried about having enough money to buy food or where you will be sleeping next month. Why should this normal anxiety be reason for sending someone on expensive therapy treatment? It might turn anxiety into depression, a much worse ailment. The acid test would be to apply the libertarian paternalists' choice principle. Let the unemployed be allowed to choose between the eight sessions of CBT or the money equivalent. Any bets which most would choose? The trouble is that the 'architecture of choice' is not designed that way.

The Labour government was considering whether some disability claimants should have CBT before going on 'employment support allowance', which an official described as 'an eight-week period which prevents people going into long-term disability'. Who will determine who 'needs' CBT? Soon, the powers that be will be saying that, unless people take a CBT course, they will lose entitlement to benefits. And will taking a CBT course be treated confidentially? Or will the fact that, as a result of their 'weakness', they have been on such a course be passed on to potential employers?

There is nothing wrong with therapy *per se*. What is dubious is its use by the state as an integral part of social policy. It is part of the panopticon state, used to create 'docile minds' and to deter subversive thoughts, such as that the menial, low-status precarious jobs pushed in the direction of unemployed people *should* be rejected. Only if people are allowed to reject them will the creators of such jobs be pressured to improve them or to do without them because they are unworthy of human endeavour.

Workfare and conditionality

Part of the libertarian paternalism agenda is to make social policy more 'conditional', providing state benefits as long as recipients behave in ways set by the state, ostensibly in their best interests. This includes programmes that require people to accept jobs or training after a short period of benefit entitlement or lose benefits and risk a permanent blot on their record, held somewhere in an online database.

The precariat is being offered several variants of 'labourfare', misnamed workfare (for a predictive critique, see Standing, 1990). One form is to make benefits so unattractive that people will not want to take them and will take almost any job instead. This is the view of Lawrence Mead, an American libertarian invited by Downing Street to advise the British government immediately after it was elected in 2010. His view of claimants is that 'government must persuade them to *blame* themselves' (Mead, 1986: 10, emphasis in original). In another form the idea is that anybody who becomes unemployed, or who has been unemployed for a few months, will be offered a job, which they must accept or lose their benefits. These ideas have been around for a very long time, harking back to Speenhamland, the Poor Law and the workhouse.

Language is used to shape perceptions. The UK Coalition government has argued that its 'workfare' plans are intended 'to break the habit of worklessness'. Nobody has demonstrated that the unemployed, or others in need, have such a 'habit'. There is considerable evidence that the reasons many people are unemployed or on the labour market margins have nothing to do with any such habit. Many have too much 'work' to do that labourists do not recognise as work, such as caring for frail relatives or children. Many have episodic disabilities.

To break the alleged habit, it was announced that jobseekers would be required to take 30-hour-a-week jobs for four weeks, as a mandatory work activity. If they refuse to take or fail to complete the placement, benefits will be stopped for three months. The intention is to make unemployment a contractual arrangement – working for benefits with a contract with the state. The underlying motive was exposed when the jobs the unemployed would be required to do were revealed – litter clearing and removing graffiti from walls.

The *Welfare White Paper* of November 2010 asserted that there was a 'national crisis' of benefit dependency, supposedly shown by the fact that 4.5 million people were receiving 'out-of-work' benefits. Iain Duncan Smith, the Minister of Work and Pensions, claimed that nearly 3 million jobs had gone to immigrants in the past decade, partly because many Britons were 'addicted' to social security benefits. This compressed two claims into one deduction. Migrants could have taken jobs because they had particular skills or were prepared to work for lower wages or because, in an open flexible labour market, they happened to be in the right place at the right time. Some may even have gained jobs precisely because they were not citizens and could be dismissed or abused with impunity. Some could have come with experience that young British workers had not had a chance to acquire because they were young. Some could have displaced older workers presumed by employers to be less efficient. All these hypotheses are possible. To make a direct link from the existence of social benefits to migrants 'taking British jobs' is simply prejudice.

The other claim, that millions of Britons are 'addicted' to state benefits, was another prejudicial statement. Millions are receiving benefits due to high unemployment, low earnings by many in temporary and part-time jobs – the precariat – or disability, illness, frailty and so on. The government should have addressed the poverty, unemployment and precarity traps many people face, none of which are the fault of those described as addicted to benefits.

The well-known 'poverty trap' will remain as long as means testing remains, even if the tapering of benefit loss with income gain is made less steep. The 'unemployment trap' will also remain. The more wages fall at the lower end of the labour market, the higher the earnings replacement rate will be if unemployment benefits are to remain adequate for survival. Meanwhile, the 'precarity trap' is worsening. If jobs are generated in one place while the unemployed are living in a deprived area somewhere else, and if those jobs are low paying and temporary or part-time, benefit recipients take a big risk in going for them. They have to travel, which is costly, they risk jeopardising a network of family, friends and places that give life meaning and identity, and they must give up benefits that may have taken months to obtain in the first place. And they are expected to do all this when those jobs may last no more than a few weeks.

Part of the precarity trap is that the jobs some may be forced to take will generate hostility to jobs in general. It is a middle-class prejudice to think the jobs the unemployed are driven to take are conducive to good working habits and labour commitment.

Workfare in the United Kingdom will expand the precariat. It will put hundreds of thousands into temporary jobs deliberately made unattractive to ensure people will not want to stay on them. If the placements were real jobs, paying a pittance would also make it harder for others doing similar jobs to bargain for decent wages. But, as with all workfare schemes, there should be no presumption that placements will be 'real jobs'. It is also unclear how a four-week forced job will 'break' a habit of worklessness. It could do the reverse, making many people sullen and resentful. And doing an enforced full-time job will prevent people from searching for a real job.

Workfare schemes do not cut public spending either. They are expensive, involving high administrative costs and low-productivity 'jobs'. Their main intention is rather to massage the level of unemployment down, not by creating jobs but by discouraging the unemployed from claiming benefits. Research in the United States found that the fall in welfare rolls after the introduction of similar schemes in the 1990s was due primarily to people withdrawing from the labour force, without having jobs. The policy was impoverishing.

Workfare advocates ignore basic economics. A market economy needs some unemployment, for efficiency and anti-inflationary reasons. It is not just the unemployed themselves who adjust expectations and aspirations as they search but others who adjust their behaviour to the existence of unemployed people competing or considering avenues for improving their lives.

While social democrats and labourists laid the ground for workfare, they have come up with a variant that, if taken literally, would be catastrophic. They argue that all unemployed should be 'guaranteed' a job and that this at a stroke will give substance to the 'right to work'. In effect, they want to maximise labour and jobs, which they see as conferring rights and the means of achieving happiness and social integration. This interpretation flies in the face of evidence that many obtain little pleasure from their jobs. They are obliged to do repetitive, inane or dirty and onerous tasks that they do for one reason, to earn income to subsist and help their dependants to do so.

Responding to the UK government's workfare proposals, Douglas Alexander, the Labour Party's Shadow Work and Pensions Secretary, came out in favour of stricter incapacity benefit tests and the Danish model of guaranteeing jobs and obliging people to take them or lose benefit. 'This is a form of conditional welfare', he said, 'Real guarantees of work, but real sanctions if the offer is not taken up'. Alexander claimed the difference between this stance and the government's was that the government had adopted the American model of cutting benefits without ensuring a job was available. He was responding to criticism from a former general secretary of the Labour Party that the party appeared to side with the 'feckless poor' against 'the hard-working squeezed middle'. But it might be more principled politics to think through the policy in terms of what it means for the precariat.

Workfare advocates place labour above work. Pushing everybody into jobs leads to the Soviet trap: Eventually the unemployed are dubbed parasitic while resentful workers lessen their effort, which led to the wry joke, 'They pretend to pay us, we pretend to work'. Long before that, Alexis de Tocqueville in 1835 put the matter succinctly when saying that guaranteeing everybody a job would lead either to government taking over almost the entire economy or to coercion. He would have had no difficulty in seeing which way it is going.

Demonising the precariat

Since the Great Recession began, governments have stepped up their demonisation of the victims of the global market economy. Four groups have been targeted – 'migrants', 'welfare claimants', 'criminals' and the 'disabled'.

The tendency to demonise migrants is global, as if they are some form of alien species. A worst scenario case would be an outbreak of mass deportations, with populist politicians fanning the fears of the domestic precariat. One hopes there is enough sense to prevent anything like that. Fortunately, there are also hefty costs to put off the zealots. One study (Hinojosa-Ojeda, 2010) estimated that mass deportation of 'illegal' migrants from the United States would cost more than the Iraqi and Afghan wars combined. But fear of deportation makes undocumented migrants accept lower wages and worse labour conditions.

In the United Kingdom, as in many countries, national newspapers have fanned anti-migrant feelings. As they are much more read than local papers, people read about migrant problems, even though their area may have none. While only 10 per cent of people in the United Kingdom are immigrants, the average Briton believes the figure is 27 per cent. National media pinpoint the exceptional. The same is true of 'benefit scroungers'. A single case is picked up and everyone in the country reads about it, imagining it could be just down the road.

If we read just *local* newspapers, most people would not hear about that case or generalise from it. The globalisation and commodification of communications give power to those who want to demonise. Thus a government can cite two examples to suggest that most of the unemployed suffer from 'a habit of worklessness', and readers can be led to believe that these two cases represent millions.

Another demonised group are 'criminals'. We saw earlier how the state is criminalising more and more people. Many are merely people who cannot function well in a market society. Others are criminalised by accident. Public employment services have become agents for conformity and social discipline that may push some unemployed to break the rules. Doctors are being turned into labour disciplinary agents, required to report on whether their patients are employed or employable. This may lead to 'convictions', for idleness or fraud. The precariat is exposed to unpleasant, insecure wage labour, which it would be understandable to want to escape from or rebel against. The penal system curbs that tendency and raises the cost of doing so. With more sophisticated monitoring coming along, more may be caught and socially branded.

In some countries, prisoners are banned from being able to vote in elections. The United Kingdom's Labour government repeatedly delayed lifting the ban, in violation of European Union law, and a proposal to do so by the new Coalition government was heavily defeated in a free parliamentary vote. A few other countries also ban prisoners from voting, and many US states ban former prisoners as well, a form of life sentence that actively fosters civic disengagement.

In general, demonisation is easier in societies characterised by systemic economic insecurity and anxiety. Insecurity makes it easier to play on fears, 'unknown unknowns' and images created and manipulated by visual and linguistic artists hired to do precisely that. This leads to what should be the biggest fear of all.

Thinning democracy and neo-fascism

What should worry all those who believe in democratic values and freedom is that, with the commodification of politics, there is a 'thinning' of democracy, with fewer people belonging to mainstream political parties and low turnouts in most elections. This thinning is hitting progressive parties particularly hard.

In the United Kingdom, an audit of political engagement showed that in early 2010 only one in ten potential voters was 'politically committed', while one in ten was 'alienated and hostile' (Hansard Society, 2010). The biggest group, one in four, consisted of the 'disengaged, distrustful'. Only 13 per cent could name their member of parliament. The disengaged were mainly young (under 35) and working class – the precariat. The report said the alienated/hostile group were 'extraordinarily difficult to engage and it would be unrealistic to hope that they can be converted to voters'. The bored/ apathetic group would also be hard to motivate to vote. More of the disengaged were inclined to vote Labour than Conservative but were turned off by what was on offer.

Thin democracy, sporadic voting by youth and the drift to the right go together. In the European Union elections of 2009, average turnout was 43 per cent, the lowest since 1979. Left-of-centre parties did badly almost everywhere. Labour took 16 per cent of the vote in the

United Kingdom. Right-wing parties did well everywhere. Socialists were crushed in Hungary, while the extreme right-wing Jobbik won almost as many seats. In Poland, the ruling centre-right Civic Platform won. In Italy, the centre-left gained 26 per cent of the vote, seven percentage points less than in the 2008 general election before the crisis, against 35 per cent for Berlusconi's People of Liberty Party. In the German elections of 2009, there was a record low turnout of 71 per cent; the right did well. Everywhere, the social democrats were in retreat.

One problem is that politicians are now sold as brands, while class-based politics has been debased, partly because the social democratic project could not survive globalisation. A result is sound-bite and image-based politics, based on a shared acceptance of the neo-liberal economic framework. This is bound to erode support for social democracy.

There seemed one exception, the United States in 2008, where Barack Obama managed to mobilise young Americans hoping for a progressive agenda. Regrettably, he was packaged and oversold. His social networking adviser came from Facebook; another adviser created an 'Obama brand' through clever marketing tools, with a logo (sunrise over stars and stripes), expert viral marketing (Obama ringtones), product placement (Obama adverts on sports video games), a 30-minute infomercial and a choice of strategic brand alliances (Oprah for maximum reach, Kennedy family for gravitas, hip-hop stars for street cred). Afterwards, Obama was given the Association of National Advertisers' Marketer of the Year Award. Company adverts copied him: Pepsi's 'Choose Change', IKEA's 'Embrace Change' and so on.

This is commodified politics, buying and selling fleeting images and buzzwords, preferring symbols over substance. There is deep alienation in having costly public relations and advertising selling a transcendental campaign involving a man as a brand surrounded by images of freedom and change without substance.

Obama won against weak Republican opposition, in the midst of a disastrous war and an economy on the edge of meltdown. He could have risked attacking the neo-liberal project. Instead he backed the International Monetary Fund, which had been a primary culprit in its hubris, bailed out the banks and appointed Larry Summers as his principal economic adviser, the man who devised the policy responsible for the sub-prime housing crisis. Obama never tried to reach out to the precariat, even though many in it had been hopeful that he would do so. The social democratic imagination could not empathise with real predicaments.

In the United States and elsewhere, anger grew at some of the corrupt aspects of the globalisation era. Recall the systemic use of subsidies. Naomi Klein among others has called the globalisation era 'crony capitalism', revealing itself not as a huge 'free market' but as a system in which politicians hand over public wealth to private players in exchange for political support. Ironically, far-right groups captured the anti-corporatist backlash. If the state has been captured by cronyism, why should anyone support a 'strong state'? Old-style social democrats are unable to respond with conviction because they accepted the neo-liberal construction and did nothing to support the precariat that grew in its shadow. The fact is that subsidies to capital were used for political and economic ends. The crude reasoning was that if a politician or party did not give subsidies to powerful interests, such as 'media barons', others would. If subsidies were not given to financial investors and 'non-doms' (rich individuals claiming to be domiciled elsewhere for tax purposes), other countries would entice them away. A generation of social democrats went along with that crude opportunism, losing all credibility in the process.

There are more worrying trends than a social democratic project on its last legs. Insecure people make angry people, and angry people are volatile, prone to support a politics of hatred and bitterness. In Europe, left-of-centre parties have been punished by the electorate for allowing inequality and insecurity to rise while going towards a workfare state. Far-right parties have grown, openly appealing to the fears of those made most insecure.

Italy led the way. The alliance forged by Berlusconi was aimed at the precariat – the Italian part of it. The political ethos deserves to be called 'neo-fascism'. Underlying it is an alliance between an elite outside the mainstream of society – epitomised by Berlusconi himself, Italy's richest man who owns the country's leading commercial TV stations – and the lower middle class and those fearful of falling into the precariat. The day after being re-elected in 2008, Berlusconi announced his intention to 'defeat the army of evil', by which he meant rid the country of 'illegal migrants'. Playing on people's fears around law and order, he instigated a series of authoritarian measures. Roma camps were demolished and Roma were fingerprinted; parliament legalised vigilante patrols; the period during which asylum seekers could be held in 'identification and expulsion centres' was extended to six months; a policy was introduced to turn back migrants at sea in the Mediterranean before they could land, sending them to caged internment centres in Libya. Berlusconi and his colleagues called the judiciary 'a cancer' and dismissed parliament as 'a useless entity'. No wonder Italy is called an illiberal democracy.

Racist attacks in Rome spread, legitimised by the re-election as mayor in 2010 of Gianni Alemanno, a former neo-fascist activist. Several social scientists noted that the young thugs perpetrating the racist attacks were less ideological than their predecessors of the 1930s and more interested in personal identity, opposing anybody perceived to be different. Another change was an emphasis on alcohol, linked to a shift from the fixation with a *bella figura* to a peculiar pride in losing control. Claudio Cerasa, author of *The Taking of Rome*, a book on the rise of the political right, described Alemanno as a product of neo-fascism, not a cause. In 2007, a year before he was first elected, a quarter of Rome's schoolchildren voted for *Blocco Studentesco*, an affiliate of the far-right *CasaPound*. It was the mood of the times.

What is happening in Italy is beginning elsewhere too. In France, President Nicolas Sarkozy, a right-winger who had already taken a tough line on immigration as interior minister, notably after the 2005 riots in the *banlieues* of Paris and other French cities, wasted no time in copying Berlusconi. In 2009, thousands of migrants were summarily deported, and in 2010 large numbers of Roma were expelled to Romania and Bulgaria. President Sarkozy was playing to his core voters. Part of the precariat was turning to the far right. The white working class and older members of the precariat voted for the National Front in March 2010 regional elections, the Front winning 17.5 per cent in the twelve regions where it had candidates in the second round. After Sarkozy's UMP party (*Union pour un*

Mouvement Populaire) was soundly beaten by a disoriented left-of-centre coalition, he moved further to the right. In a 2010 poll, a third of UMP voters said they would support joint electoral pacts with the National Front.

The extreme right has made inroads in many European countries. The biggest shock to the political mainstream was the Swedish election in late 2010, when the far-right Swedish Democrats made big gains while the iconic Social Democrats had their worst result for decades. It symbolised the end of the famed 'Swedish model'. Elsewhere too, far-right groups with xenophobic messages were making progress. The ugly Jobbik party, with its black uniforms and jackboots, made inroads in Hungary. In the Netherlands, the Freedom Party advanced in the June 2010 election, demanding limits on immigration, a reduction in red tape for small businesses, lower taxes and more elderly care. There, and in Denmark, where the populist Danish People's Party won a further tightening of the most draconian immigration laws in Europe, a Liberal-led government is dependent on anti-immigrant parties for survival. In Austria, the far-right Freedom Party took more than a quarter of votes in provincial elections in Vienna in October 2010, nearly doubling its support from 2005.

In the United Kingdom, the British National Party briefly caused a scare, sweeping to wins in the EU elections in 2009, only to implode due to the crassness of its leader. It would be too sanguine to think the undercurrents that led to its surge in popularity will be washed away. Other equally unpleasant groups such as the English Defence League have picked up the space, while some centrist figures have not been averse to stirring anti-migrant sentiments.

The policies pursued by most European governments have created an environment conducive to populism. The United Kingdom is no exception. By favouring flexible labour markets, it has allowed the precariat to grow without responding to its insecurities or fears. It has shifted social protection decisively towards means testing, which gives priority to those most in need while pushing long-standing 'citizens', who might be near-poor, towards the back of the queue for benefits, including housing.

Low-income deprived communities blighted by de-industrialisation breed antisocial behaviour; their inhabitants are surrounded by squalor and suffer from relative deprivation. As such areas attract a disproportionate number of migrants and low-income ethnic minorities, the 'white' or 'citizen' inhabitants experience multiple fears, chiefly of losing what little they have. Condemning them for their reactions and behaviour, when flexible labour markets and means testing create those conditions, is a false morality. The responsibility lies with policy makers, whose policies have fostered tensions and engendered extremism.

The Labour government responded with populist measures, launching pilot schemes to pay unemployed migrants to go home with one-way plane tickets, using a private commercial crime services company, and announcing a plan to help 'traditional communities', a euphemism for assisting low-income white neighbourhoods. Governments elsewhere have also turned to populist approaches.

In the United States, the Tea Party movement began in 2009 after TV commentator Rick Santelli called for a display of outrage against President Obama's financial plans. Those who joined the Tea Party were anti-government, demanding low taxes and free markets. The initial target was the Democrats, but Republicans deemed insufficiently committed to tax cuts and smaller government were also threatened. The Republican National Committee in 2010 was forced to adopt a rule urging party leaders to support candidates who could prove right-wing credentials by passing ten criteria set by the Tea Party.

Elite interests have flirted with the Tea Party. It has attracted the support of groups tied to oil companies and Wall Street (Fifield, 2010). Elements of the elite are coalescing with elements in the dwindling working class and the precariat, the one funding and ensuring media coverage, the others providing the foot soldiers and voters. Unless mainstream parties offer the precariat an agenda of economic security and social mobility, a substantial part will continue to drift to the dangerous extreme.

The Tea Party's first national convention contained much talk of illegal immigration and opposition to 'the cult of multiculturalism' and 'Islamification'. T-shirts had slogans such as 'I'll keep my freedom, my guns and my money'. The Birthers were there, claiming Obama was an alien imposter. Like the British National Party in England, the Tea Party accused immigrants of swamping America's Judeo-Christian values. 'This is our country', a delegate said to wild cheers, 'Take it back!' There was nobody at hand to say it had not been taken away.

The Tea Party is neo-fascist, wanting a small social state and authoritarian government. It consists predominantly of 'angry white men and women' affected by loss of jobs and dwindling living standards. Two-thirds of the jobs that went in the two years after 2008 were 'blue-collar' jobs held by men. Angry whites are judgemental about 'giving money' to people, and polls show that white men have become more conservative. Support for 'gun rights' rose from 51 per cent in 2008 to 64 per cent in 2010.

Glen Beck, a Fox News presenter hailed by the American right, is a self-confessed former cocaine addict and alcoholic who calls himself a 'borderline schizophrenic'. He pitches to those with little education or political knowledge. In his bestseller *Glen Beck's Common Sense*, he addressed the reader as follows:

> I think I know who you are. You are a person of "strong beliefs", with a "warm heart". You work hard, you're not reckless with money, you're worried about what the economy means for your family. You're not a bigot, but you stopped expressing opinions on sensitive issues a long time ago because you don't want to be called a racist or a homophobe if you stand up for your values and principles. You don't understand how the government can ask you to make more sacrifices just so that bankers and politicians can reap the benefit. Dear reader, Glen Beck can help you. He will stand up with you and say, "Don't tread on me".

Beck has become a multimillionaire celebrity. The fringe has become the mainstream. The old political mainstream has not had an alternative narrative to offer, beyond hoping for economic growth and jobs. It has had no answer to rising insecurity and inequality; unimpressed, the progressive part of the precariat stayed away from the polling stations in the midterm elections of 2010.

In Japan, the precariat is also split; large numbers of angry people, mostly young men, are joining groups dubbed by the media as the Net Far Right because members are organised via the internet and gather together only for demonstrations. Most hold low-paying, part-time or short-term contract jobs. According to sociology professor Kensuke Suzuki, 'These are men who feel disenfranchised in their own society. They are looking for someone to blame, and foreigners are the most obvious target' (Fackler, 2010). The largest group, with over 9,000 members in 2010, is called *Zaitokukai*, an abbreviation for its full cumbersome name – Citizens Who Will Not Forgive Special Privileges for Koreans in Japan. Such groups have been stepping up hostile demonstrations against migrants and say they model themselves on the US Tea Party.

Unless the commodification of politics is checked, we will see a further thinning of democratic involvement, particularly on the part of the progressive part of the precariat. Politics is now dominated by market practitioners. An eerie example was the 2010 Ukrainian presidential election, won by Victor Yanukovich, a man linked to the country's oligarchs and with criminal convictions for theft and assault. The oligarchs put up funds to hire a firm to sell him to the voters. It was led by a US Republican Party strategist, Paul Manafort, whose firm had been employed as advisers to several US presidents. Before they began work, Yanukovich was languishing in the polls, having been rejected in 2004. They repackaged him. Meanwhile, the consultancy firm founded by David Axelrod, Obama's political adviser, was aiding the other main candidate, as was John Anzalone, who also worked for the Obama campaign.

Three things are noteworthy about this bizarre election in a European country of 50 million people. It exemplified the commodification of politics; it was foreign commodification consistent with a mutant form of globalisation; and it involved a criminal elite, funding its interests in the form of a candidate. Meanwhile, huge numbers of Ukrainians advertised their votes for sale on the internet. The US Republican company outscored the US Democrat company.

The global commodification of politics should particularly worry the precariat. Probably the most regressive development in the United States, and by implication elsewhere given how its legal rulings become global precedents, was the 2010 Supreme Court ruling in *Citizens United vs Federal Election Commission*. The Court decided that any corporation, trade union or trade association could make unlimited contributions to political campaigns, on the peculiar grounds that they had the same rights as individuals to participate in elections. It was no surprise that the subsequent midterm Congressional elections were dominated by ferocious 'attack ads', funded by bodies set up to conceal where the money came from. Funds for right-wing candidates went up sixfold, most going to candidates who campaigned in favour of tax cuts, more subsidies to corporations, weaker environmental protection, reversal of healthcare reform and a tougher stance on migration and immigrants.

At a stroke, the ruling eroded a democratic principle, that each citizen has an equal right to vote and an equal weight in the process. The biggest loser is the precariat. For whereas corporations will put money into campaigns for the elite and the salariat, while the weakened unions will support their core employees, there is no powerful interest to represent the precariat. Not yet.

In sum, the precariat must be worried by the surge of neo-fascism and the pressure for a smaller social state. At present, it cannot resist. Some whose social and economic situations place them in the precariat have been politically infantilised. They are so anxious and insecure that they are easily seduced to support populist and authoritarian actions towards those depicted as a threat. Many in the precariat have lost (or fear losing) what little they had and are lashing out because they have no politics of paradise to draw them in better directions.

Conclusions

The precariat is depicted as needing monitoring, therapy and coercion to take jobs. But the libertarian paternalist solution of workfare is a means of disrupting any attempt to build occupational careers, as is therapy when used as social policy. The diagnosis of mental incapacity and the prognosis of therapy combine to accentuate feelings of precariousness. These are not policies to appeal to the uneasiness and anger in the precariat. The reverse is more likely.

Surveillance is permeating all institutions of society. At each point it will engender sousveillance or a counterculture, and this in turn will have a feedback effect inducing tighter surveillance. Surveillance cannot rest once it has been legitimised. It can only be stopped by active resistance, by class-based action.

Surveillance fosters aggression and suspicion of motives. If a man is caught on CCTV patting a young girl on the cheek, is it a sign of kindness or predatory sexual intent? If there is doubt, it will justify checks, as a precaution. You can never be too safe. A protector is never far from being a controller. A consequence will be withdrawal of normal acts of friendship. The same ambivalence and distancing tendency feed into businesses. Application of timekeeping, workplace attendance and efficiency audits are instruments for penalising nonconformists, who may be the most innovative and creative minds. Above all, surveillance chips away at civic friendship and trust, making people more fearful and more anxious. The group with most reason for that fear and anxiety is the precariat.

The utilitarianism that underpins the neo-liberal state boils down to a creed about making the majority happy while making the minority conform to the norms of the majority, through sanctions, nudges and surveillance. It is the tyranny of the majority brought to a new level of intensity. The utilitarians could get away with it as long as they were dealing with a small underclass and as long as incomes were, at worst, stagnant in the lower end of society. Once the precariat grew and incomes started to fall sharply, anger at the utilitarian agenda and the host of inequalities was bound to become explosive.

7

A politics of paradise

It is time to revisit the great trinity – freedom, fraternity and equality – in developing a progressive agenda from the perspective of the precariat. A good start would be a revival of republican freedom, the ability to act in concert. Freedom is something that is disclosed in collective action.

The precariat wants freedom and basic security. As the theologian Kierkegaard put it, anxiety is part of freedom. It is the price we pay for liberty and can be a sign that we have it. However, unless the anxiety is moderated, anchored in security, stability and control, it risks veering into irrational fears and incapacity to function rationally or to develop a coherent narrative for living and working. This is where the precariat is today, wanting control over life, a revival of social solidarity and a sustainable autonomy, while rejecting old labourist forms of security and state paternalism. It also wants to see the future secured in an ecological way, with the air clean, pollution in retreat and species revived; the precariat has most to lose from environmental degradation. And it is stirring in wanting to revive republican freedom, rather than the alienating individualistic freedom of the commodified.

Although the precariat is not yet a class-for-itself, it is a class-in-the-making, increasingly able to identify what it wishes to combat and what it wants to construct. It needs to revive an ethos of social solidarity and universalism, values rejected by the utilitarians. Their smugness was captured by a leader in the influential *Financial Times* (2010b), which stated bluntly, 'Universality is a wasteful principle'. On the contrary, it is more important than ever. It is the only principle that can reverse growing inequalities and economic insecurity. It is the only principle that can arrest the spread of means testing, conditionality and paternalistic nudging. It is the only principle that can be used to retain political stability as the world adjusts to the globalisation crisis that is leading to a decline in living standards for the majority in the industrialised world.

For the precariat, twentieth-century labourism is unattractive. For its time, the social democratic project was progressive, but it came to a dead end with dour Third Wayism. Social democratic politicians feared to mention inequality, let alone address it, embraced flexible insecure labour and disregarded liberty, advancing the panopticon state. They lost credibility with the precariat when they depicted themselves as 'middle class' and made the life of nonconformists harder and more insecure. It is time to move on.

There is a need for a new politics of paradise that is mildly utopian and proudly so. The timing is apt, for a new progressive vision seems to emerge in the early years of each century. There were the radical romantics of the early nineteenth century, demanding new freedoms, and there was a rush of progressive thinking in the early twentieth century, demanding freedom for the industrial proletariat. It is already late, but the discrediting of labourism alongside the moral bankruptcy of the neo-liberal model of globalisation is a moment of hope for an emancipatory egalitarianism geared to the precariat.

In thinking what that would look like, it is well to reflect that what seems impossible today has a habit of becoming not just possible but eminently practicable. In his preface to the 1982 edition of *Capitalism and Freedom*, originally written in 1962 when monetarism and neo-liberalism were still being mocked, the arch-monetarist Milton Friedman commented, 'Our basic function is to develop alternatives to existing policies, to keep them alive and available until the politically impossible becomes the politically inevitable' (Friedman, 1982: ix). This is where progressive thinking stands today.

A first task is to assert what has been denied by the labourists and neo-liberals. People should be trusted to think and act in their best interests, and should be trusted to respect others. They should not be treated as lazy, potential criminals, law breakers or inherently selfish. The libertarian paternalist nudgers should be told to mind their own business and their architectures of choice; the panopticon should be rolled back. Proper education and 'quality time' are the way to help people make their own decisions. Contrary to what libertarian paternalists say, most people do not make sub-optimal decisions because they are overwhelmed by information; they make them because they do not have the time or energy to sift the relevant information, do not have access to affordable expert advice and do not have Voice to exercise their choices.

The same could be said about jobs. The fact that there is an aversion to the jobs on offer does not mean that masses of people do not want to work. There is overwhelming evidence that almost everybody wants to work. It is part of the human condition. But it does not follow that everybody should be in jobs or treated as suffering from a 'habit of worklessness' if they are not.

The precariat is faced by systematic insecurity. It is oversimplifying to divide it into a 'good' precariat and a 'bad' one. However, there is a part that wants to confront the insecurities with policies and institutions to redistribute security and provide opportunities for all to develop their talents. This part, probably overwhelmingly youth, does not look back fondly to the labourist employment security of the pre-globalisation era.

The 'bad' precariat, by contrast, is fuelled by nostalgia for an imagined golden age. It is angry and bitter, seeing governments bailing out banks and bankers, giving subsidies to favoured elites and the salariat, and allowing inequality to rise, at their expense. It is drawn to populist neo-fascism, lashing out at governments and demonising those who seem favoured by them. Unless the aspirations of the 'good' precariat are addressed, more will be dragged into the circles of the 'bad'. If that happens, society will be threatened. It is happening.

The precariat's foremost need is economic security, to give some control over life's prospects and a sense that shocks and hazards can be managed. This can be achieved only if income security is assured. However, vulnerable groups also need 'agency', the collective and individual capacity to represent their interests. The precariat must forge a strategy that takes account of this twin imperative.

Make denizenship fair

The precariat is made up of many types of denizen, with different but limited bundles of rights. It would gain if disparities were reduced and if rights were properly defended. Every part of the precariat has an interest in enhancing the rights of other denizens, even if some political groups try to turn one group against another. 'Denizens unite!' would not be a bad slogan. And it is vital to remember that it is not just migrants who have denizen status. Increasingly, the state is converting more citizens into denizens.

Most egregiously, it is taking away rights from the 'criminalised'. This is a form of double jeopardy. Unless a crime is overtly political, or if a legal process has ruled that someone should not have the right to vote, there is no justification for taking away political rights or social rights. Given the state's tendency to imprison and criminalise more people, this issue deserves greater public debate.

Migrants are the primary denizens. There have been various proposals to create a process by which they could gain citizenship with a full range of rights, including 'citizenisation', decoupling status from nationality. A concept of 'residenceship' would integrate migrants better, since they would automatically become citizens after a certain period, rather than be 'naturalised'. This contrasts with the idea of 'permanent permits'; while protecting against arbitrary deportation, these would merely confirm denizens as outsiders. Universality is about overcoming such distinctions in a globalising world. As it is, governments have been increasing the conditions necessary to enjoy even denizen status. In countries that have adopted 'citizenship tests' for those wishing to settle, the precariat should demand that anybody wishing to take political office should pass them too. Better still would be to abolish them as fraudulent, since their main objective is to raise barriers to entry.

Among the most needed reforms affecting denizens are those related to the right to practice, the right to work in the sphere of one's competence and 'calling'. Millions are denied that right, through licensing and other means. Liberalising occupations would open them to migrants otherwise relegated to the precariat. Germany may by chance take a lead here. In October 2010, the labour minister said that to attract more skilled migrants Germany would introduce a law recognising foreign qualifications. This is an *ad hoc* response to a global challenge. What is needed is an international accreditation system, whereby governments and occupational bodies establish standards of qualification and mutual recognition, so that those qualified in skills in one country can more easily practise them in other countries. In most occupations, there is no need for licensing. An accreditation system could require practitioners to show potential purchasers of their services proof of qualification, which would allow the *caveat emptor* (buyer beware) principle to apply fairly.

Migrants, most of all asylum seekers, lack mechanisms to represent their interests. An egalitarian strategy would demand that representative bodies be given space in which to operate and be assisted financially. In 2010, a British campaign called Strangers into Citizens lobbied for an 'earned amnesty' for the undocumented after five years. If two years after registering they were in a job and spoke English, they would automatically receive citizenship. One could quibble with this, but state-legitimised bodies are needed to represent all groups of denizens as they struggle to obtain *de jure* and *de facto* rights.

Many others lose economic or social rights by virtue of a past demeanour or some action resulting in a concealed record blemishing their character, without their knowing or being in a position to refute it. Tony Blair once said that nobody who had not done anything wrong should be concerned with the advance of surveillance. This is a wretched perspective. One reason is that we do not know what is being collected on any of us or whether it is correct or incorrect. The precariat is most in need of protection and must demand that *de facto* denizenship is rolled back.

Recovering identities

The precariat is at the centre of the turmoil around multiculturalism and personal identities. A defining feature of all denizens is absence of rights. Citizenship is about the right to possess an identity, a sense of knowing who one is and with whom one has shared values and aspirations. The precariat has no secure identity. But in a globalising world, we cannot run away from multiculturalism and multiple identities.

States must allow for multiple identities; everybody is a denizen of some sort in having rights within some self-regulated identities and not in others. Each identity brings distinctive bundles of 'rights'. Thus a person has an identity as an adherent to a religion or as an atheist, which gives rights within a community that others do not possess (rights to certain holidays, a right to pray or not to pray, etc.). The crucial tests come with mechanisms of hierarchy, oppression and excommunication, and with ensuring that the exercise of any community right does not impinge on the rights or identity of others.

Even more crucial for the precariat are rights that come from belonging to a particular occupational identity. If a person is a plumber or a nurse, they should have rights accorded to every member of their occupation, including the right to state that they are qualified and approved by their peers. However, it is a different matter to say that someone not accepted by their peers should not have the right to practise, which is how many people are being tipped into the precariat. This is why occupational identity must be based on an accreditation system, not licensing geared to competitiveness, and why it must rest on democratic governance structures within occupational bodies in which all interests can participate (on how, see Standing, 2009). Occupational democracy is central to twenty-first-century freedom.

Turning to the political side of identity, modern neo-fascism is vehemently against acceptance of others' identity and culture. Neo-liberals also oppose the idea of identity on the grounds that individuals in a market society have no common identity. They presume a common personhood, a melting pot of folk, as implicit in the US and French constitutions. Both postures are unhelpful, to put it mildly. It would be better to assert that we can and do have multiple identities, and we need to construct institutions and policies to defend and enhance them.

The precariat is most exposed to a crisis of identity. It must not desert multiculturalism or the legitimation of multiple identities. However, it must do more, in that it must have its interests represented in all identity structures and institutions. This is not a plea for a new form of corporatism. It is a call for the precariat to become a class-for-itself.

Rescuing education

The commodification of education must be combated by those being processed to join the precariat. The spectre of teacherless universities backed by panopticon techniques should be banished by democratic and transparent regulation, involving professional associations and laws specifying that tertiary learning, as well as other levels, should not be 'teacherless'.

Determination of content should be restored to the professionals – teachers and academics – while the 'customers', the students, should have a voice in shaping the structure and objectives of education. And the precariat should be enabled to gain a liberating education on a continuing basis, not simply be subject to human capital preparation. This is not being idealistic or naïve. Of course, students do not know what is best for them. None of us do. What is needed is a governance system that balances the forces moulding the process. At present, the commodifiers are in full control. This is terrifying.

There needs to be a reversal of the dumbing down involved in 'human capital' schooling. In the United States, experts refer to a lost capacity to read and a 'massified' attention deficit syndrome. The United States is not unique. Liberating education for its own sake must be restored to primacy and the commodifiers must be resisted. We cannot remove them altogether but a balance in favour of liberating education must be institutionally achieved.

Those who want universities to serve entrepreneurialism and business and to foster a market perspective should heed the great intellectuals of the past. As Alfred North Whitehead, the philosopher, put it, 'The justification for a university is that it preserves the connection between knowledge and the zest of life, by uniting the young and the old in the imaginative consideration of learning'.

Earlier, John Stuart Mill, speaking on being installed as Rector of St Andrew's University in 1867, stated, 'Universities are not intended to teach the knowledge required to fit men for some special mode of gaining their livelihood. Their object is not to make skilful lawyers, or physicians or engineers, but capable and cultivated human beings'. The commercial rejection of this principle is something that the precariat must taunt into retreat. The philistines must be stopped.

There is another more pragmatic issue. A partial answer to the status frustration arising from youths being formally over-educated for the available jobs would be to make degrees 'leisure goods' (rather than investment goods). People could be encouraged to gain degrees over a longer time, by facilitating sabbaticals for more people during the course of their adulthood and not putting so much emphasis on going straight from secondary school to university.

The precariat may dream of a sort of 'universitisation' of life, a world in which to learn selectively and broadly at all times. For that, it must have a feeling of greater control over time and access to a public sphere that enhances education as a slow deliberative process.

Work, not just labour

It has become an article of the creed of modern morality that all labour is good in itself – a convenient belief to those who live on the labour of others.

WILLIAM MORRIS (1885), *Useful Work Versus Useless Toil*

Work must be rescued from jobs and labour. All forms of work should be treated with equal respect, and there should be no presumption that someone not in a job is not working or that someone not working today is an idle scrounger. It is not idleness that damages society. Really idle people may damage themselves, if they dissipate their lives. But it costs society much more to police and punish the tiny minority than would be gained by forcing them to do some low-productivity job. Moreover, a little idleness would not be bad. How do we know that one person's apparent idleness is not his moment of repose or contemplation? Why do we feel it necessary to presume and condemn? Some of the greatest minds in history had spells of idleness, and anybody who has read Bertrand Russell's essay *In Praise of Idleness* should be ashamed to demand frenetic labour from others.

One should not lose a sense of proportion. Labour is needed; jobs are needed. It is just that they are not the be-all-and-end-all of life. Other forms of work and time uses are just as important.

John Maynard Keynes, the greatest economist of the twentieth century, forecast that by now people in rich societies would be doing no more than 15 hours a week in jobs. Before him, Karl Marx predicted that, once the level of productivity enabled society to serve its material needs, we would spend our time developing our human capabilities. In the late nineteenth century, William Morris, in his visionary *News from Nowhere*, saw a future in which people would be unstressed, working on their enthusiasms and being inspired to reproduce nature, thriving in association with their neighbours. None of them foresaw the insatiable drive for consumption and endless growth set by a commodifying market system.

Now is the time to assert that pushing everybody into jobs is the answer to the wrong question. We must find ways of enabling all of us to have more time for work that is not labour and for leisure that is not play. Unless we insist on a richer concept of work, we will continue to be led by the folly of measuring a person's worth by the job they are doing and by the folly that job generation is the mark of a successful economy.

The precariat has most to gain. It does a disproportionate amount of work that is not labour and is forced to do much work that is neither productive nor enjoyable. Let us have better statistics that reveal how much work is being done. We could then mock those who claim or imply that anybody not in an identifiable 'job' is lazy or a welfare scrounger. Let us start with statistics on how much time the precariat spends in dealing with state bureaucrats and other intermediaries.

Full labour commodification

Contrary to the labourist declaration that 'Labour is not a commodity', there should be full labour commodification. Instead of forcing people into jobs, lowering their wages and those of others affected by the downward pressure they exert, people should be attracted by proper incentives. If there are jobs, as is claimed, and if nobody comes forward to fill them, then let the price rise until either the person offering the jobs thinks they are not worth the price (wage) he or she is prepared to pay or people are sufficiently attracted to fill them. Let governments apply the same rules to the labour market as they claim to do for other markets. For proper commodification, the price must be transparent and fully monetised. This means phasing out those fancy enterprise benefits and converting them into benefits that can be bought by market choice. Respecting principles of social solidarity can be handled separately. Non-monetary benefits are a major source of inequality and are contrary to efficient labour markets. The precariat has no prospect of obtaining them. They go to the salariat and a dwindling privileged minority of core workers. To encourage marketisation, they should be taxed at a higher rate than money earnings; at the moment they are often a means of tax avoidance. And payment systems should be transparent in being linked to the application of skill, effort and time. It is relevant that research shows that workers are more content if paid an hourly rate, which is the most transparent method of all.

Proper commodification is a *progressive* move. Consider the classic practice of maternity leave, from the perspective of social equity and the position of the precariat. If a woman is a salaried employee, she can receive pay and leave from an employer, with most of the wage being paid by the government. In the United Kingdom, women receive statutory maternity pay for up to 39 weeks and leave of up to a year. There is also paternity leave for 2 weeks, and either parent can take unpaid time until the child is five years old. Bearing in mind that employers are compensated by the government for most of the cost of maternity and paternity pay, it is a regressive benefit, favouring the salariat to the detriment of the precariat. While appealing for a labourist, how many low-income earners are in a position to receive it? It was only in 2009 that the UK Equality and Human Rights Commission *proposed* dropping the qualifying period of employment for entitlement. But many women in the precariat will be out of a job at some time during their pregnancy. They would then be unlikely to obtain a new job and so would not have access to maternity leave benefits. The precariat should have the same entitlements as everybody else. Universality does matter.

This leads to the next demand: Jobs should be treated as *instrumental*, a proper commercial transaction. Those claiming they are a primary source of happiness, and that those reluctant to partake in the delights of jobs should be coerced to do so for their long-term happiness, should be told to mind their own business. For most in the precariat, jobs are not the road to nirvana. To be told they are the source of happiness is to make them something they were never meant to be. Jobs are created because somebody wants something done. Or at least that is what they should be created for. Let them be properly commodified. If this is the rule of a free market economy, then let it apply to all commodities.

Occupational freedom

The precariat wants to develop a sense of occupation, merging forms of work and labour in ways that facilitate personal development and satisfaction. The demands of labour and jobs are intensifying, and just as many valuable forms of work are being done in sub-optimal stressful circumstances, so play is helping to squeeze out leisure. One of the great assets of tertiary society is *time*.

Instead of treating jobs as instrumental, we are told to treat them as the most important aspect of life. There are many forms of work outside jobs that can be more satisfying and socially valuable. If we say having a job is necessary and defines our identity, jobholders will feel stressed if they fear losing not just a job but their perceived social worth, status and living standard.

In late 2009, the *Wall Street Journal* ran a comment by Alan Blinder, a former vice-chairman of the US Federal Reserve, in which he wrote that Americans had 'only three things on their mind right now: jobs,

jobs and jobs'. He gave no evidence to support this insight. But if a
majority can only attain something close to security by holding onto
jobs, then obviously jobs will be paramount and stressful. It is not
being utopian to say this is unhealthy and unnecessary. We must stop
making a fetish of jobs.

It is not even clear that economic growth in rich countries requires
more jobs, as shown by evidence of 'job-less growth' and even 'job-
loss growth'. And trying to raise growth through artificial job creation
may be ecologically destructive. After all, jobs and labour tend to go
with resource use and depletion, whereas other forms of work tend to
be reproductive and resource preserving.

In shifting from jobs, the right to *work* must be strengthened; the
way to do this is to make it easier to enable people to undertake work
that is not labour and to equalise the opportunity to do so. While
the need for such work is growing, those best placed to do it are
the affluent because they have the time or can purchase it. This is a
concealed form of inequality because those with advantages are best
placed to accumulate additional advantages.

In the United States, the post-2008 recession prompted a growth
in work that was not labour. The irony went unnoticed. For instance,
thousands logged onto Volunteernyc.org, a volunteer work clearing
house. In part, this was in response to President Obama's call for more
public service; reviving community spirit was back in favour. We may
wish that to be so. Yet no political party has a strategy for providing
incentives or opportunities for such work. The rush to do it testifies
to a desire to work on socially worthwhile activities. Losing jobs can
be liberating. In this, to be in the precariat is a two-sided experience.
Being tied to a job is the hell of the jobholder society, as feared by

Hannah Arendt (1958). The organic belonging becomes sclerotic, stultifying. But being economically insecure is no better, leaving the precariat unable to take up volunteering or other social work. Their debts and precariousness prevent it.

The rush to volunteering testifies to a desire to do activities that we would regard as work if we had not been subject to decades of indoctrination implying that work equals jobs. Both Polanyi ([1944] 2001) and Arendt understood this, but neither could take the recognition into the policy sphere. Polanyi lamented commodification, Arendt lamented jobholderism, but neither had a vision of how to achieve a work-and-leisure society. In the wake of the globalisation crisis, there is an opportunity to move forward.

Some of the names of emerging NGOs are encouraging – New York Cares, 'Big Brothers, Big Sisters', Taproot Foundation and so on. Professionals, out of jobs that had used only a restricted range of their talents and aspirations, have found outlets to put dormant talents and interests to work. Think too of the NGO in New York called Financial Clinic, which arranges for experts to advise low-paid workers on financial management. These are proficians who might otherwise fall into the precariat.

Government has played its part. Among the growing organisations were AmeriCorps, which takes young volunteers for a year, Teach for America, which sends college graduates to teach in low-income-area schools, and Volunteernyc.org, New York's public service site. By mid-2009, US non-profit organisations had 9.4 million employees and 4.7 million full-time volunteers. And firms were allowing regular employees time off for public service. This may presage a new social pattern but must have displacement effects. For instance, 10,000 lawyers were laid off in the United States in the first quarter of 2009, and many were induced to do *pro bono* work for public interest groups, at nominal fees. In March 2009, the US Congress passed the Edward Kennedy Serve America Act, a sweeping reform of the national service programme launched in 1993. This effectively tripled the size of AmeriCorps, which turned 7 million people into community volunteers in the following year. The Act distinctively mobilised older Americans through 'encore fellowships', giving them 'second careers' in education, health care and non-profit management. A survey in January 2009 by AARP, which represents Americans aged over 50, found that nearly three-quarters of old agers wished to give time to social work rather than money.

Besides volunteering, there are many forms of neighbourhood and care work initiatives. Most people in modern society feel that they can devote too little time to care, for their relatives, friends and community, and receive too little from others when in need. Let us call it work and build it into our sense of occupation.

In sum, occupational freedom requires an equal opportunity for the precariat and others to undertake a wide range of work and labour in building their own sense of occupational career, without the state making a particular form of labour somehow morally and economically superior to others.

Work rights

The precariat should demand that the instruments of so-called 'labour rights' be converted into the means of promoting and defending work rights. Increasingly, people doing work are not employees, and it is artificial to define employees in complex ways just to enable them to have labour-based entitlements. Work rights should include rules on acceptable practice *between* workers and *within* occupational communities as well as between 'labour' and 'capital'. The precariat is at a disadvantage in these respects; a regime of 'collaborative bargaining' to give it Voice is required to complement regimes of collective bargaining between representatives of employers and employees, an issue to which we will return.

The precariat should also demand construction of an international work-rights regime, beginning with an overhaul of the International Labour Organisation, a bastion of labourism. How this could be done is dealt with elsewhere (Standing, 2010). Without a proper global body, the Voice of the precariat will be muted or ignored.

All work that is not labour needs to be made part of work rights. For instance, if people are expected to deal with financial management and make decisions on how they spend money, rather than being subject to paternalistic nudging by the state, they should have access to affordable information and professional advice, and enough quality time to deal with them.

The work of care is still not a sphere of rights backed by legislation and instruments of social protection. This is vitally important for women in the precariat, particularly as the triple burden grows. But it is also important for men, as more realise the potential of involving themselves in care and in other forms of work that are not labour. A work-rights agenda here would involve thinking of the care provider, the care recipient and intermediaries, all of whom can easily suffer from exploitation, oppression and self-exploitation.

Work as social activity should also become a zone of rights. We have seen how volunteering and community work have been spreading, particularly since 2008. The risk is that it could become a privileged activity for a minority and an instrument of workfare for others. Moreover, retirees and underemployed employees are effectively subsidised if they enter a market for services that are also provided by workers who depend on the income from doing that work as labour. In those circumstances, the presence of volunteers reduces the economic opportunities of the precariat.

Finally, work rights encompass ethical codes. Every occupational community should have such codes, and most would wish to impose them on their members. Sadly, some powerful occupations, such as accountants, long lacked them, allowing their greedy elites to rake in large incomes by putting ethical considerations aside and demeaning the lower ranks in their broader working communities. Occupations that lacked a tradition of collective ethics, such as bankers, conspicuously contributed to the financial crisis. The precariat must insist that ethical codes become part of every occupational community and economic activity.

Combating workfare and conditionality

Unless the precariat makes a nuisance of itself, its concerns will be ignored in utilitarian democracies. A tyranny of the majority may come about simply because the precariat is unorganised or overlooked because of its disjointedness and lack of Voice in the political process. This is currently the situation. As a result, policies that please the median voter and those who finance politics usually prevail. To combat this, the precariat must be institutionally represented and demand that policies meet ethical principles. At present there is an institutional vacuum, which a few valiant NGOs try to fill, at best sporadically.

Consider workfare, as introduced in the United States, the United Kingdom, Sweden, Australia, Germany and elsewhere. Essentially, the unemployed must accept designated jobs or forfeit benefits, possibly being marked for life as a 'scrounger' on some dataveillance system. The employed majority may think this is fair, though they would not accept it if applied to themselves (or their children). Unfortunately, in a utilitarian situation, the unfairness will be ignored or dismissed. A majority will be happy.

The state is delegating job placement activities to commercial providers, paying them by the number of unemployed placed in jobs or by the measured reduction in claimant numbers. This commercialisation of what was once a public service sets up several moral hazards. It depersonalises to the point of making it neither a service nor public but merely a commodifying transaction. The intermediary is a firm, and in a market economy a firm exists with one overriding mandate, to make profits.

Imagine the scenario. An agent wants a man put in a job quickly, to increase the agent's own income. There is a job paying a minimum wage at the other end of town; it is unpleasant but it is a job. The man says he cannot accept it because of the travel and other costs, because the long hours would make it difficult for him to spend time with his family or because it does not accord with the skills he has spent his adult life developing. He is promptly recorded as having refused a job. Under the new rules in the United Kingdom, which copy US schemes, if he refuses three such jobs, he will lose entitlement to benefits for three years. This will not be based on due process or a fair hearing but solely on a decision by the commercial agent, who is accuser, judge and jury. The state is happy because welfare rolls are cut. The man has no proper right of appeal against the penalty imposed on him, which may threaten his life as a functioning citizen and blot his record, putting him in a precarity trap.

Nobody versed in basic principles of justice would accept such a procedure for themselves or for their relatives. But as long as it is not their problem, or as long as such rules are not brought to their attention so that they are obliged to reflect on this sort of unfairness, the drift will continue.

Similarly, the UK government contracted out medical examinations for incapacity benefits to a firm called Atos Origin; it promptly declared that three-quarters of claimants were fit to labour and would thus have their benefits reduced by a third. While most claimants would probably have been too intimidated to object on their own, some areas had groups to represent claimants; within months there were numerous appeals, 40 per cent of which were successful. Doctors told the BBC (British Broadcasting Corporation) they were under pressure to do quick cheap checks and declare patients fit.

Islington, a low-income borough of London, has a voluntary Islington Law Centre that reported a success rate in appeals of 80 per cent (Cohen, 2010). Such bodies should be an integral part of public policy, funded by government. And claimants should be represented inside the agencies, so that the chance of abuse of the vulnerable is reduced. After all, making appeals is risky, costly and time consuming. Not everywhere is like Islington, with its local community of lawyers and activist journalists.

The precariat must demand that democratic transparent principles should be applied at every stage of policy development and implementation. Conditionality and commercialised social policing must be rolled back as being alien to freedom, universalism and respect for nonconformity. If jobs are so wonderful, people should be drawn to them, not driven into them. And if services are so vital, then let education and affordable access be the means by which everybody can obtain them.

Associational freedom: The precariat's *agency*

This leads back to the nature of freedom. It is not an ability to do what we want, even allowing for the caveat that it should do no harm to others. Freedom comes from being part of a community in which to realise freedom in the exercise of it. It is *revealed* through actions, not something granted from on high or divined in stone tablets. The precariat is free in the neo-liberal sense, free to compete against each other, to consume and to labour. It is not free in that there is no associational structure in which the paternalists can be rebuffed or the oppressive competitive drive held in check.

The precariat needs collective Voice. The EuroMayDay movement is just a precursor, activities of primitive rebels preceding the emergence of collective action. Now is the time for bodies that represent the precariat on a continuing basis to bargain with employers, with intermediaries such as brokers and with government agencies most of all.

As a first task, recovering control over privacy is an imperative. The precariat lives in public spaces but is vulnerable to surveillance and undemocratic nudging. It should demand regulations to give individuals the right to see and correct information that any organisation holds on them, to require firms to inform employees, including outworkers, if any security breach occurs affecting them, to require organisations to undergo annual information-security audits by an accredited third party, to put expiry dates on information and to limit use of data profiling on the basis of some probability of behaviour. Data protection and freedom-of-information laws have been a step in the right direction but do not go far enough. Active Voice is required. The precariat must mobilise around an agenda to recover and strengthen privacy and the right to correct misinformation.

The precariat will grow angrier about the ecological destruction taking place around it. Deniers of man-made climate change have mobilised the extreme right and populism to depict government efforts to limit pollution as a plot to extend state power. The precariat should be wise to that. But it is being frightened by the prospect of fewer jobs, which are presented as the source of income security, and slower growth, which is depicted as somehow trickling down to them. In rich countries, the precariat is told that raising production costs would accelerate the transfer of jobs to poorer nations. In developing countries, it is told that measures to reduce energy use would slow job generation. Everywhere the precariat is told it must accept the *status quo*. It needs to realise that the problem is the primacy given to jobs rather than to the environment. To reverse that, we need to be less dependent on job generation.

The precariat Voice in the sphere of work and labour is weak. In principle, trades unions could be reformed to represent precariat interests. But there are several reasons for thinking this is unlikely. Trade unions lobby and struggle for more jobs and a larger share of output; they want the economic pie to be bigger. They are necessarily adversarial and economistic. They make gestures to the unemployed, to those doing care work and to 'green' issues. But whenever there is a clash between the financial interests of their members and social or ecological issues, they will opt for the former. Progressives must stop expecting unions to become something contrary to their functions.

A new type of collective body will have to take up the challenge of 'collaborative bargaining' (Standing, 2009). Such bodies will need to consider the full range of work and labour activities that the precariat has to undertake and its social aspirations. They must develop a bargaining capacity vis-à-vis employers, labour brokers, temporary agencies and an array of state bodies, notably those dealing with social services and monitoring activities. They must also be able to represent the precariat in dealings with other groups of workers, because its interests are not the same as those of the salariat or core employees, who may have labour unions to speak for them. And they must be associations that facilitate social mobility, providing structured communities in which mobility can be more orderly and feasible than at present.

One problem is escaping from the neo-liberal trap, based on the claim that any collective body of service providers distorts the market and should be blocked on antitrust grounds. Fortunately, there are promising models emerging in several countries. One is worker cooperatives, modernised to allow for more flexible involvement.

A Polanyian message is that associations emerging to help 're-embed' the economy in society following the globalisation crisis should allow nonconformity, to accommodate the precariat while enhancing egalitarianism. The principles of cooperativism have something to offer in this respect. Intriguingly, before his election as UK Prime Minister, David Cameron announced an intention to allow public sector workers, except the police, courts and prison services, to run their organisations as worker cooperatives, negotiating contracts with the relevant government department. This would move towards a modern form of guild socialism and turn over the management of occupations to occupational associations. Challenges to be overcome would include transparency, over-tendering, accountability once contracts were negotiated, and governance of rules on distribution of income, labour opportunities and internal promotions. Problems would also arise in jurisdiction and relations with other services. How would a service deal with labour-saving technical change?

On launching the idea in February 2010, Cameron cited examples such as call centres, social work, community health and nursing teams, hospital pathology departments, and rehabilitation and education services in prisons. This list prompts several questions. How large should the group be that is designated as a 'worker cooperative'? If all National Health Service hospitals in a local authority area were selected as a group, problems would arise in determining what share of income would go to groups with widely different earnings and technical skills. Would the share be paid on a *pro rata* basis, depending on relative earnings at the outset? Or would the rule be equal shares, regardless of skill or amount of time spent doing the work? If the cooperative unit were smaller, confined just to doctors, nurses or pathology departments, then internal rules might be simpler, but any internal change might have implications for individuals in the group. For that reason, changes offering a better or less costly service might well be resisted or simply not considered.

The difficulty with integrated social services is determining the monetary value of particular parts of it. Do doctors deserve 70 per cent of the value of medical services and nurses the remaining 30 per cent? Or should it be 60–40 or 80–20? One could say the shares should be determined democratically, in that government departments would bargain with the cooperatives. But just stating that should prompt us to think of the potential spheres of negotiation, including transaction costs. There would be legitimate tensions between related occupational groups. Think how nursing auxiliaries would react if the allocation for nursing services was split 70–30 in favour of registered nurses. Nevertheless, the proposal is a move towards collaborative bargaining. It recognises that, in a tertiary society, we exist not just as individuals but as willing members of groups, with a sense of identity. It harks back to nineteenth-century friendly societies and 'mutuals', and to the occupational guilds.

To work well there would have to be a strong floor of rights, so as to facilitate flexibility and give sufficient income security to induce people to be amenable to changes in organisation and their own personal profile. One under-appreciated drawback of the old employment security model was that, because benefits and income rose with duration in the service, firm or organisation, people clung to jobs when it would have been personally and organisationally advantageous for them to move. The gilded cage too often became a leaden cage. The cooperative principle is laudable but it must not become another means of stifling occupational mobility.

Besides cooperatives, another form of agency that would serve the precariat is an association of temporary workers. There are several variants. The Freelancers' Union, set up for 'permalancers' (permanent freelancers or temporaries) in New York, provides a wide range of services to individual members. Another variant, which is based on legislative help, is the freelance editors' association in Canada (Standing, 2009: 271–3). A third model might be something like SEWA (the Self-Employed Women's Association of India). Others are emerging and should be supported by progressive politics. They will give new meaning to associational freedom.

Above all, flexible labour markets and the overbearing state mean the precariat needs Voice inside policy agencies. The salariat knows how to defend itself against bureaucrats and complex administrative procedures. It can raise its voice. But the precariat is disadvantaged. While many in it are just insecure, others have additional disadvantages. For example, in the United Kingdom, two out of every five on incapacity benefit are said to be mentally ill. Add the poorly educated and migrants with limited command of the language, and their need for advocates and pressure groups inside policymaking structures can be appreciated. They need to be able to contest unfair dismissals, unpaid or underpaid benefits, deal with debt and resolve problems while negotiating their way around increasingly complex procedures seemingly designed to make it as hard as possible to qualify for and obtain benefits.

Reviving equality

In the twentieth century, inequality was seen in terms of profits and wages. For social democrats and others, redistribution was to be achieved by controlling the means of production, through nationalisation, and obtaining a greater share of profits through taxation, which could then be redistributed in state benefits and public services.

That model fell into disrepute and socialists are in despair. In a collection of essays on *Reimagining Socialism* by American socialists who saw the means of production going to China, Barbara Ehrenreich and Bill Fletcher (2009) wrote: 'Do we have a plan, people? Can we see our way out of this and into a just, democratic, sustainable (add your own favourite adjectives) future? Let's just put it on the table: We don't'.

They should take heart. The egalitarian ethos has moved on. The baton is being picked up by the precariat, the rising class in a tertiary society where means of production are nebulous and dispersed, and often owned by workers anyhow. Every Transformation has been marked by a struggle over the key assets of the era. In feudal societies, the peasants and serfs struggled to gain control of land and water. In industrial capitalism, the struggle was over the means of production, the factories, estates and mines. Workers wanted decent labour and a share of the profits in return for conceding control of labour to managers. But in today's tertiary society, progressive struggle will take place around the unequal access to and control of five primary assets.

They can be summarised as economic security, time, quality space, knowledge and financial capital. The progressive struggle will be about all five. We know the elite and salariat have most of the financial capital and that they have gained vastly more income without any evidence that they are more astute or hard working than their predecessors. Their affluence makes a mockery of claims of a meritocracy. Control of the income from financial capital means they can buy more of the privatised quality space, squeezing the commons on which the precariat and others rely, and they can have control over their own time that others can only dream of.

There is no magic bullet for redistributing all the five assets. In each case, institutional changes, regulations and bargaining will be required. However, one policy that has been discussed for many years would help in all respects. Before considering how the precariat could obtain a greater share of the five key assets, let us define the key idea and give the ethical rationale for it.

A basic income

The proposal has already been a theme of precariat demonstrations and has a long history with many distinguished adherents. It has gone under many names: The most popular is a 'basic income' but others include a 'citizen's grant', 'social dividend', 'solidarity grant' and 'demogrant'. While we will use the most popular name, a variant is proposed here that takes account of two desirable objectives that have not been part of the argumentation so far.

The core of the proposal is that every legal resident of a country or community, children as well as adults, should be provided with a modest monthly payment. Each individual would have a cash card entitling them to draw a monthly amount for basic needs, to spend as they see fit, with add-ons for special needs, such as disability. In most rich countries, it would be less radical than it may appear, since it would mean consolidating many existing transfer schemes and replacing others that are riddled with complexity and arbitrary and discretionary conditionality.

Such a basic income would be paid to each individual, not to a larger contestable group, such as 'the family' or 'household'. It would be universal in being paid to all legal residents, with a waiting period for migrants, for pragmatic reasons. It would be in the form of cash, allowing the recipient to decide how to use it, not in a paternalistic form, such as a voucher for food or other predetermined items. It must promote 'free choice', not be a means of nudging. It should be inviolable, in that the state should not be able to take it away unless a person ceases to be a legal resident or commits a crime for which denial is a specified penalty. And it should be paid as a *regular* modest sum, not as a lump sum payment along the lines of the 'baby bond' or 'stakeholder grant' intended under the United Kingdom's Child Trust Fund, which raises 'weakness-of-will' and other problems (Wright, 2006).

The grant would be unconditional in behavioural terms. There are laws, courts and due process to deal with questionable behaviour. They should not be mixed up with a policy to provide basic security. If they are, neither security nor justice will be provided. In principle, cash transfers liberate; they give economic security with which to make choices about how to live and develop one's capacities. Poverty is about unfreedom as well as about not having enough to eat, not enough clothing and an inadequate place to live. Imposing conditions, whether behavioural or in terms of what the recipient is permitted to buy, is an act of unfreedom. Once it is accepted, what is to stop policy makers going to the next step? They can easily think they know what is best for someone who is income-poor and less educated. Conditionalists will tend to extend conditions and tighten how they operate until they become coercive and punitive. A basic income would go in the other direction.

A basic income would not be quite like a negative income tax, with which it is often compared. It would not create a poverty trap, in which as income rises the benefit is lost, acting as a disincentive to labour. The person would retain the basic income regardless of how much is earned from labour, just as it would be paid regardless of marital or family status. All earned income would be taxed at the standard rate. If the state wanted to limit the amount going to the affluent, it could claw it back through higher tax on higher incomes.

The objections to a basic income have been reviewed extensively, notably in an international network formed in 1986 to promote debate. Originally called BIEN (Basic Income European Network), it changed its name at its Barcelona Congress in 2004 to BIEN (Basic Income Earth Network) to reflect the fact that a growing number of its members were from developing countries and other countries outside Europe. By 2010, it had flourishing national networks in many countries, including Brazil, Canada, Japan, Mexico, South Korea and the United States as well as in Europe.

The main claims made against an unconditional basic income are that it would lower labour supply, could be inflationary, would be

unaffordable, would be used by populist politicians and would be a
'handout', a reward for sloth and a tax on those who labour. All of
these have been answered in the BIEN literature and by other scholarly
work. However, in thinking of the advantages of basic income for the
precariat in terms of the key assets (and how to pay for it), we will
respond to some of those criticisms here.

Philosophically, a basic income may be thought of as a 'social
dividend', a return on past investment. Those who attack it as giving
something for nothing tend to be people who have been given a lot
of something for nothing, often having inherited wealth, small or
vast. This leads to the point elegantly made by Tom Paine (2005) in
his *Agrarian Justice* of 1795. Every affluent person in every society
owes their good fortune largely to the efforts of their forebears and
the efforts of the forebears of less affluent people. If everybody were
granted a basic income with which to develop their capabilities, it
would amount to a dividend from the endeavours and good luck of
those who came before. The precariat has as much right to such a
dividend as anybody else.

A desirable step towards a basic income is integration of the tax
and benefit systems. In 2010, a development moving the United
Kingdom towards a basic income came from what many would have
thought an unlikely direction. The Coalition government's plans for
radical reform of the tax-benefit system recognised that the system
of fifty-one benefits that the previous government had built up, many
with different eligibility criteria, was befuddling and rife with moral
hazards linked to poverty and unemployment traps. In amalgamating
state benefits into two – a Universal Work Credit and a Universal Life
Credit – it would have been possible to advance tax-benefit integration

and facilitate a more orderly tapering of withdrawal of benefits as earned income rose. Integration could create the circumstances for a basic income to emerge. Sadly, the work and pensions minister, a Catholic, was persuaded to force benefit recipients to labour, ushering in workfare and allowing commercial agents to have control. But integration would be a step towards rebuilding a system of social protection with a universalistic base.

Redistributing security

The asset of security has several elements – social, economic, cultural, political and so on. We are concerned here with the economic dimension. Chronic insecurity is bad in itself and is instrumentally bad, affecting the development of capacities and personality. If this is accepted, then there should be a strategy to provide basic security. The precariat is stirring precisely because it suffers from systemic insecurity.

One can have too much security or too little. If one has too little, irrationality prevails; if one has too much, a lack of care and responsibility prevails. An emphasis on security may become reactionary, resisting change and justifying regressive controls. However, basic economic security would still leave existential insecurity (we worry about those we love, our safety and health, etc.) and development insecurity (we want to develop our capacities and live a more comfortable life, but must take risks to do so). And a sense of stability is required in order to be rational, tolerant and compassionate. Basic security must be assured, not something that can be taken away at someone's discretion without just and proven cause.

Utilitarians and neo-liberals ignore the need for universal economic security as a means of enabling people to internalise principled behaviour. They tend to see people who are failures of a market society as a collective 'other'. Thinking of targeting a group of people called 'the poor' is to pity and condemn in roughly equal measure. 'They' are deserving, undeserving or transgressing, to be benevolently helped, reshaped or punished, according to how we good folk judge them. To talk of 'the poor' is to talk of pity, which is akin to contempt, as David Hume taught us. 'They' are not like 'us'. The precariat's retort is that they are us or could be at any time.

Thinking of universal basic security is to shift the mind away from pity to social solidarity and compassion. Social insurance was about producing security in an industrial society. It could not work now and did not work very well then. But the principle of solidaristic security was laudable. It has been lost in the plethora of targeted schemes seeking to weed out the 'undeserving'. What does it matter if 0.5 per cent of the people are lazy? Should policies be designed with the 0.5 per cent in mind or to give security and freedom to the 99.5 per cent, so that society has a more relaxed, less anxious life? Many control policies that politicians, their advisers and bureaucrats devise may appeal to prejudiced minds and gain votes, but they are costly and largely counterproductive. It costs the taxpayer much more to force a few unproductive people into unproductive jobs than just to let them drift, if that is really what they want. It would be better to offer disinterested advice, as a service, not as a thinly disguised sanction.

The vast majority would not be content to live off just a basic income. They want to work and are excited by the possibility of improving their material and social living. To hound a tiny minority for their 'laziness' is a sign of our weakness, not our merit. In that regard, a little experiment conducted in the backstreets of London in 2010 had heart-warming lessons. Some homeless vagrants were each asked what they most wanted; their dreams were modest, as befitted their situation. The money to fulfil those dreams was provided without conditions; a few months later, nearly all of them had ceased to be homeless and a burden on the local authorities. The savings for taxpayers of giving that money amounted to fifty times the cost of giving it.

Basic security is, first, having moderate, not extreme, *uncertainty*; second, knowing that if something went wrong there would be affordable and behaviourally acceptable ways of *coping*; and third, having affordable and behaviourally tolerable ways of *recovering* from a shock or hazard. In a market society with conditional welfare schemes, costly private options and little social mobility, those conditions do not exist and must be constructed. The starting point for the precariat is dealing with uncertainty, since they are faced by uninsurable 'unknown unknowns'.

The need for multi-layered *ex ante* security (as contrasted with the *ex post* security offered by social insurance, which deals with specific contingency risks) is thus a reason for wishing the good society of the future to include an unconditional basic income. Those affluent politicians lucky enough to have lived off private welfare all their lives should be told that having 'welfare for life' is what everybody deserves, not just them. We are all 'dependent' on others, or to be precise we are 'interdependent'. It is part of the normal human condition, not some addiction or disease. And providing fellow human beings with basic security should not be made conditional on some moralistically determined behaviour. If certain behaviour is unacceptable, it should be made a matter of law, subject to due process. Linking social protection to conditionality is to bypass law, which is supposedly the same for all.

Basic security is an almost universal human need and a worthy goal for state policy. Trying to make people 'happy' is a manipulative ruse, whereas providing an underpinning of security would create a necessary condition for people to be able to pursue their own conception of happiness. Basic economic security is also instrumentally beneficial. Insecurity produces stress, which diminishes the ability to concentrate and learn, particularly affecting those parts of the brain most associated with the working memory (Evans and Schamberg, 2009). So, to promote equal opportunity, we should aim to reduce differences in insecurity. More fundamentally, psychologists have shown that basically secure people are much more likely to be tolerant and altruistic. It is chronic socio-economic insecurity that is fanning neo-fascism in rich countries as they confront the delayed downward adjustment of living standards brought about by globalisation.

This leads to a first possible modification of the proposal for a basic income (see also Standing, 2011). We know that the globalised economy produces more economic insecurity and is prone to volatility, and that the precariat experiences uninsurable fluctuations in economic insecurity. This creates a need for income stability and for automatic economic stabilisers. The latter role used to be played by unemployment insurance and other social insurance benefits, but these have shrivelled. If a basic income were seen as an 'economic stabilisation grant', it would be an egalitarian way of reducing economic volatility. It would be more efficient and equitable than conventional monetary and fiscal policy as well as all those deplorable subsidies that foster inefficiency and a host of deadweight and substitution effects.

The value of the basic income card could be varied counter-cyclically. When opportunities for earning were high, its value could be lower, and when recessionary conditions were spreading it could be raised. To avoid political misuse, the level of the basic income could be set by an independent body, including representatives of the precariat as well as of other interests. This would be equivalent to the quasi-independent monetary bodies set up in recent years. Its mandate would be to adjust the core value of the basic income grant according to economic growth and its supplementary value according to the cyclical condition of the economy. The point is to redistribute basic security from those with 'too much' to those with little or none.

Redistributing financial capital

There are many ways of paying for basic income or stabilisation grants. The contextual point is that inequalities are greater than for a long time, in many countries greater than at any time. There is no evidence that such inequality is necessary. But more is due to the high returns to financial capital. The precariat should obtain a share.

Rich country governments missed an opportunity to reduce inequality following the shock to the banking system. When they bailed out the banks with citizens' money, they could have taken a permanent citizens' interest share of the equity, requiring a public-interest representative on the board of directors of all banks, or all receiving public assistance. When the banks started making profits again, some would have flowed back to the public who had effectively invested in the banks. It is not too late to do something like this.

Two reforms would help. First, subsidies to capital and to labour should be phased out. They do not benefit the precariat and are inegalitarian. Had one-half of the money spent on bailing out the banks been allocated to economic stabilisation grants, a decent monthly grant could have been provided to every citizen for years (Standing, 2011). Other subsidies are distortionary and contribute to inefficiency.

Second, ways must be found to redistribute part of the high returns to financial capital, returns that bear no relationship to the labour of those now profiting from its strategic position in the global economy. Why should people with particular skills – always accepting they are skills – live a vastly better economic life than others who have different skills?

Rich countries must come to terms with being *rentier* economies. There is nothing wrong with investing capital in emerging market economies and with receiving fair dividends from the investment. This side of globalisation should give rise to a win-win situation but only if some of the dividends are distributed to the citizens and denizens of the investing country.

Sovereign wealth (or capital) funds, which already exist in forty countries, are a promising way of doing that. If the income accruing to such funds could be shared, the precariat would gain a means of control over their lives. It is all very well for economists to claim that jobs will come in non-tradable sectors. What we are learning is that most activities are tradable. Expecting jobs to be the means by which inequality is reduced is whistling in the wind. Jobs will not disappear. To think otherwise is to accept the 'lump of labour fallacy'. But many if not most will be low paying and insecure.

Capital funds can be used to accumulate financial returns to help pay for a basic income. There are precedents. The Alaska Permanent Fund, established in 1976, was set up to distribute part of the profits from oil production to every legal resident of Alaska. It continues to do so. It is not a perfect model, since its governance can result in the relative neglect of the precariat or tomorrow's Alaskans relative to today's. But, like the Norwegian Fund, it provides the nucleus of a capital fund mechanism that could be used to finance a modest basic income, however it might be called.

The precariat would also benefit from so-called 'Tobin taxes', levied on speculative capital transactions. There are arguments for believing that reducing short-term capital flows would be beneficial in any event. And then there are ecological taxes, designed to compensate for the externalities caused by pollution and to slow or reverse the rapid depletion of resources. In short, there is no reason to think a universal basic income is unaffordable.

Internationally, the recent legitimation of cash transfers as an instrument of development aid is promising. They were first accepted as short-term schemes for post-shock situations, as after earthquakes and floods. Later, as noted earlier, conditional cash transfer schemes swept Latin America. Donors and aid agencies have come round to them. Cash transfers, stripped of their phoney conditionality, should become the main form of aid, to ensure the aid raises living standards and is not used for regressive or corrupt purposes.

We should think afresh about the global redistribution of income. A book by jurist Ayelet Schachar (2009), *The Birthright Lottery*, has argued for a citizenship tax in rich countries to redistribute to people in poor ones, treating the material benefits of citizenship as property, an inheritance. This is akin to Paine's argument. It may be too utopian for immediate implementation. But it builds on the insight that citizenship is not a natural right, since borders are arbitrary. It conjures up a link between earmarked taxes and redistribution via basic transfers to those 'unlucky enough' to be born in low-income parts of the world. The only reason for thinking it utopian today is that in a globalising market society we are all expected to be egotistical, not global citizens.

So, there should be no qualms in saying that there are ways of funding moves towards a basic income in both rich and developing countries. The challenge is political; only if the precariat can exert enough pressure on the political process will what is possible become reality. Fortunately, as it exerts that pressure, evidence is accumulating of the beneficial effects of basic cash transfers in countries that only a few years ago would have been regarded as places where a basic income would be impossible.

Gaining control of time

A basic income would also give people more control over their *time*. And it would be an answer to the libertarian paternalists. They believe that people cannot make rational decisions because they are faced by too much information. In that case, they should favour policies that would provide people with more time in which to make rational decisions. People also need time to do work-for-labour and other forms of work that are not labour. Let us slow down. We need a Slow Time Movement, along the lines of the Slow Food Movement; both are integral to localism.

There are few levers to enable people to slow down. Instead, fiscal and social policy 'rewards' labour and penalises those who opt for less labour. People who wish to labour less are doubly penalised, not only in receiving lower earnings but also in losing entitlement to so-called 'social rights', such as pensions.

A basic income, delinked from labour, would be decommodifying in that it would give people a greater capacity to live outside the market and be under less pressure to labour. But it could increase the amount of labour by allowing people to move in and out of the labour market more easily. In other words, it might induce more labour but would do so in conditions of greater security and independence from market pressures. A basic income would also enable citizens to accept low wages *and* to bargain more strongly. If they judged that a certain amount was all that a potential employer could afford, they might take the job as long as they had enough on which to live.

It is the need to regain control over time that is so important. We need it to make decisions on risk management. Some libertarian paternalists claim that education fails to improve people's ability to make good decisions, justifying their nudges and use of sticks that look like carrots. However, a UK survey found that investors identified lack of time as the main barrier to managing risks (Grene, 2009). Risks can be explained so that people can make rational choices. Doctors can communicate risk to patients as part of the delivery of 'informed choice'. Statistical findings can be brought to people's attention. Financial service professionals could be obliged to accept a broader definition of risk and to engage with consumers to enable them to make more rational decisions, through a 'risk communication and recognition tool'. The point is that people need time in which to weigh up risks, as long as policies ensure the appropriate information is made available.

This recalls one of the worst precarity traps. The precariat is faced with a time squeeze from declining returns to labour and from pressure to do more work-for-labour and work-for-reproduction, partly because they cannot afford to pay for substitutes. Anxious and insecure, to the point of being 'spent', they have to do an excessive amount of work-for-labour and are unable to digest and use information that comes their way. A basic income would give them greater control of their time and thus help them to make more rational decisions.

Recovering the commons

Finally, there is the maldistribution of public quality space. This has two relevant dimensions. Most informed people recognise the frightening ecological threat posed by global warming, pollution and the disappearance of species. Yet much of the elite and upper parts of the salariat do not really care. Their affluence and connections can ensure they are not touched. They can retreat to their islands in clear blue sea and their mountain retreats. They want high rates of economic growth to augment their incomes and wealth, never mind the ecological destruction caused by resource depletion. It is the precariat that is naturally the green class in arguing for a more egalitarian society in which sharing and reproductive, resource-conserving activities are prioritised. Rapid growth is only needed in order to retain the grotesque inequalities that globalisation has produced. Just as we need to slow down in order to reduce the stress of frenzied labour and consumption, we also need to do so to reproduce nature.

The precariat must also struggle for a viable commons; it needs a rich public space. Perhaps the most revealing acts of former UK Prime Minister Margaret Thatcher – that architect of neo-liberalism so revered by successors Tony Blair and David Cameron – were the mass sales of council housing and playing fields and other facilities attached to state schools. That cut the public space for low-income citizens and denizens.

Three decades later the policy culminated in the austerity measures of 2010. Hundreds of public libraries are set for closure, just as they have been across the United States. These are precious public places for the precariat. Sports funding for state schools is targeted for huge cuts, with after-school clubs facing devastation. Other public facilities are being cut or will be priced out of range. And urban zoning of residence will become more systemic. The sale of council housing created a shortage of affordable rental accommodation for low-income earners in towns and cities. Rents for private accommodation rose, increasing the sums paid out in housing benefit to low-income earners. When the government looked for fiscal savings, housing benefit was an easy target. It plans to restrict benefit levels to the cheapest 30 per cent of homes in an area and cap the amount a family can receive.

The reforms are bound to drive low-income earners out of high cost, high-living-standard areas, in what the Mayor of London, a Conservative, called 'social cleansing' and the Archbishop of Canterbury called 'social zoning'.

Perversely, the move will make the labour market more chaotic. As low-income and relatively uneducated people concentrate in low-income areas, job opportunities will concentrate in higher-income areas. Pockets of poverty and unemployment will become zones or even ghettos, just as the *banlieues* of Paris are centres of deprivation, insecurity, unemployment and survival crime, and just as South African cities, zoned under apartheid, remain fragmented into heavily guarded gated areas and the seething anger of the townships.

There is also need for more secure public spaces in which the precariat can congregate and develop public civic friendship. The public sphere needs to be revived. Sociologist and philosopher Jürgen Habermas, lamenting the fragmentation of the public sphere, has harked back to the eighteenth century of London's coffee houses, the salons of Paris and Germany's 'table talks'. His view, infused with nostalgia, is that the public sphere was killed by the welfare state, mass media, public relations and the undermining of parliamentary politics by political parties. Implicit is a belief that if only we had well-informed coffee-house denizens, democracy would revive.

There is something in this, in that while the precariat is the emergent class populating the modern coffee houses, pubs, internet cafes and social networks, there is a *deliberative* deficit. Habermas depicted the internet as generating an anarchic wave of fragmented circuits of communication that could not produce a public sphere. Fair enough. But he is too pessimistic. The precariat may be offered a fragmented public sphere, but it may fight for one where deliberative democracy can be revived. And a basic income can help even here.

Leisure grants

A worrying aspect of the jobholder society is the loss of respect for leisure in the Greek sense of *schole*. That loss of respect goes with civic privatism and an individualism based on crude materialism. For the health of society and for ourselves, we need mechanisms to reverse the trend.

Thin democracy, the commodification of politics, and the power of public relations and elite money risk strengthening a tyranny of the majority and an unhealthy denigration of nonconformity. As a counter-movement, the precariat needs mechanisms to generate *deliberative* democracy. This promotes values of universalism and altruism, since it encourages people to think along 'veil of ignorance' lines and to depart from the standpoint influenced by their position along the social and economic spectrum. However, deliberative democracy requires active participation, which cannot be done by distracted people fed a diet of sound bites and platitudes. It requires debate, eye contact, body language, listening and reflection.

In ancient Athens, a stone device called a *kleroterion* was used to select a random 500 people to make policy, out of 50,000 citizens. It was undemocratic, in that women and slaves were excluded. But it resembles deliberative democracy. Research by James Fishkin, Bruce Ackerman and others indicates that public discussions often lead away from populist views. One experiment in recession-hit Michigan led to a rise of support for higher taxes, in the case of income tax from 27 to 45 per cent. In such experiments, the biggest changes in opinion come from those gaining most knowledge. It does not mean the changes are always desirable. But it does indicate that deliberation makes a difference. Earlier psychological experiments found that those with basic economic security are more altruistic, tolerant and egalitarian than those who are economically insecure, and that group deliberation around related propositions led to even more support for providing people with a guaranteed floor of security (Frohlich and Oppenheimer, 1992).

Some advocate the use of the internet to conduct deliberative democracy, through polls. It has been used in Greece and China for a few projects, such as to determine how a local infrastructure fund should be allocated in Zeguo, China. It is being considered as a safety valve for social pressures. However, while using the internet would be intriguing, it cannot replace the concentration involved in public physical participation.

It is thus worth considering one interim variant of basic income grants, which could help turn the precariat away from populism. This is to require everybody entitled to a basic income grant, when they register eligibility, to make a moral commitment to vote in national and local elections, and to participate in at least one local meeting a year convened to discuss topical political issues. Such a commitment should not be legally binding, with sanctions; it should merely be a recognition of civic responsibility, as befits an ethos of emancipatory egalitarianism.

Even without the moral commitment, a basic income would be an instrument for encouraging deliberative democracy. Thin democracy is likely to be captured by elites or populist agendas. If democracies are less corrupt than non-democracies, as Transparency International estimates, then pro-participatory measures would strengthen democracy. And, presuming a linear relationship between degree of democracy and corruption, this would diminish corruption. With low turnout, it is more likely that entrenched candidates will win. The precariat and proficians, reflecting their more nomadic way of life, are more likely to switch to politicians regarded as trustworthy. Many elections are decided by who does not vote. This cannot be a good outcome.

Work-and-leisure grants can be related to the new enthusiasm for 'localism'. The desire for devolution under the rubric of a 'post-bureaucratic age' is seductive, favoured by both social democrats and conservatives. In the United Kingdom, the Conservatives cleverly invented the term Big Society, a vague euphemism that seems to embrace localism and a greater role for civic society and voluntary work. The think-tank Demos also emphasised localism in its pamphlet *The Liberal Republic* (Reeves and Collins, 2009), which linked it to 'a self-authored life' in which individual autonomy is paramount in shaping one's version of the Good Life.

There are troubles ahead. Localism may go with social zoning, with affluent areas gaining to the detriment of others. It neglects the need for associational freedom rather than just individual autonomy, which would leave the precariat at a disadvantage. Civic society can be dominated by the affluent and well connected. And localism could usher in more paternalism. Already it is being linked to measures to promote 'pro-social behaviour'. An idea is to let citizens vote on how money should be spent in their neighbourhood in return for doing voluntary work or attending public meetings. This form of conditionality threatens principles of democracy. Voting is a universal right and the objective should be to increase deliberative democracy, not create insiders and outsiders. Moreover, localism could only succeed if people were civically engaged, and linking entitlement to a grant to a moral commitment to participate in democratic activity would be a better way forward.

An intention that should appeal to progressives is to raise the voting level, bearing in mind that where that happens the propensity to support liberal or progressive values rises. Brazil has compulsory voting, which may be why there has been little support for neo-liberalism there. A large number of poor, who pay little tax but gain from state benefits, push politicians to the left in social policy. So progressives should want to increase voter turnout, a reason for them to support leisure-conditional grants. Obligatory voting could be why Brazil may introduce a basic income before other countries and why a commitment to do so was passed into law in 2004.

There is a precedent for linking political participation to basic income grants. In 403 BC in Athens, citizens were given a small grant as a token for their participation in the life of the *polis*. To receive it was a badge of honour and an inducement to take responsibility in the conduct of public affairs.

Conclusions

The precariat may soon find it has many more friends. It is worth recalling the famous admonition attributed to Pastor Martin Niemöller on the rise of the Nazis in 1930s Germany.

They came first for the Communists,

and I didn't speak up because I wasn't a Communist.

Then they came for the trade unionists,

and I didn't speak up because I wasn't a trade unionist.

Then they came for the Jews,

and I didn't speak up because I wasn't a Jew.

Then they came for me

and by that time no one was left to speak up.

The warning is relevant because the dangerous class is being led astray by demagogues like Berlusconi, mavericks like Sarah Palin and neo-fascists elsewhere. While the centre-right is being dragged further to the right to hold its constituents, the political centre-left is giving ground and haemorrhaging votes. It is in danger of losing a generation of credibility. For too long, it has represented the interests of 'labour' and stood for a dying way of life and a dying way of labouring. The new class is the precariat; unless the progressives of the world offer a politics of paradise, that class will be all too prone to listen to the sirens luring society onto the rocks. Centrists will join in supporting a new progressive consensus because they have nowhere else to go. The sooner they join, the better. The precariat is not victim, villain or hero – it is just a lot of us.

BIBLIOGRAPHY

Aguiar, M. and Hurst, E. (2009), *The Increase in Leisure Inequality, 1965–2005*, Washington, DC: AEI Press.

Amoore, L. (2000), 'International Political Economy and the Contested Firm', *New Political Economy*, 5(2): 183–204.

Arendt, H. (1958), *The Human Condition*, Chicago, IL: University of Chicago Press.

—([1951] 1986), *The Origins of Totalitarianism*, London: André Deutsch.

Asthana, A. and Slater, C. (2009), 'Most Parents Can't Find Enough Time to Play with Their Children', *Observer*, 2 August, p. 17.

Atkins, R. (2009), 'Europe Reaps the Rewards of State-Sponsored Short-Time Jobs', *Financial Times*, 29 October, p. 6.

Autor, D. and Houseman, S. (2010), 'Do Temporary-Help Jobs Improve Labor Market Outcomes for Low-Skilled Workers: Evidence from "Work First"', *American Economic Journal: Applied Economics*, 3(2): 96–128.

Bamford, J. (2009), *The Shadow Factory: The Ultra-Secret NSA from 9/11 to the Eavesdropping on America*, New York: Doubleday.

Barber, S. (2010), 'Jobless Migrants Living in Shanty Towns Offered Free Flights Home', *Observer*, 7 February.

Bennett, C. (2010), 'Do We Really Need Advice on How to Deal with Boomerang Kids?' *Observer*, 3 January, p. 25.

Bentham, J. ([1787] 1995), *Panopticon; or The Inspection-House*, reprinted in M. Bozovich (ed.), *The Panopticon Writings*, London: Verso, pp. 29–95.

Bernstein, R. (2009), 'Don't Trust Anyone Under 30?', *New York Times*, 14 January.

Beveridge, W. (1942), *Social Insurance and Allied Services*, London: HMSO.

Blinder, A. (2009), 'How Washington Can Create Jobs', *Wall Street Journal*, 17 November, p. 16.

Bloomberg Business Week (2005), 'Embracing Illegals', *Bloomberg Business Week*, 18 July.

Bourdieu, P. (1990), *The Logic of Practice*, Cambridge, UK: Polity Press.

—(1998), 'La précarité est aujourd'hui partout' ['Precariousness is Everywhere Nowadays'], in *Contre-feux*, Paris: Raisons d'agir, pp. 96–102.

Browne, J. (2010), *Securing a Sustainable Future for Higher Education*, London: The Stationery Office.

Bryceson, D. B. (ed.) (2010), *How Africa Works: Occupational Change, Identity and Morality*, Rugby: Practical Action Publishing.

Bullock, N. (2009), 'Town Halls Find Fresh Angles to Meet Recession',
   Financial Times, 23 December, p. 2.
Carr, N. (2010), *The Shallows: What the Internet Is Doing to Our Brains*,
   New York: Norton.
Centre for Women in Business (2009), *The Reflexive Generation: Young
   Professionals' Perspectives on Work, Career and Gender*, London: London
   Business School.
Chan, W. (2010), 'The Path of the Ant Tribe: A Study of the Education
   System That Reproduces Social Inequality in China', paper presented at the
   Seventh East Asia Social Policy Conference, Seoul, 19–21 August.
Chellaney, B. (2010), 'China Now Exports Its Convicts', *Japan Times Online*,
   5 July. Available at http://search.japantimes.co.jp/print/eo20100705bc.html
   [accessed 2 December 2010].
Choe, S.-H. (2009), 'South Korea Fights Slump through Hiring, Not Firing',
   International Herald Tribune, 2 April, pp. 1, 4.
Coase, R. H. (1937), 'The Nature of the Firm', *Economica*, 4(16): 386–405.
Cohen, D. (2009), *Three Lectures on Post-Industrial Society*, Cambridge,
   MA: Massachusetts Institute of Technology Press.
Cohen, N. (2010), 'Now, More than Ever, the Poor Need a Voice', *Observer*,
   7 October, p. 33.
Coleman, D. (2010), 'When Britain Becomes "Majority Minority"', *Prospect*,
   17 November.
Collison, M. (1996), 'In Search of the High Life', *British Journal of Criminology*,
   36(3): 428–43.
Crawford, M. (2009), *Shop Class as Soulcraft: An Enquiry into the Value of Work*,
   New York: Penguin.
Dench, G., Gavron, K. and Young, M. (2006), *The New East End: Kinship,
   Race and Conflict*, London: Profile Books.
De Waal, F. (2005), *Our Inner Ape*, London: Granta Books.
Dinmore, G. (2010a), 'Tuscan Town Turns Against Chinese Immigrants',
   Financial Times, 9 February, p. 2.
—(2010b), 'Chinese Gangs Exploit Niche Left by Mafia', *Financial Times*, 29
   June, p. 5.
Doerr, N. (2006), 'Towards a European Public Sphere "from Below"? The Case
   of Multilingualism within the European Social Forums', in C. Barker and
   M. Tyldesley (eds), *Conference Papers of the Eleventh International
   Conference on 'Alternative Futures and Popular Protest', vol. II*, Manchester:
   Manchester Metropolitan University.
Dvorak, P. and Thurm, S. (2009), 'Slump Prods US Firms to Seek a New
   Compact with Workers', *Wall Street Journal*, 20 October, pp. 14–15.
The Economist (2007), 'Changing How Japan Works', *The Economist*,
   29 September, p. 70.

—(2009), 'Public Sector Unions: Welcome to the Real World',
The Economist, 12 December, p. 46.

—(2010a), 'Too Many Chiefs', *The Economist*, 26 June, p. 72.

—(2010b), 'Dues and Don'ts', *The Economist*, 14 August, p. 62.

—(2010c), 'The Biology of Business: Homo Administrans',
The Economist, 23 September.

Ehrenreich, B. (2009), *Smile or Die: How Positive Thinking Fooled America and the World*, London: Granta.

Ehrenreich, B. and Fletcher, B. (2009), 'Reimagining Socialism', *The Nation*, 23 March.

Elger, T. and Smith, C. (2006), 'Theorizing the Role of the International Subsidiary: Transplants, Hybrids and Branch Plants Revisited', in A. Ferner, J. Quintanilla and C. Sánchez-Runde (eds), *Multinationals, Institutions and the Construction of Transnational Practices: Convergence and Diversity in the Global Economy*, Basingstoke: Palgrave Macmillan, pp. 53–85.

Environmental Justice Foundation (2009), *No Place Like Home: Where Next for Climate Refugees?* London: Environmental Justice Foundation.

Equality and Human Rights Commission (2010), *Inquiry into the Meat and Poultry Processing Sectors: Report of the Findings and Recommendations*, London: EHRC.

Esping-Andersen, G. (1990), *The Three Worlds of Welfare State Capitalism*, Cambridge, UK: Cambridge University Press.

Evans, G. W. and Schamberg, M. A. (2009), 'Childhood Poverty, Chronic Stress, and Adult Working Memory', *Proceedings of the National Academy of Sciences*, 106(16): 6545–9.

Fackler, M. (2009), 'Crisis-Hit South Koreans Living Secret Lives with Blue-Collar Jobs', *International Herald Tribune*, 8 July, p. 1.

—(2010), 'New Dissent in Japan Is Loudly Anti-Foreign', *New York Times*, 29 August, p. A6.

Fauroux, R. (2005), *La lutte contre les discriminations ethniques dans le domaine de l'emploi [Combating Ethnic Discrimination in Employment]*, Paris: HALDE.

Federal Communications Commission (2010), *National Broadband Plan: Connecting America*, Washington, DC: Federal Communications Commission.

Fifield, A. (2010), 'Tea Party Brews Trouble for Both Sides as Protest Recoils on Right', *Financial Times*, 28 January, p. 5.

Financial Times (2010a), 'Britain's Growing Inequality Problem', *Financial Times*, 28 January, p. 14.

—(2010b), 'Osborne Preaches One Nation Austerity', *Financial Times*, 5 October, p. 16.

Fiszbein, A. and Schady, N. (2009), *Conditional Cash Transfers: Reducing Present and Future Poverty*, Washington, DC: World Bank.

Florida, R. (2003), *The Rise of the Creative Class, and How It's Transforming Work, Leisure, Community and Everyday Life*, London: Basic Books.

—(2010), 'America Needs to Make Its Bad Jobs Better', *Financial Times*, 6 July, p. 11.

Forrest, R. and Kearns, A. (2001), 'Social Cohesion, Social Capital and the Neighbourhood', *Urban Studies*, 38(12): 2125–43.

Foucault, M. (1977), *Discipline and Punish: The Birth of the Prison*, London: Penguin.

Freeman, R. (2005), 'What Really Ails Europe (and America): The Doubling of the Global Workforce', *The Globalist*, 3 June. Available at http://www.theglobalist.com/storyid.aspx?StoryId=4542 [accessed 6 December 2010].

Friedman, M. (1982), *Capitalism and Freedom*, Chicago, IL: University of Chicago Press.

Friedman, M. and Kuznets, S. (1945), *Income from Independent Professional Practice*, New York: National Bureau of Economic Research.

Frohlich, N. and Oppenheimer, J. A. (1992), *Choosing Justice: An Experimental Approach to Ethical Theory*, Berkeley, CA, and Los Angeles, CA: University of California Press.

Gibney, M. J. (2009), *Precarious Residents: Migration Control, Membership and the Rights of Non-Citizens*, New York: Human Development Reports Research Paper 2009/10, United Nations Development Programme.

Giridharadas, A. (2009), 'Putting the Students in Control', *International Herald Tribune*, 7–8 November, p. 2.

Goldthorpe, J. H. (2007), *On Sociology*, second edition, Stanford: Stanford University Press.

—(2009), 'Analysing Social Inequality: A Critique of Two Recent Contributions from Economics and Epidemiology', *European Sociological Review*, 22 October. Available at http://esr.oxfordjournals.org/content/early/2009/10/22/esr.jcp046. abstract [accessed 2 December 2010].

Goos, M. and Manning, A. (2007), 'Lousy and Lovely Jobs: The Rising Polarisation of Work in Britain', *Review of Economics and Statistics*, 89(1): 118–33.

Gorz, A. (1982), *Farewell to the Working Class: An Essay on Post-Industrial Socialism*, London: Pluto Press. [Original published as *Adieux au proletariat*, Paris: Galilée, 1980.]

Green, H. (2010), *The Company Town: The Industrial Edens and Satanic Mills That Shaped the American Economy*, New York: Basic Books.

Grene, S. (2009), 'Pension Investors Fail to Get the Message', *FT Report - Fund Management*, 27 July, p. 3.

Grimm, S. and Ronneberger, K. (2007), *An Invisible History of Work: Interview with Sergio Bologna*. Available at http://www.springerin.at/dyn/heft_text. php?textid=1904&lang=en [accessed 2 December 2010].

Haidt, J. (2006), *The Happiness Hypothesis*, London: Arrow Books.

Hankinson, A. (2010), 'How Graduates Are Picking Up the Tab for Their Parents' Lives', *The Observer*, 31 January.

Hansard Society (2010), *Audit of Political Engagement 7: The 2010 Report*, London: Hansard Society.

Hardt, M. and Negri, A. (2000), *Empire*, Cambridge, MA: Harvard University Press.

Harris, P. (2010), 'Can Geoffrey Canada Rescue America's Ailing Schools? Barack Obama Hopes So', *The Observer*, 10 October.

Hauser, M. D. (2006), *Moral Minds: How Nature Designed Our Universal Sense of Right and Wrong*, New York: Harper Collins.

Hewlett, S. A., Jackson, M., Sherbin, L., Shiller, P., Sosnovich, E. and Sumberg, K. (2009), *Bookend Generations: Leveraging Talent and Finding Common Ground*, New York: Center for Work-Life Policy.

Hinojosa-Ojeda, R. (2010), *Raising the Floor for American Workers: The Economic Benefits of Comprehensive Immigration Reform*, Washington, DC: Center for American Progress, Immigration Policy Center.

Hinsliff, G. (2009), 'Home Office to Unveil Points System for Immigrants Seeking British Citizenship', *Observer*, 2 August, p. 4.

Hobsbawm, E. J. (1959), *Primitive Rebels: Studies in Archaic Forms of Social Movement in the 19th and 20th Centuries*, Manchester: Manchester University Press.

House, F. (2009), *The Business of Migration: Migrant Worker Rights in a Time of Financial Crisis*, London: Institute for Human Rights and Business.

Howker, E. and Malik, S. (2010), *Jilted Generation: How Britain Has Bankrupted Its Youth*, London: Icon Books.

Human Rights Watch (2010), *From the Tiger to the Crocodile: Abuse of Migrant Workers in Thailand*, New York: Human Rights Watch.

Internal Displacement Monitoring Centre (2010), Available at http://www. internal-displacement.org [accessed 2 December 2010].

Izzo, P. (2010), 'Economists Believe Many Jobs Won't Return', *Wall Street Journal Europe*, 12–14 February, p. 7.

Johal, A. (2010), 'Precarious Labour: Interview with San Precario Connection Organizer Alessandro Delfanti', 11 September. Available at http://www. rabble.ca/blogs/bloggers/amjohal/2010/09/precarious-labour-interview-san-precario-connection-organizer-alessan [accessed 3 December 2010].

Kellaway, L. (2009), 'Why My Friend's Job Delivers without Paying a Packet', *Financial Times*, 13 July, p. 10.

Kerbo, H. R. (2003), *Social Stratification and Inequality*, fifth edition, New York: McGraw Hill.

Kingston, J. (2010), *Contemporary Japan: History, Politics and Social Change since the 1980s*, Hoboken, NJ: Wiley-Blackwell.

Knox, M. (2010), 'Union Takes on Labor Over "Cheap" Foreign Workers',
    Sydney Morning Herald, 12 February, p. 1.

Kohn, M. (2008), *Trust: Self-Interest and the Common Good*, Oxford: Oxford
    University Press.

Kosugi, R. (2008), *Escape from Work: Freelancing Youth and the Challenge to
    Corporate Japan*, Melbourne: Trans Pacific Press.

MacDonald, R. and Shildrick, T. (2007), 'Street-Corner Society: Leisure Careers,
    Youth (Sub)Culture and Social Exclusion', *Leisure Studies*, 26(3): 339–55.

Maher, K. (2008), 'More in US Are Working Part-Time Out of Necessity',
    Wall Street Journal Europe, 10 March, p. 10.

Mallet, V. (2009), 'Soup Kitchen Queues Lengthen as Families Ignore Plight of
    Jobless', *Financial Times*, 14 May, p. 4.

Maltby, L. (2009), *Can They Do That? Retaking Our Fundamental Rights in the
    Workplace*, New York: Portfolio.

Marcuse, H. (1964), *One Dimensional Man: The Ideology of Industrial Society*,
    London: Sphere Books.

Martin, P. (2009), *Sex, Drugs and Chocolate: The Science of Pleasure*, London:
    Fourth Estate.

Mayhew, L. (2009), *Increasing Longevity and the Economic Value of Healthy
    Ageing and Working Longer*, London: Cass Business School, City University.

McGovern, P., Hill, S. and Mills, C. (2008), *Market, Class, and Employment*,
    Oxford: Oxford University Press.

Mead, L. (1986), *Beyond Entitlement: The Social Obligations of Citizenship*,
    New York: Free Press.

Mitchell, T. (2010), 'Honda Presses Staff not to Strike', *Financial Times*,
    31 May, p. 1.

Morrison, C. (2010), 'The Relationship between Excessive Internet Use and
    Depression: A Questionnaire-Based Study of 1,319 Young People and Adults',
    Psychopathology, 43(2): 121–6.

Mouer, R. and Kawanishi, H. (2005), *A Sociology of Work in Japan*, Cambridge,
    UK: Cambridge University Press.

Nairn, G. (2009), 'Telework Cuts Office Costs', *FT Report - Digital Business*,
    12 March, p. 4.

National Equality Panel (2010), *An Anatomy of Economic Inequality in the UK:
    Report of the National Equality Panel*, London: Centre for Analysis of Social
    Exclusion and the Government Equalities Office.

Needleman, S. (2009), 'Starting Fresh with an Unpaid Internship', *Wall Street
    Journal*, 16 July, p. D1.

Nink, M. (2009), 'It's Always about the Boss', *Gallup Management Journal*,
    25 November.

Obinger, J. (2009), 'Working on the Margins: Japan's Precariat and Working
    Poor', *Electronic Journal of Contemporary Japanese Studies*, 25 February.

OECD (2010a), *International Migration Outlook 2010*, Paris: OECD.

—(2010b), *A Profile of Immigrant Populations in the 21st Century: Data from OECD Countries*, Paris: OECD.

Paine, T. ([1795] 2005), *Common Sense and Other Writings*, New York: Barnes & Noble, pp. 321–45.

Parliamentary and Health Service Ombudsman (2010), *Fast and Fair? A Report by the Parliamentary Ombudsman on the UK Border Agency* (fourth report), London: The Stationery Office.

Peel, Q. (2010), 'German Popular Perception Fuels Furious Debate on Immigration', *Financial Times*, 2 September, p. 4.

Pigou, A. C. ([1952] 2002), *The Economics of Welfare*, New Brunswick, NJ: Transaction Publishers.

Polanyi, K. ([1944] 2001), *The Great Transformation: The Political and Economic Origins of Our Time*, Boston, MA: Beacon Press.

Reeves, R. (2010), 'Why Money Doesn't Buy Happiness', *Observer Magazine*, 25 April, p. 48.

Reeves, R. and Collins, P. (2009), *The Liberal Republic*, London: Demos.

Reidy, G. (2010), 'Young, Single and Labouring Round the Clock', *NYT Business*, 7 September, p. 13.

Richtel, M. (2010), 'Hooked on Gadgets, and Paying a Mental Price', *New York Times*, 7 June, p. 1.

Rigby, R. (2010), 'The Careerist: What You Know Has a Shorter and Shorter Lifespan', *Financial Times*, 22 February, p. 12.

Royle, T. and Ortiz, L. (2009), 'Dominance Effects from Local Competitors: Setting Institutional Parameters for Employment Relations in Multinational Subsidiaries: A Case from the Spanish Supermarket Sector', *British Journal of Industrial Relations*, 47(4): 653–75.

Saltmarsh, M. (2010), 'Far from Home and Miserable in Sweden', *International Herald Tribune*, 8 September, p. 3.

Sawhill, I. and Haskins, R. (2009), *Creating an Opportunity Society*, Washington, DC: Brookings Institution.

Schachar, A. (2009), *The Birthright Lottery*. Harvard, MA: Harvard University Press.

Sen, A. (1999), *Development as Freedom*, Oxford: Oxford University Press.

Sennett, R. (1998), *The Corrosion of Character: The Personal Consequences of Work in the New Capitalism*, New York: Norton.

Shildrick, T., MacDonald, R., Webster, C. and Garthwaite, K. (2010), *The Low-Pay, No-Pay Cycle: Understanding Recurrent Poverty*, York: Joseph Rowntree Foundation.

Si, L. (2009), *The Ant Tribe: An Account of the Agglomerate Settlements of University Graduates*, Guilin: Guangxi Normal University Press.

Simonian, H. (2010), 'Adecco Rejects Slowdown Fears', *Financial Times*, 12 August, p. 11.

Sklair, L. (2002), *Globalization: Capitalism and Its Alternatives*, Oxford: Oxford University Press.

Soysal, Y. (1994), *The Limits of Citizenship*, Chicago, IL: University of Chicago Press.

Standing, G. (1989), 'Global Feminization through Flexible Labor', *World Development*, 17(7): 1077–95.

—(1990), 'The Road to Workfare: Alternative to Welfare or Threat to Occupation?', *International Labour Review*, 129(6): 677–91.

—(1999a), 'Global Feminization through Flexible Labor: A Theme Revisited', *World Development*, 27(3): 583–602.

—(1999b), *Global Labour Flexibility: Seeking Distributive Justice*, Basingstoke: Macmillan.

—(2009), *Work after Globalization: Building Occupational Citizenship*, Cheltenham, UK, and Northampton, MA: Edward Elgar.

—(2010), 'Global Monitor: The International Labour Organization', *New Political Economy*, 15(2): 307–18.

—(2011), 'Responding to the Crisis: Economic Stabilisation Grants', *Policy & Politics*, 39(1): 9–25.

Tabuchi, H. (2010), 'Japan Accused of Violating Migrant Workers' Human Rights', *New York Times*, 21 July, p. B1.

Tavan, C. (2005), *Les immigrés en France: une situation qui évolue [Immigrants in France: An Evolving Situation]*, INSEE Première, No. 1042, September.

Thaler, R. and Sunstein, C. (2008), *Nudge: Improving Decisions About Health, Wealth, and Happiness*, New Haven and London: Yale University Press.

Thompson, E. P. (1967), 'Time, Work-Discipline and Industrial Capitalism', *Past and Present*, 38(1): 58–97.

Tomkins, R. (2009), 'The Retreat of Reason', *FT Weekend*, 23–24 May, pp. 24–9.

Tulgan, B. (2009), *Not Everyone Gets a Trophy: How to Manage Generation Y*, San Francisco, CA: Jossey-Bass.

Turque, W. (2010), 'D. C. Students Respond to Cash Awards, Harvard Study Shows', *Washington Post*, 10 April, p. B1.

Uchitelle, L. (2006), *The Disposable American: Layoffs and Their Consequences*. New York: Alfred Knopf.

Ueno, T. (2007), ' "Precariat" Workers Are Starting to Fight for a Little Stability', *Japan Times Online*, 21 June.

UKBA (2010), *Points Based System Tier 1: An Operational Assessment*, London: The Stationery Office.

Virtanen, M., Ferrie, J. E., Singh-Manoux, A., Shipley, M. J., Vahtera, J., Marmot, M. G. and Kivimäki, M. (2010), 'Overtime Work and Incident Coronary Heart Disease: The Whitehall II Prospective Cohort Study', *European Heart Journal*, 31: 1737–44.

Wacquant, L. (2008), 'Ordering Insecurity: Social Polarization and the Punitive Upsurge', *Radical Philosophy Review*, 11(1): 9–27.

Weber, M. ([1922] 1968), *Economy and Society*, Berkeley, CA, and Los Angeles, CA: University of California Press.

Wilkinson, R. and Pickett, K. E. (2009), *The Spirit Level: Why More Equal Societies Almost Always Do Better*, London: Allen Lane.

Willetts, D. (2010), *The Pinch: How the Baby Boomers Took Their Children's Future – and Why They Should Give It Back*, London: Atlantic.

Willsher, K. (2010), 'Leaked Memo Shows France's Expulsion of Roma Illegal, Say Critics', *Guardian*, 14 September, p. 20.

Wong, E. (2009), 'China Confronts Backlash from Its Mass Exports of Labor', *International Herald Tribune*, 21 December, p. 16.

Working Families (2005), *Time, Health and the Family*, London: Working Families.

Wright, E. O. (ed.) (2006), *Redesigning Distribution: Basic Income and Stakeholder Grants as Cornerstones for an Egalitarian Capitalism*, London: Verso.

Zolberg, A. (1995), 'Review of Y. Soysal, Limits of Citizenship', *Contemporary Sociology*, 24(4): 326–9.

INDEX

Page numbers with 'b' shows information found in a box.

Ackerman, Bruce   311
Adecco   56–7, 84
agency   288–93
Agrarian Justice (Paine)   298
Aguiar, Mark   219
Alemanno, Gianni   257
Alexander, Douglas   250
alienation   33–41
alternative medicine   120
altruism   311
anger   33–41, 265
anomie   33–41, 109
Ant Tribe   125
anxiety   33–41, 265
Anzalone, John   262
apprenticeships   17b, 39, 102,
        123–5, 208
architecture of choice   228, 239,
        241–2, 245
Arendt, Hannah   200, 282
Arizona law SB1070   159, 166–7
associational freedom   288–93
associations, occupational   291
asylum seekers   153, 157–8, 160,
        164–5, 256, 272
Atos Origin   287
atypical labour   54, 69
Australia   67, 154, 162, 175
Austria   258
Axelrod, David   262

baby boomers   113–14, 127
bag lady syndrome   108, 144

banausoi   21, 200
basic income   295–303,
        305–8, 311
Bauerlein, Mark   119
BBVA   86
Beck, Glen   261
Belgium   67
benefits   19–20, 55–6
    and the disabled   141
    health care   87
    unemployment   77–9, 135, 161,
        173, 182
    and wages   70–1
    women and   102
Bentham, Jeremy   228–9
Berlusconi, Silvio   118, 315
    on immigrants   7, 165, 256–7
BIEN (Basic Income European
        Network/Basic Income Earth
        Network)   172
Birthright Lottery, The (Schachar)
        297–8
Blair, Tony   233, 272, 309
Blinder, Alan   280
boredom   32, 243
Bosson, Eric   166
brain   31
Brazil   314
breadwinners   70, 102, 106–7, 109
British Airways   86
Brown, Gordon   176
Bryceson, D. B.   35
Buffett, Warren   134

call centres   27, 291
Cameron, David   239, 291, 309
Can They do That? (Maltby)   237
Canada   136, 194
capital funds   304–5
Capitalism and Freedom
        (Friedman)   269
care work   105, 147, 215
careers, leisure   222
cash transfers   305
    see also conditional cash
        transfers (CCTs)
CCTs (conditional cash transfer
        schemes)   241–2
Cerasa, Claudio   257
Channel 4, call centre
        programme (UK)   27
charities   90
children, care for   205
China   47
    and contractualisation   63
    criminalisation   150
    deliberative democracy   312
    education   125
    immigrants to Italy   8
    invasion of privacy   231
    migrants   154, 163, 174, 179,
        182–3, 185–6, 191–3
    old agers   142
    Shenzhen   229, 236
    and time   198
    wages   70
    youth   130
    see also Chindia
China Plus One   47
Chindia   43, 46–9, 142
    see also China
Chrysler Group LLC   74
circulants   153, 156
*Citizens United vs Federal Election
        Commission* (US)   263

civil rights   19, 160–1
class, social   13–14, 114–15
Coase, Ronald   29
Cohen, Daniel   97, 113, 119
collaborative bargaining   290
collective attention deficit
        syndrome   218
commodification
    of companies   49–51
    of education   115–23
    and globalisation   49
    labour   278–80
    of management   69
    of politics   253, 255, 262–3
    re-   71
conditional cash transfers
        (CCTs)   241–2
    see also cash transfers
conditionality   241, 307
    and basic income   302–3
    and workfare   246–51, 285–8
connectivity, and youth   217–19
contract status   59, 61, 63, 76,
        87, 104
contractors, independent/
        dependent   26
contractualisation   63
counselling for stress   216
Crawford, Matthew   119
credit   75
crime   23, 222
criminalisation   24, 252, 271
crystallised intelligence   145
cultural rights   23

de Tocqueville, Alexis   250
de-industrialisation   9, 64
debt, and youth   126–7
Delfanti, Alessandro   133
deliberative democracy
        311–12, 314

denizens 23, 159–64, 173, 192, 201, 270–3
Denmark 258
dependent/independent contractors 26
deskilling 29, 55, 68, 212
developing countries 20, 70, 93, 103, 112, 137, 163, 179–85
disabled people 148–9, 251
discrimination
  age 145
  disability 137
  gender 104, 211
  genetic profiling 235–6
  and migrants 169, 173
disengagement, political 42
distance working 65–6, 91
dole (UK) 77
Duncan Smith, Iain 247
Durkheim, Emile 34

economic security 260, 270, 294, 296, 299–300, 302
The Economist 29–30, 56, 88, 96, 235
economy, shadow 95–7
education 16, 115–23, 221–2, 274–6
Ehrenreich, Barbara 35, 294
elites 12, 37, 41–2, 68, 85, 89
  criminality 262
  and democracy 313
  ethics 285
  Italian 256
  and the Tea Party (US) 260
empathy 38–9, 236
employment agencies 56–7
employment security 17b, 18, 28–9, 53, 87–9, 200
Endarkenment 120
Enlightenment 41, 120
enterprise benefits 19–20
environmental issues 267

environmental refugees 158
Esping-Andersen, G. 70
ethics 39–40, 204, 285
ethnic minorities 147–8
EuroMayDay 2–6, 288
European Union (EU) 2, 67, 252–3
  and migrants 160, 166
  and pensions 138
  see also individual countries
export processing zones 180

Facebook 218, 230, 232
failed occupationality 35
family 42, 44, 75–6, 103, 112, 217
fear, used for control 55
fictitious decommodification 70
financial capital 294–5, 303–6
financial sector jobs 67–8
financial shock 2008–9 *see* Great Recession
Financial Times 76, 93, 207, 268
firing workers 52–3
Fishkin, James 311
Fletcher, Bill 294
flexibility 30
  labour 40, 52–76, 96, 112–15
  labour market 9, 207, 293
Ford Motor Company 71–2, 74
Foucault, Michel 150, 229
Foxconn 48–9, 74, 179, 236
  see also Shenzhen
France
  criminalisation 150
  de-industrialisation 64
  education 119
  leisure 222
  migrants 162, 166, 172–3, 194
  neo-fascism 257
  and old agers 145
  pensions 136
  shadow economy 96

Telecom   18
   youth   112–13
fraternity   20, 37, 267
freedom   267, 280–3, 288
freelance *see* temporary employment
freeter unions   15
Friedman, Milton   66, 269
functional flexibility   62–5, 88
furloughs   61, 85–6

gays   109
General Motors (GM)   73–4, 92
genetic profiling   235
Germany   15
   de-industrialisation   64
   disengagement with jobs   42
   migrants   154–5, 162, 171–2, 194
   pensions   136
   shadow economy   96
   temporary employment   25, 59
   wages   69
   and women   106
   youth and apprenticeships   123–4
Glen Beck's Common Sense (Beck)   261
Global Transformation   43, 45–52,
      155, 197
globalisation   8–11, 45–52, 200, 255
   and commodification   44
   and criminalisation   150–1
   and temporary employment   57
Google Street View   230
Gorz, André   12
grants, leisure   311–14
Great Recession   4, 84–5, 107, 251
   and education   122
   and migrants   174
   and old agers   142
   and pensions   138
   and youth   128
Greece   89, 96, 200, 312
grinners/groaners   102, 135–47

Habermas, Jürgen   310
Haidt, J.   40
Hamburg (Germany)   5
happiness   242–3, 280, 302
Hardt, M.   223
Hayek, Friedrich   66
health   86, 102, 214–15, 231
Hitachi   144
Hobsbawm, Eric   6
hormones   235
hot desking   91
Howker, Ed   111
Human Rights Watch   181
Hungary   254, 258
Hurst, Erik   219
Hyatt Hotels   55

IBM   65, 236
identity   16
   digital   232–3
   work-based   16, 20–1, 39, 273–4
Ignatieff, Michael   150
illegal migrants   165–8
In Praise of Idleness (Russell)   243, 277
income security   17b, 52, 76
independent/dependent
      contractors   26
India   85, 142, 151, 163, 174, 186–7,
      191–2
   see also Chindia
individuality   4, 32, 209
informal status   11, 118, 200
inshored/offshored labour   51, 63
International Herald Tribune   36
internet   31, 217–19, 238, 263,
      310, 312
   surveillance   231, 237
interns   27, 61, 128–30
invasion of privacy   229–33, 289
Ireland   89, 132
isolation of workers   65

Italy
    education   118
    neo-fascism   256-7
    pensions   136
    Prato   6-8
    and the public sector   89, 91
    shadow economy   96
    and temporary employment   57
    youth   110

Japan   2, 51
    and Chinese migrants   190
    commodification of
        companies   51
    and migrants   175-6
    multiple job holding   205
    neo-fascism   261-2
    pensions   136
    salariat   28
    subsidies   144
    and temporary employment
        25, 55-8, 69-70
    and youth   113, 126-7
job security   17b, 18, 87-8

Kellaway, Lucy   143
Keynes, John Maynard   277
Kierkegaard, Søren   267
Klein, Naomi   255
knowledge   54, 201, 214-15, 294

labour   21-2, 188-92, 276-8
labour brokers   56-7, 188, 289-90
labour flexibility   40, 52-76
labour intensification   205-6
labour market flexibility   9
labour security   17-18, 17b, 53
Laos   190
lay-offs see furloughs
Lee Changshik   36
legal knowledge   214

legal processing   85
Legal Services Act of 2007 (UK)
        (Tesco Law)   68
leisure   21-2, 219-24 see also play
lesbians   109
Liberal Republic, The   313
Lloyds Banking Group   86
localism   307, 313-14
long-term migrants   171-4
loyalty   99, 128

McDonald's   55
McNealy, Scott   118
Malik, Shiv   111
Maltby, Lewis   237
Manafort, Paul   262
management, commodification of   69
Mandelson, Peter, Baron   117
Maroni, Roberto   165
marriage   110-11, 157
Martin, Paul   243
Marx, Karl   277
masculinity, role models for
        youth   109-11
Massachusetts Institute of
        Technology   117
Mayhew, Les   139
Mead, Lawrence   246
mergers, triangular   51
Mexico   155
Middle East   186
migrants   3-4, 24, 42, 153-5, 251
    and basic income   295
    and conditionality   246
    denizens   159-64, 270-3
    government organised   184-5
    internal   185
    and queuing systems   176-9
    and recession   174-5
Mill, John Stuart   275
Morris, William   276-7

Morrison, Catriona   219
multinational corporations   45,
     47, 157
multitasking   32, 217

National Broadband Plan   232
near-sourcing/shoring   61
Negri, A.   233
neo-fascism   42, 253, 256–7, 263,
     270, 274, 302
Netherlands   67, 140, 150, 192, `
     194, 258
New Thought Movement   35
New York Times   119, 205
News from Nowhere (Morris)   277
Niemöller, Martin   314
non-refoulement   158
Nudge (Sunstein/Thaler)   238–9
nudging   239, 244, 265, 268–9, 284,
     289, 296, 307
numerical flexibility   53–62

Obama, Barack   125, 239, 254–5
Observer, The   33
occupations
     associations of   291
     dismantling of   66–9
     freedom in   280–3
     obsolescence in   212
offshored/inshored labour   51, 63
old agers   93, 135–47
old-age dependency ratio   138
Organisation for Economic
     Co-operation and
     Development (OECD)   45
origins of the precariat   2–6
outsourcing   49, 56, 60, 62–4, 71, 80,
     84–5, 90

Paine, Thomas   298, 306
panopticon society   228–42
Parent Motivators (UK)   240

part-time employment   25, 60, 86–7,
     106, 110, 140
Pasona   56
paternalism   28, 48, 236, 246, 264,
     267–9, 284, 306–7
     nudging   239, 244, 265, 268–9,
     284, 289, 296, 307
pensions   71–3, 114, 136–9, 141
PepsiCo   236
personal deportment skills   210
Philippines   187
Phoenix, University of   122
Pigou, Arthur   201, 214
play   21–2, 194, 201, 219, 235, 243
pleasure   243
Polanyi, K.   282, 291
political engagement/
     disengagement   33, 253
Portugal   89, 96
positive thinking   35, 148
Prato (Italy)   6, 8
precariat (definition)   10–21
precariatisation   28–30
precariato   15
precarity traps   81–3, 126–8, 194,
     222, 248, 308
pride   38
prisoners   228, 252
privacy, invasion of   229–33, 289
private benefits   19–20
productivity, and old age   145
proficians   12–13, 25, 282
proletariat   10–12
protectionism   46, 92
public sector   86–91

qualifications   162
queuing systems   176–9

racism   167, 172, 193, 257
Randstad   84
re-commodification   71

recession *see* Great Recession
refugees 153, 157–9, 164
regulation 44, 66–7, 145, 295
Reimagining Socialism (Ehrenreich/
    Fletcher) 294
remote working 65–6, 91
rentier economies 45, 304
representation security 17b, 53
retirement 71–2, 139–42
rights 19, 150, 250, 270–3, 279
    see also denizens
risk management 307
Robin Hood gang 5
role models for youth 109–10
Roma 165–6, 256–7
Rossington, John 170
Rothman, David 150
Russell, Bertrand 243, 277
Russell, Lucie 110
Russia 150, 198

salariat 12–14, 23, 28–9, 41–2, 51,
    54, 63–4
Santelli, Rick 259
Sarkozy, Nicolas 118, 166, 257
Sarrazin, Thilo 172
Schachar, Ayelet 306
Schneider, Friedrich 96
Schwarzenegger, Arnold 122
seasonal migrants 168–70
security, economic 270, 294, 296,
    299–300, 302
self-employment 26, 140, 162
self-esteem 36
self-exploitation 33, 210
self-production 19
self-regulation 39, 66
self-service 214
services 67–8, 108
*Sex, Drugs and Chocolate: The Science
    of Pleasure* (Martin) 243
sex services 108

sexism, reverse 211
shadow economy 95–7, 161
Shenzhen (China) 229, 236
    see also Foxconn
Shop Class as Soulcraft
    (Crawford) 119
short-time compensation schemes 94
side-jobs 205
skill reproduction security 17b
skills 286, 304
    development of 51, 53, 77
    personal deportment 210
    tertiary 208–12
Skirbekk, Vegard 145
Smarsh 238
Smile or Die (Ehrenreich) 35
Smith, Adam 121
snowball theory 134
social class 13–14, 114–15
social factory 64, 202, 228
social income 18–20, 69–76, 86,
    103, 113
social insurance 38, 177
social memory 20, 39, 221
social mobility 39, 97–8, 260
social networking sites 236
    see also Facebook
social rights 23
social worth 36
sousveillance 231–2
South Africa, and migrants 155,
    167–8
South Korea 25, 94, 104, 129–30
space, public 289, 309–10
Spain
    BBVA 86
    migrants 161
    and migrants 175
    pensions 136
    and the public sector 94
    shadow economy 96
    temporary employment 59–60

Speenhamland system   93, 246
staffing agencies   56, 84, 189
state benefits   19–20
status   11, 38, 55, 59–60, 159–60
status discord   16
status frustration   16, 37, 109, 115,
          132, 134–5, 152, 194, 212, 276
stress   33, 206, 243–4
subsidies   61, 91–5, 144–6, 303–4
suicide, work-related   29, 48, 99, 179
Summers, Larry   255
Sun Microsystems   118
Sunstein, Cass   239
surveillance   231–4, 264–5, 272, 289
    see also sousveillance
Suzuki, Kensuke   262
Sweden   98, 136, 188–9, 192, 233,
          258
symbols   4

Taking of Rome, The (Cerasa)   257
taxes   43
    and citizenship   306
    France   136
    and subsidies   96
    Tobin   305
    United States (US)   312
Tea Party movement   259–60
technology
    and the brain   31
    internet   310, 312
    surveillance   231–4
teleworking   65
temporary agencies   56–7, 59, 290
temporary employment   25, 84
    associations for   293
    Japan   15
    and numerical flexibility   55–9
    and old agers   143
    and the public sector   87
    and youth   112

tertiarisation   64–5
tertiary skill   208–12
tertiary time   200, 204
tertiary workplace   202–3
Tesco Law (UK)   68
Thailand, migrants   180
Thaler, Richard   239
therapy state   244–6
Thompson, E. P.   197
time   197–200, 306–8
    labour intensification   205–6
    tertiary   200, 204
    use of   64
    work-for-labour   206–8
titles of jobs   29–30
Tobin taxes   305
Tomkins, Richard   120
towns, company   229, 236
toy-factory incident   185
trade unions   2–3, 17b, 263
    and migration   155
    public sector   88
    and youth   132–3
    see also yellow unions
training   207–9, 212
triangular mergers   51
triangulation   57
Trumka, Richard   133
trust relationships   14, 50
Twitter   218

Ukraine   262–3
undocumented migrants   154–5,
          160–1, 165–8
unemployment   245
    benefits   77–9, 135, 161
    insurance for   302
    voluntary   210
    youth after recession   132
uniforms, to distinguish employment
          status   55

unions
    freeter 15
    yellow 56
    see also trade
United Kingdom (UK) 174–8
    benefit system 298
    Channel 4 call centre
        programme 27
    company loyalty 128
    conditionality 247–9, 287–8
    criminalisation 150–1
    de-industrialisation 64
    disabled people 251–2
    and education 115, 117, 120, 122
    financial shock (2008–9) 84–6,
        122
    labour intensification 205–6
    Legal Services Act (2007)
        (Tesco Law) 68
    leisure 222
    migrants 155, 162, 169, 174–5,
        193–4, 251
    neo-fascism 258
    paternalism 240, 242
    pensions 73, 136
    and the public sector 90–1
    public spaces 309
    and regulation of occupational
        bodies 67
    shadow economy 96
    and social mobility 97–8
    and subsidies 92, 94
    temporary employment 24, 58–9
    as a therapy state 244
    women 106–7, 279
    workplace discipline 238
    youth 110, 130
United States (US)
    care for children 215
    criminalisation 150–1
    education 116–17, 119, 233–4

ethnic minorities 147
    financial shock (2008–9) 84–5
    migrants 154, 159, 161–2, 193–4
    neo-fascism 258–60
    old agers 140–1, 145–6
    pensions 73, 89, 136
    public sector 90
    regulation of occupational
        bodies 67
    social mobility in 97–8
    subsidies 92, 94
    taxes 311–12
    temporary employment 58–9
    volunteer work 281–2
    wages and benefits 73–4
    women 106–7
    youth 129, 132
universalism 268, 288, 311
University of the People 117
University of Phoenix 122
unpaid furloughs 61
unpaid leave 86
uptitling 29
utilitarianism 150, 228, 244, 265

value of support 19
Vietnam 46, 188–90
voluntary unemployment 210
volunteer work 140, 281–3
voting 252–3, 314

Wacquant, L. 227
wages 9, 13–14, 19
    and benefits 70
    family 103
    flexibility 69–76, 113
    individualised 103
    and migrants 182
    and temporary workers 55, 57
    Vietnam 46
    see also basic income

Waiting for Superman
    (documentary)   119
Wall Street Journal   60, 280
Walmart   56, 183
Wandering Tribe   125
Weber, Max   11, 13
welfare claimants   287
welfare systems   75
Wen Jiabao   179
Whitehead, Alfred North   275
Williams, Rob   107
wiretapping   233
women   102–11
    and care work   215
    CCTs (conditional cash transfer
      schemes)   241–2
    labour commodification   279
    and migration   156
    multiple jobholding   205
    reverse sexism   211
work   200–2, 276
    and identity   273–4
    and labour   21–2
    right to   250, 281, 283–5
    security   17b

work-for-labour   206–8, 307–8
work-for-reproduction   213–17
work–life balance   202
worker cooperatives   291–3
workfare   246–51, 285–8
working class   10, 12
workplace   202–3, 209, 223, 225
    discipline   234–8
    tertiary   202–3

Yanukovich, Victor   262
yellow unions   56
youth   102, 112–15, 146, 270
    commodification of
      education   115–23
    connectivity   217–19
    and criminality   222
    generational tension   131
    and old agers   140
    precarity traps   126–8
    prospects for the future   133–5
    and role models   109–10
    streaming education   123–6

zero-hour contracts   61